CW01213157

SEAS OF PLENTY

SEAS OF PLENTY

MARITIME TRADE INTO ENGLAND
AND WALES c. 1400–1540

IAIN SODEN

AMBERLEY

First published 2024

Amberley Publishing
The Hill, Stroud
Gloucestershire, GL5 4EP

www.amberley-books.com

Copyright © Iain Soden, 2024

The right of Iain Soden to be identified as the Author of this work has been asserted in accordance with the Copyright, Designs and Patents Act 1988.

ISBN 978 1 3981 2289 5 (hardback)
ISBN 978 1 3981 2290 1 (ebook)

All rights reserved. No part of this book may be reprinted or reproduced or utilised in any form or by any electronic, mechanical or other means, now known or hereafter invented, including photocopying and recording, or in any information storage or retrieval system, without the permission in writing from the Publishers.

British Library Cataloguing in Publication Data.
A catalogue record for this book is available from the British Library.

1 2 3 4 5 6 7 8 9 10

Typesetting by SJmagic DESIGN SERVICES, India.
Printed in the UK.

CONTENTS

Acknowledgements 7
Introduction 9
    England and The Libelle; *Goods In.*

1 Movers and Shakers 19
    Travellers; Slavery; Merchants and passengers;
    Over the horizon; Some Englishmen abroad;
    Royal influence – civil wars and trade wars.

2 'Cherysshe Marchandyse' 46
    Spain and Flanders; Portugal; Brittany;
    Scotland and Ireland; Wales; Brabant, Zeeland and
    Hainault; Iceland; The Italian city-states – Genoa,
    Florence, Venice; The Baltic; The Hanseatic League.

3 Sea Lanes and Sailing Routes 107
    Arrivals from the south; Arrivals from the north;
    Crewing and victualling; Life at sea;
    The choice of port-destination.

4 Destination England and Wales 141
    The many ways to market; Contemporary views.

Seas of Plenty

5 West Coast Ports   153
Lancashire and Cheshire; North Wales; South Wales; Gloucestershire/Avon; Somerset; North Devon; North Cornwall.

6 South Coast Ports   170
South Cornwall; South Devon; Dorset; Hampshire; Isle of Wight.

7 Channel Coast Ports   194
Sussex; Kent.

8 London, East Anglia and the North-East   208
London; Essex; Suffolk; Norfolk; Lincolnshire; Yorkshire; Durham and Northumberland.

9 Sating Appetites   229
Gascony and beyond – the wine trade; Wines from further afield; Silks, velvets and furs; Metal and timber; Spices; Ceramics; Glass; Fine arts and music; War Booty.

10 A Permanent Heavy Swell   263
Xenophobia; Piracy; Shipwreck; Lighthouses.

11 The Rise of an English Merchant Fleet   296
A census of ships; The Flanders Galleys affair; Endings and continuity

Notes   315
Bibliography   338

ACKNOWLEDGEMENTS

I began notes for this book around 2010 before going off on one of life's tangents involving a decade's distraction. It therefore contains ideas developed over many years and ends up very much a personal reflection, not an academic treatise. After four decades as a professional field archaeologist, the scholarship relies more on a long view than perhaps any professional edge. I gratefully acknowledge the colleagues who have accompanied me, too many to list by name.

I record first and foremost my debt to my wife and my sons for their encouragement. My wife has been my constant companion and my welcoming haven in every storm. To my parents I record my lifelong thanks.

To my old friend and colleague Joe Prentice go my thanks for his friendship and advice over thirty years. To Sara Elin Roberts I record my appreciation for her kind correspondence over more than a decade – and her help with medieval Welsh. I thank Andy Isham for his maps and Alex Bennett at Amberley for the finished product.

Thanks go to the following for permission to reproduce images: The Victoria and Albert Museum, London; Bram Janssens of STAM-Stadsmuseum Gent; Ulrike Fladerer of Städel Museum, Frankfurt am Main; Mathias Böhm of the Austrian National

Library; Emil Lundin of Uppsala University Library; Birmingham Museums Trust; Ali Wells of the Herbert Art Gallery and Museum, Coventry; Museum of London Archaeology and Steve Parry, their former CEO; Sara Elin Roberts and Jonathan Pinsent. To the late Walton Hudson of Waterfoot, Rossendale, Lancashire, I tip my hat for his photographs from *circa* 1932–60, and I also thank Skears Photographic, Northampton, for their scanning. I include dates to all photos where known.

I count as key to this volume the anonymous writer of *The Libelle*. It is a shame he cannot see that his apparently struggling England of *circa* 1435 became the centre of a global trading empire, still surprising people in a challenging world after 600 years.

The Earth is The Lord's, and the fullness thereof.

INTRODUCTION

Here too on our little reef display your power,
This fortress perched on the edge of the Atlantic scarp
The mole between all Europe and the exile-crowded sea
                                    W. H. Auden, 'Prologue'[1]

For thousands of years Britain has been an island. As an island nation, however insular our ways, we have always had to look outwards; we have a compulsion to sail and to travel, and the sea fascinates us. Our tastes seek external stimuli, and our hunger is for the new, the exotic – and, when we are successful, external comparisons through which we can relate the nature and extent of our success. Our maritime fringe is in fact a considerable gulf and is far more than just a border, being ingrained in the national psyche.

This is a book about people making very difficult sea journeys and experiencing the joy and relief of arrival, although they were not always appreciated by their hosts. Maritime travel to England and Wales brought great personal perils but considerable mercantile rewards. This is not a book generally about archaeological finds, other than in passing; rather it concerns the people who imported those objects and their travels, often undertaken at huge personal and financial risk. Nor is this a book about our exports – English wool and woollen cloth, tin or lead. The holds of the foreign ships which took away our wool came loaded with all that England desired from afar, from a continent that was usually beyond the experience of most ordinary Englishmen; and arguably this was far more exciting than the weaver's loom or the dyer's vat, although the ships supplied both with what they needed to weave and colour England's cloth for export.

The fifteenth-century Dominican friar Brother Felix Fabri is perhaps the most effusive chronicler of maritime adventures in his generation, and his written experience of life aboard Venetian galleys in the 1480s is without parallel, but he is unusually concise when he sums up the contemporary experience: 'A journey by sea is subject to many hardships. The sea itself is very injurious to those who are unaccustomed to it, and very dangerous on many accounts; for it strikes terror into the soul; it causes headache, it provokes vomiting and nausea; it destroys appetite for food and drink; it causes extreme and deadly perils, and often brings men to a most cruel death.'[2]

We will encounter the irrepressible Felix Fabri again later in this volume, for he wrote erudite prose about the people he met and the mariners and rowers with whom he shared a deck – and in whose calloused hands he placed his life. His humanity stands out in a fifteenth-century world of cargos and port-duties, diplomatic (and very undiplomatic) dealings, piracy and shipwreck.

This book looks at the perilous fifteenth and sixteenth century journeys undertaken, and the hardy mariners and merchants who undertook them, to get bulk raw materials, foodstuffs and luxuries here in huge quantities: food and wine to our tables, opulent cloth into our wardrobes, raw materials to our workshops, weapons to our armies; satisfying hunger, thirst and the urge to enjoy more of the bounty which the earth clearly had to offer beyond our shores. Merchants came in fragile ships on tempestuous seas against a backdrop of piracy, widespread racism and an ever-present threat of violence. We will also chart the gradual change that took place as official foreign fleets, regularly beaten up, depleted by sequestration and cajoled by growing tariffs, tolls and increasing risk, gave way to personal ventures – and, even by the 1520s, an English merchant navy of sorts.

England and The Libelle

When, around 1435, an anonymous Englishman composed a poem entitled *The Libelle of Englysshe Polycye* (hereafter simply the *Libelle*), he bemoaned a dire deficit in the national balance of trade, but in doing so he evinced every emotion, good and bad, that went with belonging to this island race.[3] He believed in his fellow Englishmen and their ability to enrich the country by their trade:

> Here beginneth the Prologue of the processe of the Libelle of Englysshe Polycye, exhortynge alle Englande to keep the see environ and onely the narrowe see, shewynge what profete cometh thereof and also what worshype and salvation to England and to alle Englyshe menne.[4]

Medieval borders flowed quite freely at times, and languages often spanned them. Late medieval Europe was a mélange, with its constituent kingdoms, dukedoms and counties all having specific regional and cultural identities which were not really those of their countries, each markedly different one from another. England and Wales were not dissimilar in this regard.

In England in the fifteenth and sixteenth centuries perhaps the biggest internal differences were still felt between the English nation and its older Celtic cousins, where a distinct identity (and language) persisted, even as close as Cornwall. Wales, across the often unruly western 'marcher' counties, remained stubbornly different and occasionally restive, and independent Scotland was separated by a wide borderland populated by 'reivers', who were fiercely independent and changed allegiance on a whim. To be from Northumberland or Cumbria, Lancashire or Durham was often to simply stand apart, speaking a strong local dialect; in Wales and Cornwall, they spoke another language altogether. What kept them together to some extent, however, was the bountiful but unforgiving sea. All to north and south were surrounded by that same gulf, to cross which involved taking ship and venturing 'abroad'. What one might say is that the longer the journey, especially when the cargo was successfully delivered and dispersed, the more interesting its story.

Materials and finished items crossed mountains, seas and rivers. Many travelled hundreds of miles, and in some cases thousands. On horseback, on foot, by wagon and aboard ship they came, tied, bagged, wrapped or crated up, in great leaps (at 8–10 knots maximum) from port to port and then market to market. The variety of vessels available to the merchants and shippers who sought to supply this island with its needs can be found elsewhere: from the navis (ship) come its cousins the carrack, galea (galley), batella (small boat), carvela (caravel), balingera (barge), scapha (skiff), spurancea (spinace), woodbush, ketch, picard and even the lowly cog. There is little guarantee that what a word meant in one port meant the same a few miles away. Many thousands of words have been expended in discerning one from another and delineating the pedigree of each ship type.[5] Even more has been written on the growing corpus of excavated ships, boats, hulks, broken shells and scattered pieces, from whole ships sunk in silt to reused ribs and sternposts built into harbour wharves and estuarine bulwarks everywhere from Studland to Sandwich, from Newport to Guernsey, from Bremen to Stockholm to Gdansk and back.[6]

The *Libelle*, the poem that runs as a thread though this book, is an embittered and angry work which was written in 1435, 1436

Introduction

or 1437, at a nadir in English trading fortunes. The anonymous author indulged himself in a diatribe about what today might be called the balance-of-trade deficit. It may sound an unpromising subject, more suited to the *Financial Times*, but its author set it out in verse and, liberally sprinkling it with his own embittered brand of bile and invective, muttered what he thought of foreign fripperies imported into this country, to the detriment of sensible taste, home-grown producers and the market. Outrage came naturally to him. His was certainly an England in a rare and deep trading rut.[7] He was part of a widespread opposition to all things foreign; an opposition which made for some despicable receptions to foreign traders. When occasionally a proper welcome was extended by contemporaries, it shines out.

However, the author of the *Libelle* also exhorted his countrymen 'to keep thys regne in rest cherysshe marchandyse, keep them (adm) yralte that we be maysteres of the narrow see'.[8] He entertained something of a siege mentality about his Englishness but did recognise that our insularity is very special to our national identity, employing an enduring metaphor:

> Keepe then the see abought in special, whiche of England is the rounde wall, as though England were lykened to a cite and the wall environ were the see. Keep then the see, that is the wall of England.[9]

In the 1430s, during a century of war against our nearest neighbour, the country struggled to retain Aquitaine and Calais, the last English possessions in France. Then to both north and south of this knotty, very un-neighbourly problem a trade crisis was born. A growing understanding between France and Burgundy (Flanders) threatened the balance, and by the Treaty of Arras in 1435 they excluded England. Wealthy Gent (or Ghent), in what is now Belgium, described English Calais as a thorn in its side. There followed a dramatic slump in trade out of most English ports for up to three years. Wool exports collapsed and England was unable to reach agreement with its neighbours.

In all this Southampton remained buoyed by economic success, but even that town struggled. Safe-conduct passes were abused and bribery was rife. The *Libelle* pleaded for 'gode governance'.[10]

Goods In

No one was singled out for special treatment in the *Libelle*'s brand of invective. All imports were scrutinised; it did accept the import of staple foodstuffs and other such items, but only begrudgingly. To read it in full is to begin to appreciate the extent of fifteenth-century xenophobia, but it is also our island's shopping list to the world, providing a window on the exotic and the far-flung. This angst-ridden sideswipe at the nation's trade can be looked at alongside shipping manifests, port-books, censuses and national crises, occasionally with the added detail of archaeological data. No one should ever be surprised at the sheer range of materials, both manufactured and natural, which came into England (and to some extent Wales) from abroad to sate the country's hunger and thirst for the foreign, the sweet and spicy, and the downright difficult to obtain. Far from being the preserve of kings and the nobility, foreign goods and foodstuffs were to be found in markets all across this country, from the port-side wharves to land-locked towns and cities, appetites fed thanks to a busy road network little changed since Roman times and an equally busy waterborne trade up winding navigable rivers (especially in the eastern counties), driven by foreign merchants, English middlemen and Merchant Adventurers, entrepreneurial monasteries, civic guilds and individuals who sought to impress or simply revel in the latest tastes.

I have chosen to highlight some of the principal foreign carriers, most of whom are known by nationality, and some even by name. Documents

Introduction

Imports were carried mainly via aged Roman roads and navigable rivers like the River Nene, from King's Lynn to Peterborough and beyond. Pictured is the medieval and later bridge at Irthlingborough, Northants (2017).

and archaeology also combine to shed light on some specific markets, consumers and places that illustrate England and Wales's imports, so often organic and therefore perishable and impermanent. Late medieval England and Wales were awash with imported goods and foodstuffs, and to cover all of them would be impossible. The people of this era were hungry to stock their larders and cellars with continental produce and their Baltic timber cupboards with the manufactured goods of their neighbours, just as much then as today.

The English ports, markets and patterns of consumption chosen for comparison in this book reflect the places in which I have researched, enquired or excavated over decades – medieval towns and cities and a variety of monasteries and nunneries of numerous monastic orders, all foci in the medieval landscape.

In the Midlands, Coventry arguably presents the most interesting case among the urban centres since not only was it the fourth city of the realm by 1377 (after London, Bristol and York), but it was caught up in the governance of England during the fifteenth century.[11] A ready market for the exotic and the high-end, it became an unashamedly partisan 'Lancastrian' city, a love affair which began under Henry IV. In his son Henry V's reign, the city and its Benedictine cathedral priory helped fund the famous Agincourt campaign of 1415. In 1403, 1456 and 1459 it was host to three of only four sessions of parliament that were held outside London in the entire period 1400–1540; the fourth took place in nearby Leicester in 1413. No other city received such attention. During 1456–60, in the grip of growing civil strife, King Henry VI, Queen Margaret and the entire court virtually decamped to Coventry for long periods and the city was a whirl at the centre of Henry's febrile and ailing Lancastrian government, sucking in whatever the continent had to offer its guests. After Henry's first deposition, his usurper Edward IV held his Christmas court there in 1468. However, in the following thirty years the city went from boomtown to near basket-case before a brief revival of sorts.

Known for its soap production in the thirteenth century, Coventry's *raison d'être* became trade; it was already being dubbed 'beloved of merchants' in the 1320s.[12] However, first its international wool and later its woollen cloth trade were dependent upon imported dyestuffs and mordants carried chiefly by the Genoese. In its appetite for Lombardy woad – the dye for its sky-blue woollen cloth industry – lay the seeds of its later downfall. Archaeological work in Coventry, along with other towns and cities, highlights a populace hungry for what our European neighbours might produce, from fruit and wine to pots, pans and raw materials. Gentry, merchants, the civic authorities and monasteries all dabbled in long-distance trade, filling cellars with continental produce and stocking the drapery (which supplied the Royal Wardrobe) with shimmering silks, velvets and striking dyes of red, yellow and blue, especially the sky blue that became known as Coventry blue. Coventry offers useful insights into middle-England economic fortunes and popular appetites between 1400 and 1540.

Introduction

Meanwhile, anything could be bought in London. A huge majority of imports passed through the capital, enriching the city in the process. However, London is not the focus of this enquiry. It has never been representative of the whole country, being rather at the centre of its own economic vortex as the regular seat of government.

Archaeological enquiry at the principal ports often firstly confirms, and then expands what the histories already say and what one might expect – that they enjoyed regular overseas contact. These were the break-of-bulk points from which numerous imported goods fanned out. It is at such locations that archaeological assemblages show the greatest concentration of 'goods-in' from abroad, just before they became 'goods-out' and reached every corner of the kingdom in a far more representative scatter, along roads, rivers and trackways, guided by genteel envy, seigneurial aspiration, monastic fear of missing out and, as ever, a widespread mercantile wish to find new markets and make money. It is the archaeology of these eventual destinations, including Coventry, which indicates the extent to which England partook of what its continental neighbours, the fabled east and even the frozen north had to offer.

Sandwich, Southampton, Dartmouth, Plymouth, Falmouth, Bristol, Ipswich, King's Lynn and Boston sit at the top of a long list of ports with regular contact with our neighbours. Many more – and this book looks at some of them – had irregular contact, if only with smaller boats and a narrower range of imports, principally fish for local consumption. Most had their day in the limelight, but all were – and are still – constrained by their location, their access to the road network, existing preferences, the contacts of inland merchants and, most of all, the port facilities, not to mention the limits the sea itself placed upon each port. The sea is an unforgiving mistress.

Due to the limitations of the excavated data, this is very much a personal journey through four decades working on medieval archaeology and documents. History and archaeology are limited by which documents and sites survive, and which are selected for research. Again, the documentary choice is my own, mostly eschewing State Papers and highlighting some of the more obscure domestic and foreign records to show our trading partners' experiences of our shores and our seas. If I have misread or omitted something, the fault is mine. Greater detail always lies beneath the surface.

I

MOVERS AND SHAKERS

> *Your mind is tossing on the ocean*
> *There, where your argosies with portly sail,*
> *Like signiors and rich burghers on the flood*
> William Shakespeare, *The Merchant of Venice*,
> Act 1 scene 1

Travellers

How much English and Welsh Society knew of distant lands is difficult to gauge, but likely it was not very much – a little as hearsay, but most of it difficult to corroborate. During the thirteenth and fourteenth centuries there was a growth in what might be termed 'travel literature' in its broadest sense, but in England this amounted to fanciful tales such as the travels of the likely fictitious John Mandeville, whose author understood little of geography and believed almost anything he was told as he journeyed (or didn't journey) but recorded it anyway.[1] Others were more circumspect, such as the Irish friar Simon FitzSimon, whose more prosaic experiences within England and France are largely the result of his own observations. But these are for the most part men of their age, lacking consistency and obvious rigour in their observations.

Seas of Plenty

Traders, mariners and pilgrims were the greatest travellers of the ancient and medieval world, whether they lived in western and northern Europe, Scandinavia, or around the Mediterranean or the Holy Land, where the west met the Middle East, with another world beyond – to China, India and the Far East.[2]

Some people from these specific communities were accomplished and worldly travellers in the medieval era, but few ordinary folks in fifteenth- and sixteenth-century England and Wales travelled very great distances *routinely*. Armies of thousands crossed to France, and some occasionally travelled even further as crusaders, mercenaries or unwilling accomplices in the royal business of waging war for the realm. Plunder returned in unquantified shiploads, as did slaves and hostages in large numbers. Royal or other embassies and trade negotiators travelled as part of large groups, their passage and expenses paid by the Crown or interested nobility. Pilgrims too travelled long distances, but on tried and tested (although equally dangerous) routes. The first act of a pilgrimage was often to make a will.

Beyond these the principal travellers were merchants, along with masters, sailors, victuallers and all those who endeavoured

Tall tales of the sea abounded: a mermaid on a fifteenth-century misericord at St Lawrence's Church, Ludlow, Shropshire.

to carry people, animals and hard-bargained cargoes safely to their destinations. Mariners travelled most, and were always in great danger, but the vast majority probably saw little beyond the ports.

It is therefore highly likely that the most pervasive tales of travel to foreign lands came from the old seadogs who frequented the quaysides and taverns of three dozen English and Welsh ports and coastal towns, long after their seagoing days were done. From Chester to Bristol, Plymouth to the Solent, Winchelsea to Sandwich, Dover to King's Lynn and Boston to Newcastle, our coasts look unswervingly outwards every bit as much as they provide gateways into our interior.

Expanding one's horizons, or what one might term 'travel for the sake of it', is far from a modern preoccupation. In late medieval Europe there seems to have been a widespread curiosity and urge to become 'worldly'. Writing prolifically in the third quarter of the fourteenth century, the north Italian Christian 'humanist' Petrarch lauded the great knowledge-seeking travellers of antiquity (including legendary ones such as Odysseus and Aeneas) for their tenacious journeys. He was scathing when an old friend openly confessed his horror of any travel beyond the comforts of Paris, which he considered a kind of exile.[3] Petrarch (who was himself well-travelled) made a habit of keeping himself informed and was aware of the rise of England's star on the continent.

Generally there was wide-eyed amazement about foreign lands, as much at the preposterous as the genuine.[4] Even by the middle of the fifteenth century, tall tales of distant lands were informed at best by the earnest but often silly reports of the fictitious Mandeville's travels via southern Europe to the east and to Africa, Marco Polo's long quest in the Far East and the enduring tales of a lost Christian kingdom presided over by 'Prester John', variously located somewhere between the Hindu Kush and the

African interior.[5] There were even legendary Christian islands in the Atlantic for mariners to 'rediscover'.

There was, however, a lack of interest in cultures which held no prospect of trade or immediate profit.[6] In 1520, the great German engraver Albrecht Dürer expressed his amazement at an exhibition of Aztec treasure plundered from the New World. He was apparently unmoved by their sorry plight, reflecting a widespread indifference to foreign cultures except as a basis for trade.

Slavery

African slavery as the modern world has come to view it had hardly begun in the late medieval period. Certainly, slaves were taken and sold by most European cultures, but this was not the wholesale exchange of Africans to plantations in the New World which characterised the 'triangular trade' from the seventeenth century to the nineteenth. The Portuguese, backed by the Papacy in their search for African gold, began to take West African slaves from the middle of the fifteenth century and are thought to have shipped around 150,000 to Europe between 1450 and 1500.[7] Slavery was condemned outright in 1521 by Polydore Vergil in his *De inventoribus rerum*: 'By the Grace of God we are now nearly all brothers in Christ and citizens of the kingdom of God. While we have servants in our houses, they are not to be called slaves. Still less should slaves be possessed.' While Portugal and then Spain began their explorations of the Atlantic coast of Africa during the fifteenth century, seeking gold and a route around the Cape to the Indian Ocean, England's own Atlantic trade routes bore no comparison. It was not until the reign of Elizabeth I that England's stance on Africa changed, begging an initial appraisal and laying foundations for what would become the most heinous and reprehensible international trade in history, undertaken by most of western Europe's nations. We must be careful, however, not to transpose modern views onto the past. Each successive generation considers itself the most enlightened yet, and that seems unlikely to change.

Despite the opprobrium it might attract from parts of the church in their day, many good and bad traders alike dealt in slaves to some extent, and society did not necessarily think any worse of them for it. In continuity with the ancient world, Europeans regularly took slaves in chains when sacking cities, even as their societies were giving rise to the more enlightened views espoused by Polydore Vergil. In 1390 the English joined the French to aid the Genoese in a rare – and thus notable – joint military adventure, besieging the walled city of Tunis to help rid the Mediterranean of Barbary pirates. Although the pirates would soon return to harry shipping, the expedition was a triumph of close cooperation. Tunis fell and was brutally sacked. The English and French returned with up to 4,000 captives as slaves.[8]

It was not unheard of for mercantile families themselves to keep slaves. In 1437, Cataruccia, second wife of Michael of Rhodes, a senior mariner in the pay of Venice, and who knew England well, bequeathed her personal *'serva et sclava'* Maddelena de Rosia, whom she had bought with dowry money, to serve her brother for five years after her death. After that she was to be freed.[9] After Cataruccia's death, Michael remarried and when he wrote his own will Maddelena was described as a 'former slave'. It could be a similar story at the edges of the known world, where traders met only well-travelled merchants from even more distant spheres of influence. In the eleventh and twelfth centuries Abraham Ibn Yiju, a trader out of Fustat (Old Cairo), lived in India for seventeen years. There he married an Indian slave whom he freed and who converted to Judaism. In a wonderful turn of events, he returned to Cairo and brought decades of trading accounts and correspondence, which survived in the Cairo Genizah to be retrieved in modern times.[10]

The Renaissance brought into focus the revered classical world, which had run almost entirely on slavery. The so-called Enlightenment did not lead automatically to the discovery of a moral compass; rather it was the Industrial Revolution which gradually removed the need for enslaved muscle power and replaced it with engines and machines. It was to a growing extent steam power which relieved the lot of the slave. Former slaveowners then had the leisure to reflect on their treatment of their previous charges and a degree of shame crept in – for some, at least. For the rest, an overworked landless poor replaced the slaves, working for a pittance, and the worst excesses of the Industrial Revolution were facilitated.

Beyond the Portuguese, the northern Italian states took many slaves in the period covered by this book, often from the Black Sea coasts, and sold them mainly to the militaristic Mamluk rulers of Egypt, who maintained a steady demand. Likewise, many north Italian galleys, particularly Venetian ones, originally contained a fair number of slaves from their conquered dominions across the Adriatic and further inland, but by the early fifteenth century the number of those truly 'enslaved' was dwindling. Many were simply the sons of long-conquered peoples and acquiescent client-cities who sensed opportunity, a distinction perhaps lost on some. When they got to their destinations they mingled in the taverns and fleshpots of north-western Europe, losing plenty of money; such freedoms would perhaps have been denied to proper slaves, who were more likely to show a clean pair of heels given the opportunity. Around 1440 the rowers of Michael of Rhodes' generation lived all over Venice – mostly near the Arsenale, where the galleys themselves were built – although two-thirds of them were originally from the Adriatic coast or were Greek by birth, hailing from Rhodes.[11]

Over a period of 140 years things did change, however, and by the later fifteenth century there was a shortage of rowers in

Venice and its dominions, which were adversely affected by war and the press of a militant Islamic world. Casual remarks of the time suggest that ne'er-do-wells might also be impressed out of the gaols and into galley service. A Slavic rower's (or merchant's) tomb in the chancel of St Nicolas' Church in Upper Stoneham, Southampton, was probably financed by much-appreciated professional rowers, either long settled in Venetian pay or sailing under their own (perhaps Ragusan) flag.[12] For those who sadly died *en route* or in England during loading, there was a decent burial and a lasting memorial.

The Dominican friar Brother Felix Fabri, writing of his two pilgrimages to the Holy Land in 1480 and 1483, was in no doubt that the rowers he encountered on Venice's eastern run were slaves, drawn from Macedonia, Albania, Greece, Dalmatia and elsewhere, noting that some were Turks and Saracens and remarking on how

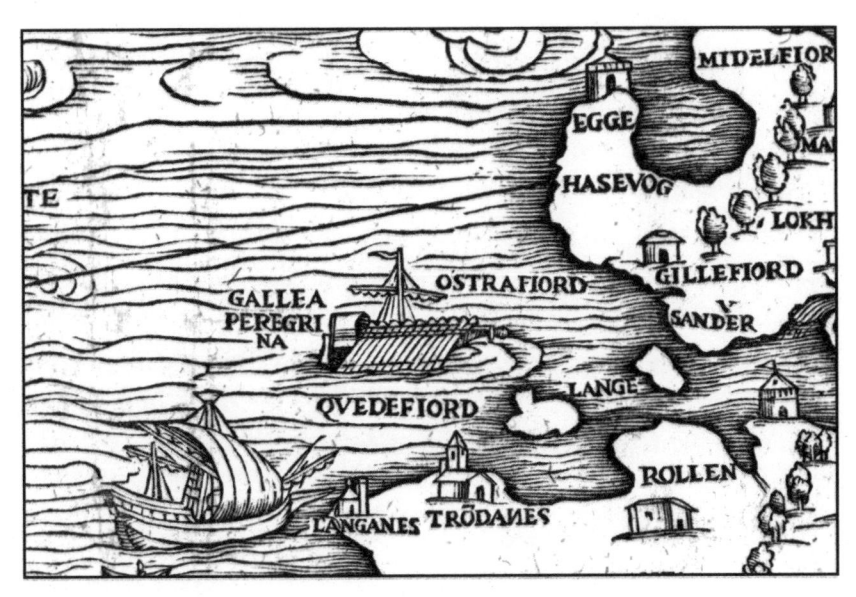

The north Italians were very fine mariners, but this 'wandering galley' may be rather off course at the mouth of a Norwegian fjord in Olaus Magnus' 1539 *Carta Marina*. Thanks to Uppsala University Library for permission to reproduce this detail.

many were polyglots: 'These galley-slaves are for the most part the bought slaves of the captain, or else they are men of low station, or prisoners, or men who have run away, or been driven out of their own countries, or exiles, or such as are so unhappy that they cannot live or gain a livelihood ashore. Whenever there is any fear of their making their escape, they are secured to their benches by chains.'

Noting that there was even an unofficial pecking order among them, he noted that 'they are all traders, and every one of them has something for sale under his bench, which he offers for sale when in harbour, and trading goes on daily amongst them'. That rowers' trading allowance, the so-called 'seamen's portion', will be discussed later in this book, as will their entrepreneurial spirit. Fabri, during his second pilgrimage, also observed that when they entered port the galley slaves carried their goods out of the ship into the marketplace to offer them for sale. They may have been under no illusion as to who was in charge, but some allowance was seemingly extended to them to better their lot, perhaps a dim light in an otherwise grim existence.

Many sailed along well-travelled sea lanes, although even the most popular routes were perilous. Each day, tides presented a fresh challenge. Thus, there was always an element of risk involved visiting one of the principal pilgrimage destinations, such as Rome, Jerusalem or Santiago de Compostela. Some land routes were available, but for an English traveller this meant merely exchanging the dangers of a long sea voyage for those of an initial overland trek across a restive and often antagonistic France.

Merchants and Passengers

Many English passengers crossed to France each day, and French passengers into England, together with other nationalities returning home. Some were part of embassies, trade delegations or royal prenuptial parties, while others were escorts to the gentry, spies (often *bona fide* merchants with additional royal instructions) or minor officials travelling under either English or French safe-conduct passes. Miscreants, too, fleeing the heavy hand of justice, might 'abjure the realm' and go into voluntary exile. They were able to choose their port of departure, with the Channel coast ports being preferred. Traitors in flight might cause the ports to be put on watch, or even closed for a time. For all these a direct crossing, embarking from the Kent coast and landing anywhere near Calais, might suffice. Alongside its notable fishing fleet, there was a regular foot-passenger service out of Rye, and another from Hythe in Kent to Calais, and this tiny port regularly supplied the English garrison at Calais right up to the reign of Henry VIII.[13] Calais had its own place in English lore even then, and thus the *Libelle* contains an exhortation to keep it (and its outer ring of strongpoints) safe in English hands, bemoaning that of late its profile had slipped,[14] just as France pressed hard to get control. Calais was finally lost in the mid-sixteenth century.

The experience of the Cistercian monk Lazarus of Padway (Padua) and his companion John (we do not know his surname) was unremarkable in that they crossed from Dover to Calais in 1471 by a regular service and returned the same way some months later, but their overall experience was far more noteworthy because on the outward leg (to Cîteaux in Burgundy) they could not land at Calais due to the military situation there, diverting instead to Boulogne. On their return journey they were delayed by adverse winds and narrowly avoided shipwreck, being blown around the coast to Sandwich. This was only a small diversion but took them perilously close to Goodwin Sands, a ships' graveyard so filled with unlucky sailors that over the centuries it has achieved international notoriety. Lazarus was evidently terrified by the whole experience.[15]

While most late medieval merchants known to us were men, there were certainly women too, of whom we even know some names. Witness the redoubtable Margery Russell of Coventry, who in 1413 received recompense for having lost £800 of goods to pirates of Santander.[16] In the Bristol customs accounts of Edward IV seven women are listed, including Elizabeth Jakes. Some, such as Joanna and Margaret Rowley, were widows acting on their dead husband's behalf, and importing wine, sugar oil, wax and woad, but there are others who made shipments in their own right. Alice Chester at Bristol was sufficiently wrapped in her city's trade that after her husband's death in 1470 she funded the construction of a dockside crane for her and her fellow citizens' benefit.[17] Foreign women took a firm hand as well, among them the Hanseatic trader Nell Bartholomuxdoghter, who shipped spice cakes ('patyns') into England, and her fellow continental trader Christiana Combemaker, whom we know simply as 'foreigner' but who, as her name suggests, ran a workshop making combs, likely of bone, to sell in England.[18] There was clearly considerable enterprise among a body of women merchants who made notable headway in a male-dominated society that took a view of the female condition that was rarely helpful and often dismissive.

Over the Horizon

It would be a strange book recounting English late medieval trade if no mention were made of Christopher Columbus in his own right. Columbus himself was an experienced Venetian sailor and was said to have been a regular visitor to Bristol from the 1470s. It has been said that there he heard stories of already discovered lands far to the west, which fired in him the desire to explore those waters himself. He was in Spanish pay when his tiny fleet of three ships found their way across the Atlantic and purportedly discovered the New World. It remains a moot point as to whether he *was* the first, and the early benefits of his 'discovery' of America are ever to be balanced against the dire health consequences of his arrival on the indigenous cultures he met. On such long voyages there was very little opportunity to import meaningful quantities of anything that might be of value to the Old World except gold or silver. Eventually such voyages would account for the introduction into Europe of tobacco, along with such staples as potatoes and tomatoes. It is unsettling to consider traditional Italian cooking without the presence of tomatoes, or English fish without chips.

Perhaps the only New World import that began to make a difference in the early sixteenth century was the pearl. Probing voyages by Amerigo Vespucci (after whom America *is* named) and early forays to the Caribbean opened the islands of Cubagna (Hispaniola and Cuba) to traders, who found oyster beds to rival anything in the Mediterranean or the Red Sea. Caribbean pearls began to arrive in Seville by 1508,[19] and the trade was quickly worth 75,000 ducats per annum to Venice, which already bought most of the European pearl stocks to sell on.

As Columbus' enquiries around Bristol suggest, England herself also had early explorers and the city was certainly in the forefront of the early search for the New World, however briefly. William Worcestre, writing in 1480, notes: 'On 15 July the ship of ... and John Jay the younger, of weight 80 tons, began a voyage from Kingroad at the port of Bristol to the island of Brazil to the west of Ireland, sailing over the sea ... and (John) Lloyd was the ship's master, the most knowledgeable mariner in all England. And news came to Bristol on Monday 1 September that the said ship had sailed the sea for about nine months [probably nine weeks], not finding the island, but was driven back by storms at sea to the port of ... in Ireland, for refitting the ship and replenishing the crew.'[20]

John Cabot, an adopted Bristolian, had settled there with his family and was something of a local celebrity, routinely recognised in the street. Like Columbus he was Venetian by birth and, in 1496 or 1497, as the Venetians themselves reported to the Signory in August of the latter year, was sent by Henry VII to seek new lands on the 'western passage'. He returned having found two 'very large and very fertile islands', including seven 'cities', 400 leagues (1,375 miles) from England. By October 1497 he had gone out and returned once more, having purportedly found the land of 'Grand Cham', a fabled ruler of China, 700 leagues (2,375 miles) distant. There he coasted for 300 leagues (1,031 miles) before landing, very diplomatically planting the flags of both England and St Mark (Venice). He was said to have seen no human beings, but when he found snares and some felled trees he and his companions returned to their ship in alarm. On their return they noted two islands off to starboard.[21] The voyage lasted three months.

It is not clear what places Cabot 'discovered' since his distances are far too short for the Caribbean. For the latter discovery the distance of 700 leagues would equate roughly to landfall near what is today St. John's, Newfoundland. Generally, this is thought to be what he saw and arguably represents his greatest achievement. For the islands seen on the way back the only real candidates are the Azores, although they formed an archipelago not unknown to Europeans at the time. The two islands with seven cities are a reference to a persistent but erroneous legend of Atlantis or Antilla – the isle of seven cities to which, long before, seven Portuguese bishops were said to have fled to escape a barbarian invasion. There they settled and their Christian descendants were said to have lived on unmolested. Like the legend of 'Prester John', a lost Christian king living in splendid isolation in India or China, the 'two islands and seven cities' myth endured and exercised the minds of travellers, gaining traction with each wishful but deluded generation.[22]

On his next voyage west, John Cabot and his company disappeared without trace. His son Sebastian claimed to have found the Northwest passage in 1509, although he probably ended up in Hudson Bay in Canada. Thereafter England quickly lost ground to the efforts of the Spanish and Portuguese, whose discoveries dominated the first half of the sixteenth century. The Pope had already established in a Bull of 1456 that Portugal was the 'preferred contractor' of the papacy in terms of exploration – sadly including slavery as an offshoot of its gold trade.[23] This ruling also gave Portugal a monopoly on trading with Saracens, excepting only weapons. It has been described as the papacy's 'Charter for Portuguese Imperialism'. Few nations took any notice, however, and eventually joined them anyway.

Some Englishmen Abroad

Three further purely English voyages of exploration warrant mention here.[24] In 1530 William Hawkins sailed the *Paul* of Plymouth (250 tons) down the west coast of Africa to Guinea to trade for ivory – but very much in the wake of the Portuguese. Then, in 1532 (roughly fifty years after William Worcestre's mention of such a place), he headed west to the coast of Brazil, a coastal land already apportioned by papal decree to Portugal – not that England took much notice. Leaving as hostage one Martin Cockeram, a native of Plymouth, he persuaded a local indigenous leader to return to England, where he became a celebrity at court. Although Hawkins returned some months later with his celebrity passenger, the Brazilian guest did not survive the journey. Fortunately, understandable fears for Cockeram's safety were not realised and he returned to tell tales of life among the indigenous peoples of Brazil.

In 1536, one Master Hore out of Gravesend took two ships, the *Trinity* (140 tons), and the smaller *Minion* to Newfoundland. Theirs was a company of 120, of which thirty were gentlemen, so it was neither a small party nor one of limited means. Misfortune followed, and although they encountered drifting icebergs and described seeing what may have been flamingos, they were unable to make the return leg in the time allotted. Their supplies dwindled and they found themselves at the point of starvation. They cast lots and resorted to cannibalism, the darkest fear of every stranded mariner. The survivors only made it back when they caught the attention of a French ship, which set them ashore at St Ives in Cornwall, no doubt damaging their national pride.

These were rare early English forays into far-flung lands, but by 1530 England had a much stronger trading fleet. Indeed, the experiences of Hawkins and Hore indicate that even small vessels were considered sufficiently capable for such long, hazardous voyages.

There is much mention in this book of the very professional and time-served foreign merchants, largely state-sponsored, who came to these islands with their holds crammed full. Alongside this, home-built shipping formed a considerable and steadily growing portion of that which used our ports throughout the period 1400–1540. Much of it passed without trace, in part because surviving documentation is scant until the Elizabethan period but also because it included a preponderance of smaller local vessels that rarely, if ever, troubled the tollhouses to record them. Few would have had official names, and their masters could barely be called merchants or travellers as they plied between neighbouring creeks, bays, coves and havens along our coasts. Smaller than cross-Channel vessels, most were perhaps of 10 to 20 tons.

We do, however, occasionally get strong glimpses of larger vessels and their masters. Eileen Power in 1937 highlighted the Celys family, whose six ships sailed out of five south- and east-coast ports, including London, in 1481, chiefly exporting wool: the *Mary* and *Mary Grace* of London, the *Christopher* of Rainham, the *Thomas* of Maidstone, the *Michael* of Hull and the *Thomas* of Newhithe.[25]

Around 1480, William Worcestre noted the ships in Bristol that had recently been built for the Bristolian merchant William Canynges (1402–74), who had 800 men working there, with 100 toiling each day in a rota. They were the *Mary Canynges* (400 tons), *Mary Redcliffe* (500 tons), *Mary and John* (900 tons), *Galliot* (50), *Catherine* (140), *Marybat* (220), *Margaret of Tenby* (200), *Little Nicholas* (140) and *Katherine of Boston* (220). He also mentions an unnamed ship of 160 tons lost off Iceland.[26] Perhaps using the same documents, Dutchman Willem Schellinks in 1661 published a list of the long-scrapped Canynges vessels but added the *Mary* (200 tons) and noted a ship in Ireland of 100 tons. He dated his list to 1474, which was the year of Canynges' death.[27]

Canynges had many concerns around our coasts and was registering his shipping in a number of different ports. Worcestre also chose to note those ships that drew over 50 tons that actually belonged to the city of Bristol in the year of his visit (1480). They were Mary *Grace* (300 tons), the *Trinity* (360 tons, and of which more later), *George* (200 tons), *Katherine* (180), *Mary Bride* (100), *Christopher* (90), *Mary Sherman* (54), *Leonard* (50), *Mary* (60) and the *George* (51). His text is incomplete and at least three others have garbled mentions.[28] We also know of the *Antony* of Bristol, from late in Edward IV's reign, which may have been one of these. It was lost in Bristol's Kingroad anchorage, a mere stone's throw from its home port, in 1488.[29]

William Canynges is without doubt the best known of the shipowners, not least since his house was also excavated some time ago, when it was discovered to be paved with fashionable encaustic tile floors which were moved to the British Museum *en bloc*. However, it is likely that every port had its equivalent of the Canynges family, each trading to some degree with the same continental partners, many of whose contacts lived in close proximity, although mostly gathered as small communities in the big towns and ports for their mutual welfare and safety. Their favour was sought by religious trading guilds and Italians and Germans were admitted regularly into such Guilds and Merchant Adventurer establishments from York to Coventry and Bristol to London.

Royal Influence – Civil Wars and Trade Wars

There were occasions when the attention of the king, whether welcome or not, changed the balance of power and the comings and goings of entire merchant fleets. For example, in 1415–18 England was at war with France and needed every ship it could get its hands on. The army in France also needed to be provisioned. King Henry V requisitioned hundreds of merchantmen from all over English ports and then doubled the number of vessels with a fleet drawn out of a dozen ports in Holland as well. This was to convey the king and his entourage to Calais and carry the troops across, while another fleet of fishing boats provisioned the army and another took his guest, Sigismund, King of Hungary and later Holy Roman Emperor, to Dordrecht. The whole exercise, out of Sandwich, had scores of merchant ships providing a ferry service for eighteen days.[30] It was perhaps, in Shakespeare's words, a 'fleet majestical'.[31]

The influence of England's kings on trade was huge. In a century which included wars with Scotland, Brittany, the Hanseatic League and France, the Wars of the Roses were almost the straw which broke the camel's back, and the stress they put on English and Welsh society was felt everywhere. Certainly the mercantile history of this country might have been more stable and resulted in greater wealth if it had not been for so much strife, but as royal and rebel armies criss-crossed the Midlands and the king reached abroad with a huge stick with which to beat his neighbours, he also tried, sometimes in vain, to maintain trading standards while giving vent to the most unpleasant xenophobia and racism against both Italians and Germans.

Such sentiments were akin to those expressed in the *Libelle* and hung around for most if not all the fifteenth century, reasserting themselves well into the sixteenth century. However, that is not to say it was all doom and gloom – there was regular and genuine inclusion of foreign merchants in civic life, as befitted their true value. They took part in civic processions and pageants, notably under Henry VIII (which also made them very visible to a restive populace). They also took part in royal occasions like coronations and even funerals, such as that of Henry VII's late queen, Elizabeth of York, who died in 1503: 'Companies of foreign merchants, French, Spaniards and Venetians, holding tapers, with the arms of their respective nations were also present.'[32] These occasions accounted for such quantities and variety of lavish cloth that they alone would have been sufficient to employ many of Italy's finest silk and velvet merchants.

Difficulty in improving trading standards was further exacerbated by the size of the war chest and the consequent parlous state of Crown and Exchequer finances. The celebrated move against France under Henry V, culminating in the 1415 battle of Agincourt and the siege of Harfleur, was hugely expensive, funded early on by Hanseatic loans and small but prominent lump sums from nobility. Sometimes cities contributed as well, predominantly London but also the likes of Coventry, where the Benedictine priory persuaded the Bishop of Worcester to open his purse.[33] Agincourt might have become *the* turning point if Henry V's successor, Henry VI, both in his minority and then in his own right as king, had not constantly waged war against France, even when the tide was turning. The result was an impoverished England for much of Henry's almost forty-year reign. Between the death of Henry IV and the last five years of Henry VI's reign, royal revenues fell annually by almost 70 per cent, while the yearly cost of financing Crown debts rose between 1433 and 1450 by 60 per cent. Despite all efforts, the books could not be balanced. Many highly regarded officials and gentlemen in royal service went unpaid for long periods and even the army was restive, needing regular war booty to keep it solvent. One case in point was Henry VI's king of arms, who went unpaid for nineteen years.[34] Only his family's relative wealth would have kept him solvent. The dearth of coinage had seemingly already set in during Henry V's reign. To speed up their manufacture, Henry V in 1422 had the *Peter* of London carry nine Norman master moneyers from Rouen to reinforce his English moneyers, who were already working flat out in the Tower of London.[35]

In the early fifteenth century the marketplace was swamped with Venetian small change, so-called 'galyhalpens', galley-ha'pennies or *soldini* – small coins barely a centimetre in diameter, carried by Venice's state-backed Flanders galleys for small purchases, and probably representing the pay or allowance of the rowers. Issued by the Doge of Venice, they were of poor silver quality compared with English coinage, which was in short supply. When the Exchequer raised the alarm, these coins sent England's customs officials into a flat spin. Strenuous efforts were made to search out galley ha'pennies and confiscate them before they left the ports; indeed, hundreds if not thousands were forfeit, but each year many more are found in excavation and by detectorists along the former routes of inbound and outbound merchandise. They go to show that the silver content of small change made little difference in the marketplace, where a coin was a coin.[36] For their part, so anxious were the Venetians to maintain good relations that they made sure that these coins were not carried on board by sailors the year after the Exchequer raised concerns.[37]

The nadir of Henry's reign in 1450 resulted in a countrywide uprising, Jack Cade's Rebellion, which the Venetians noted with some alarm: 'As that city [London] and the whole island of England is understood to be in great combustion, the galleys will run manifest risk.'[38] Amid all the national penury, it was the support of loyal nobles, gentry and those who wished to curry royal favour that kept the cash-strapped economy going. The city of Coventry, 'Lancastrian' through and through, repeatedly voted monies to the king and raised it by means of extraordinary city-wide taxes among its mercantile and artisanal community in

1424, 1430, 1434, 1444 and finally in 1461, before the fateful battle of Towton saw Henry VI exiled.

Edward IV took over a country in a parlous financial state that was not going to be easily redressed. In fact, Edward maintained a front of apparent indifference towards England's Italian partners, especially the Genoese, and the xenophobia which characterised Henry's reign merely continued. As if to underline the credentials of the coming Yorkist regime, the eminent historian and biographer of Edward IV, Charles Ross, said that Edward had some claim to be regarded as the first 'merchant king' in English history.[39] If only it were so simple! His two reigns were littered with inconsistencies and his financial policy, shot through with impractical xenophobic nonsense, came good only at the last.

Edward's two reigns were very distinct. The first, spanning 1461 to 1471, began with a focus on mopping up after the battles of Northampton (1460) and Towton (1461) left a tattered Lancastrian nobility largely leaderless but seriously disgruntled, with Henry banished to Scotland. It would take some parts of the land, such as Wales, many years to come into line, and then only with the help of a new breed of royal supporter and not a little bloodshed. Harlech, for instance, remained in revolt until 1468 when it fell to William, Lord Herbert, a relative newcomer to the king's table.

France's capture of Gascony in 1453 had created many problems of its own, and England's xenophobia was not the sole cause. In 1462 Louis XI, backing his kinswoman Margaret of Anjou (Henry VI's exiled queen), forbade the export of French goods and merchandise to England, while in a seemingly counter-productive move Edward then banned the import of Gascon wines to England, even under safe-conduct passes. This would have been terrible news for the southern ports of England and the ships' masters who had painstakingly negotiated annual French export licenses since 1453, and indeed for Gascon

French vineyards whose principal market for generations had been the thirsty English. For this reason alone, we might question how effective such restrictions were or could ever be. Indeed, despite an obvious and serious decline in the tonnage of wine landed through the 1450s and 1460s, it never dried up, devolving to intermediate foreign carriers from secondary ports. Gascon wine, bought by an Englishman, carried in a Spanish or Florentine ship and exported by a Hanseatic resident out of Bruges, is probably just one of many permutations that would not have raised an eyebrow but effectively sidestepped the royal tit-for-tat boycotts.

To consolidate England's position after the end of the Hundred Years War and the loss of Gascony, Edward negotiated thirty-year free-trade treaties with Burgundy and Brittany. These had limited success, since the terms of the former were more favourable to the Flemish, while the Bretons were also individually treating with France as their own neighbour. The marriage of Edward's sister Margaret to Charles, Duke of Burgundy in 1468 was a prestigious coup, lavishly celebrated as the wedding of the century, but the feel-good effects were neither widespread nor long lasting – and Edward had difficulties raising the dowry of 200,000 gold crowns, including 50,000 due on the wedding day itself, causing a two-month delay in the nuptials.

Edward pursued policies which were very pro-London, leaving other urban centres unheard and trailing, previous prominence counting for little. Being pro-London also meant robustly representing Londoners against Hanseatic embassies who continually lobbied for greater trading privileges, and which were supposed to grant reciprocity for Englishmen long settled as traders in the Baltic. This fine balance was usually taken by the English as a gross affront – reciprocity took the hindmost. Tit-for-tat sniping at each other's merchants was de rigueur and if widespread piracy by privateers was sanctioned, it was surely most acute between

England and the Hanse. The 1449 capture of the Hanseatic salt fleet in the Channel had been an English high-point, and meant open warfare on the high seas was inevitable. Edward IV's pressure on the Hanse made them prick up their ears and take notice. However, his heavy-handed approach alienated them more than it brought rewards. This was particularly so in the years 1470-74, when the Hanseatic presence in England was virtually withdrawn, with only Cologne breaking ranks and staying because, quite simply, the English market was too big a share of its income for it to do more than protest weakly. Cologne did, however, provide a back door to continuing negotiation with the Hanse as matters deteriorated. One contemporary chronicler stated that it was widely said 'that Edward was much to blame for harming merchandise'.[40]

Meanwhile the public purse was in a dreadful state, with the result that the wool staple at Calais compelled its foreign (often Hanseatic) customers to pay in cash, which could then be brought back to the Tower and melted down to be recast and minted into English coin. One of Edward IV's first major fiscal policies in 1464-5 had been to devalue the coinage and introduce a new series of gold coins – the ryal (or rose noble), worth 10s, and the angel, worth 6s 8d, along with half- and quarter-ryals and a half-angel (or angelet). The result was a beautiful set of new gold currency, but it came at a time when bullion was in short supply, and this remained the case. It did little to put new gold into circulation (gold ryals were the currency needed to pay the Danish Sound Toll, granting entry into the Baltic, and so they flowed out of the market with every English passage), but a consequent devaluation of the national coinage, by about 25 per cent, pushed up demand for English goods on foreign markets. It also made imports more expensive by comparison.

Florentine bankers played a major role in financing the Crown in these years, so any continuing anti-Italian stance was very unhelpful. Having lent Henry VI only £1,000 during his entire reign, Florentine loans to Edward before 1475 topped £38,000. The City of London, too, regularly gave very substantial help, pointedly aware of the king's growing favour.

If the 1440s and 1450s had seen the nadir of English xenophobia towards the Italians as Henry VI's faltering government sought scapegoats, with 'the views of hosts' putting resident foreigners under the restrictive eye of their landlords, Edward's Yorkist regime was scarcely better. In 1463, only his second year on the throne, Edward introduced an Act prohibiting the export of wool by foreign merchants. Designed to favour home-grown Englishmen in the carrying trade and boost English merchant shipping, it was a severe blow to the Italians. The following year he pronounced that finished manufactured goods from abroad, mainly clothes and metal wares, should be banned. It was another blow to the Italians, whose silks, especially from Genoa, were highly prized in England. In fact, Edward eventually became wholly cool towards Genoa, which had wasted no time at all in dealing with the short-lived government of the readepted King Henry VI during Edward's brief exile in Bruges between 1470 and 1471.

If Genoa, Florence and Venice's stars were waning over English waters, Italian commerce was far from done with English trade. In 1468 a treaty was signed with Naples which for the first time brought Neapolitan state shipping to Southampton, to lie alongside the vessels of its countrymen.

Edward's second reign, from 1471 to 1483, saw the culmination of the war with the Hanseatic League, already begun before the brief readeption of Henry VI. When it was concluded, the Hanse merchants managed to wrest numerous concessions from the Crown although Edward's pro-London stance meant he continued to take every opportunity to oppress them at the trading level. The Hanse only took occasional interest in the south and west of England, concentrating on London and the east coast where their new concessions meant that for the first time they owned outright their 'factories' in London, King's Lynn (hereafter Lynn), Boston and other port towns in a much stronger trading base. They retained primacy in Bruges, where in 1478 they opened a new headquarters. Although English interests in Antwerp markets were strengthening, it was not until the Portuguese broke the Venetian spice monopoly at Bruges and the Zwin inlet silted up in 1521 that Antwerp really came into its own.

Some debt relief was received when the late Henry VI's former queen, Margaret of Anjou, a broken woman after the deaths of her husband (in the Tower) and their son (at the battle of Tewkesbury), was ransomed by her French family after a brief stay in Westminster Abbey. That left Henry Tudor as 'thonely ympe' of his line to claim the throne for Lancaster, and he was whisked away to exile in Brittany.[41]

There was a gradual improvement in Crown finances, and by 1478 the worst was passed; there was even a surplus. One historian said of Edward that 'to rescue the crown from the financial abyss into which the Lancastrians had plunged it was no mean achievement. To die solvent was something no other English king had achieved for two hundred years.'[42] It is unlikely that England's trading partners in the Mediterranean and the Baltic would agree with the methods he used, but for their English counterparts a new generation of merchants would come to benefit.

Eleven statutes of the realm during Edward's first reign favoured English mercantile interests and those of industry. Seeking the support of such men at the start of his reign was a must after so many had followed the house of Lancaster and Henry VI, but to continue to seek their advantage over that of England's established continental partners was to assume that England's merchants and its merchant fleet were ready to take over from others who had been carrying for generations. They simply were not! In the same way, with a need for Florentine money, the king was in no position to alienate the Italians. When war with the Hanse muddied the northern waters, there was the potential for a perfect storm of anti-foreign feeling and legislation that would leave the people of England wearing rags, eating unsweetened hardtack and re-using the cast-offs of previous generations.

If England had won its war with the Hanse, which dragged on from 1468 to 1474, Hanseatic privileges would have disappeared. But in the score-draw which resulted, an embarrassed England was forced to compromise. In fact, by comparison with earlier times, in the late fifteenth century English interest in carrying Baltic trade was waning anyway. In the 1460s it was at a low ebb. At Bruges and Antwerp, tensions between Merchant Adventurers and Hanseatic traders was on the rise.

In Edward's last parliament of 1483 a poll tax was imposed upon resident foreigners, excepting Spaniards and Bretons and the Hanse, who were still feeling cocky after 1474. The Bretons were probably spared because Edward wanted Brittany to hand over young Henry Tudor, who was moved from safehouse to safehouse for twelve years.[43] There were diplomatic attempts to get Henry back and into English custody, and he made an abortive attempt to return to claim the throne. Henry was biding his time, and Brittany was mostly an unwilling negotiator.

The brief reigns of the ill-fated Edward V (1483) and the contentious Richard III (1483–85), beset by what has been described as 'hand-to-mouth financing', made little impact on the trade of the nation, other than to continue to hamper it.[44] Richard was particularly unhelpful to the Genoese, a factor which drew papal indignation (Pope Adrian IV himself was from near Genoa). Henry Tudor then returned in triumph from Brittany to become Henry VII (1485–1509), and it was this money-conscious king who turned a corner for English trade, although he too could never quite shake off a xenophobic national outlook and occasional acts of extraordinary whim that flew in the face of good trade. His confiscation of the Venetian state galleys in 1491 to ferry troops to Calais and Boulogne showed that he differed little from his Yorkist predecessors!

In 1491 Henry opened a wool staple in the Florentine city of Pisa, to the consternation of the Venetians, whose spies had seen it coming and who protested noisily. The Florentine state fleet had stopped coming to England by then, so the establishment of the staple represented an English attempt to carry to and from Florence what the Florentine state galleys had once carried for themselves. In 1491 the Venetians in London were deep in debt, so when they had their galleys sequestered, or were scurrilously implicated in a fire at the arsenal at Southampton, they could only offer weak protests.

It was during the reigns of Henry VII and his son Henry VIII (1509–47), no different to their predecessors in their tendency to bash England's neighbours, that the Hanseatic League began to look like a spent force. It had little to do with the two kings, however, and everything to do with a changing world. Once more there was a sudden influx of Venetian small change, which threatened much in the marketplace but probably did little more than ruffle the feathers of 'jobsworth' customs officials who set about confiscating whatever they found at the ports, just as their forbears had done more than a generation beforehand. Much slipped through.

If the parsimonious Henry VII husbanded his resources carefully as he steered England out of its former penury, Henry VIII squandered this legacy, continually warring against France. The 1520s saw him casting around for new shipping to bolster his own foreign ambitions, and his avarice for merchant ships stripped provincial ports of their best shipping in 1522–25, including foreign vessels.[45] Eventually, because of paranoia over French invasion, in the 1540s he built a chain of castles and blockhouses to protect ports and coastal trading centres, but all too late.[46] Henry's devaluation of the coinage, combined with rampant inflation and petulant outbursts, conspired with events on the continent to ensure the great Italian galleys dwindled. The Flemish and English markets were by then just too unpredictable, and the Mediterranean world demanded Venice's undivided attention as more local threats verged on the existential.

By the 1520s, England's own overseas trade – in its own ships – was growing. Gradually it eroded Hanseatic privileges, since there seemed little purpose in the Hanse paying lower duties than the English and undercutting the Merchant Adventurers, whose name really meant 'Merchants who ventured overseas with calculated risk' – effectively risk-taking venture capitalists. In 1538, all foreign merchants were given customs parity with the English without exception. The Hanseatic position in the Baltic never again took precedence.

In terms of politics, France and Brittany were in a dance of etiquette which saw them pool their futures in a dynastic marriage between Anne of Brittany and Francis I, King of France, in 1514, theoretically ending Breton independence. The north Italian states, meanwhile, met with disaster after disaster in their Mediterranean world, shrinking under the growing influence of an expansionist Islam. Christianity was increasingly beset with quarrelling as northern European Protestants flexed new-found liturgical muscles, with religious conflicts beginning to break out. At the same time, the papacy had put its eggs in the basket of Portuguese and Spanish exploration, seeking new souls and sources of silver and gold; the Catholic God had new worlds to conquer and religious wars to finance. In southern Germany, Catholic Bavarian cities grew aggressive and took a greater share of northern markets. Nuremburg and its neighbours became as great a trading hub as their former European cousins had at Bruges and Lübeck, by then on the frontier of the Protestant Reformation. The balance of trading power shifted markedly.

As for world geography, the discovery and increasing exploitation of the Americas simply meant that the former Baltic world gradually became a sideshow as Transatlantic trades were established by conquest and colonisation, from fishing off Newfoundland to goldmines in the Americas and pearl fisheries in the Caribbean. A new trading world simply overtook the Hanse, barely glancing back in Magellan's wake as it sailed into new ventures, new wars and new controversies.

2

'CHERYSSHE MARCHANDYSE'

The gift of being near ships, of seeing each day
A city of ships with great ships under weigh;
The great street paved with water, filled with shipping
And all the world's flags flying and seagulls dipping.
                                John Masefield, 'Biography'

'Cherysshe marchandyse' – so exhorted the embittered writer of the *Libelle*. His invective was designed to encourage, but he did so by launching a diatribe against almost all the foreign agencies that imported goods and foodstuffs into this country. He was almost certainly a merchant or trader himself, but one unprepared for the hard competition of business, in which success is never assured and often elusive. Trading privileges were hard won, often fleeting and subject to swings in national, regional or even seigneurial mood.

The writer mentions each foreign importer by nationality in a list of subjects, targets for anger and resentment, which seem to have been considerable; sometimes his thinly veiled xenophobic asides help us picture the trading nadir of early fifteenth-century England. This was a long period of fluctuating fortunes punctuated by civil war on our own soil and wars with our neighbours, who had their own conflicts with each other as well, making for very tenuous trade routes across stormy seas. There were times when supplying England with all that it needed seemed improbable.

Spain and Flanders

'Oute of Spayne,' wrote the author of the *Libelle*, came:

> Bene falcons, raysyns, wyne, bastarde and dates and liycorys, syvyle oyle and also graine. White Castell [Castilian] sope and wax is not in vayne. Iron wolle, wadmole, getefel, kydefel also (for poyntmakers [pinners] full nedefull be the ij). Saffron, quicksilver, which Spaynes marchandy is into Flanders shipped craftylye unto Bruges as to here staple fayre. The havene of Sluys they have for her repayre which is cleped the Swyne [Zwin], thru shyppes guydynge where many wessell and fayre arne abydynge ... And when these sayde marchants discharged be of marchandy in Flandres neare the sea, then they be charched again with marchandy that to Flanders layeth full rychelye fine cloth of Ipre [Ypres], that round is better than owen cloth of Courtryke [Courtrai], fine clothe of all colours, moche fustyane and also linen clothe. But ye Flemyngis, if ye be not wrothe, the grete substance of youre clothe at the fulle, ye wot ye make hit of oure Englishe wolle.[1]

The Spanish produce that made its way into England was relatively straightforward. Although in the 1430s one can see there was already direct competition with some English products, Spain's fine climate enabled production of so many fruits that were impossible to grow in England.

For England the supply of Spanish fruits and wine were paramount. Spain's raisins had a reputation which went back centuries, and its southern harvest of oranges was expected in time for Christmas. Added to these were pomegranates, lovingly known in fifteenth-century English as 'pound-garnets' in simple allusion to the look of the sliced-open fruit, with seeds like a fistful of gleaming garnets. Spanish iron and finished steel came through Bayonne in France, while the finest Spanish leather came from Cordoba, giving us the name 'cordwainer' for one who works with high-quality leather.

The mention of 'quicksilver' (mercury) may indicate a market among would-be alchemists (although it was also used in refining silver from its host lead ores). Among imports found at several southern ports and at a number of monastic sites such as Bermondsey Abbey, as well as far inland at Coventry, are small, distinctive mercury jars, usually from Spain.[2] It would seem that this, among other things,[3] could be bought directly from Spain but also in Flanders (but not necessarily from Spanish traders). The Spanish (and others) seem to have been selling to everyone, giving the English little chance to sell on and make a profit. There may also have been some price-fixing going on.

The list of Flanders' own produce into England is the most eclectic of all and is the result of Flanders not being a great producer but having the great north-European trading hub of Bruges at its head, served, as the *Libelle* indicates, through its outlying port-town of Sluys and the Zwin inlet. The powerful Hanseatic League merchants had a base at Bruges and their relative control of many north European markets meant that almost anything could be had there, although it might have passed through two or three different ships' holds to get there: 'Bere (Low Countries), bacon, osmund (Swedish iron), copper (Poland and Sweden), bowstaves (Austria and Romania), stele (both Germany and Spain), wex (Poland), pettreware, grey, pyche, tarre, borde (Danzig), flex, Coleyne threde (Cologne), fustian, canvas (probably Breton), corde, bokerame, silver plate, wegges (ingots) of silver and metalle.'

While all the trading nations of Europe sent their wares to Bruges and later (to a lesser extent) Antwerp, by means of most carriers, they also sent their merchants there to buy things for distribution and selling on back at home. Thus, Venetians or others might buy foodstuffs in Bruges to sell in England. Equally, English carriers might go to buy direct, and there was an English Merchant Adventurers' base in Antwerp from 1421, with others at Middleburg from the 1380s. Then there was established 'The English House' in Bruges, one of a collection of national establishments set up to represent traders from their own country or state as a sort of embassy or consulate – a permanent trade legation, as it were, along the lines of the Steelyard, the Hanseatic League's London headquarters. The printing pioneer William Caxton resided here for the English for some years in the 1460s, soaking up the latest advances from Germany and the Low Countries, and brought the new art of printing back when he accompanied his king, Edward IV, on his return to England after a brief exile in Bruges in 1470–71.

Bruges, like almost no other city, existed for commerce. It enriched the Hanseatic merchant class and brought wealth to its master, the Duke of Burgundy. The sister of Duke Philip the Good had married the Duke of Bedford, regent to the young (Lancastrian) Henry VI. Later, the hand in marriage of Duke Charles the Bold attracted Margaret, the sister of Edward IV, in a sumptuous wedding in 1468, securing the duke as Edward's most influential brother-in-law, a saviour in exile who eventually facilitated Edward's second reign.[4] With England wracked by civil war between the royal houses of York and Lancaster, Bruges was literally and metaphorically in bed with both sides across two generations.

The Hanse was pre-eminent at Bruges, where it maintained the most eminent of its four principal *kontors*, or trading hubs. Until 1478 the Hanse often traded out of the Carmelite friary on Ezelstraat, but in 1478 a new headquarters was completed at the eponymous 1 Oosterlingenplein (Easterlings Square). The Hanse warrants its own distinct entry in this book, although regular mention of the incomparable Bruges is an unavoidable corollary of study of both the Hanse and everybody else's trade with England. The presence of the Hanse in a few English towns is notable (for all, see below). It represented a trading association – or what we would now call a cartel – of 'German' cities and ports; however, they were not in any sense German as we understand it today. Many modern European nations had not coalesced at all, some being city-states, kingdoms, duchies, margraves and others being vassal states under another's control. The Hanse stretched from what is today Germany north-west to Norway and across the Netherlands and east to Poland, the Baltic republics and Russia. Despite this vast spread, they formed a strong and influential trading unit which 'looked after its own' and very heavily influenced northern European trade when and where it could.

Many merchants converged on Bruges at four distinct times of the year to attend the great seasonal markets: the Pask Mart in spring (Easter), the Synxon Mart in summer around St John's Day (25 June), the Balms Mart or Bammys Mart around St Remy's Day (28 October), and finally the Cold Mart in winter, before the sea lanes were affected by snow and ice and the river and canal to Sluys and Damme froze solid.[5]

Sluys, which now sits on the Dutch side of the border with Belgium, and Damme were both ports with extensive facilities, outliers to the city of Bruges, the former on the coast at the time, the latter a fully functioning inland port and a stopping point along Bruges' canalised access to the sea via the Zwin inlet. When the Zwin silted up in 1520–21 it was a catastrophe for Bruges, which saw much of its trade migrate to Antwerp, a city already on the rise. Bruges is said to have gone into a long sleep at that point (to the benefit of its unrivalled stock of surviving historic buildings).

During Bruges' fifteenth-century heyday, although canals extended right into its heart, many oceangoing ships, unless they

'Cherysshe Marchandyse'

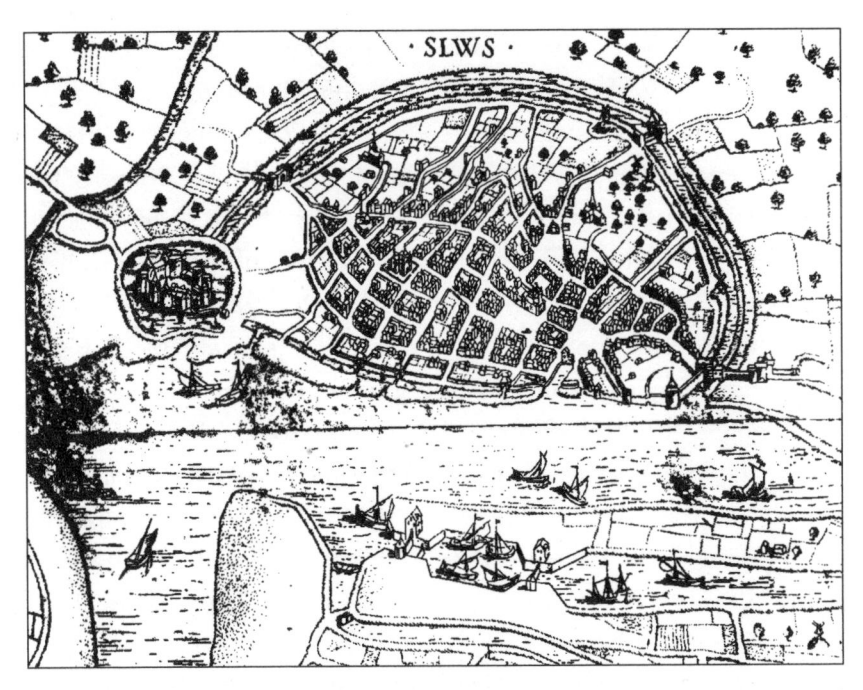

Sluys: the original port of Bruges. Tidal approach, locks, stockade (basin) and bypass channel, from a map by Marcus Geerhaerts, 1562.

were narrow in beam and drew a very shallow draught indeed, generally proceeded no further than Sluys or Damme, where berths and unloading facilities were provided. At Sluys there was also a 'stockade', or what might be better understood in maritime parlance as a 'basin'. This was useful for loading or unloading very bulky or abundant goods when a pass to proceed to Bruges was not forthcoming, either because the quantities were too great or because the vessel's passage was undesirable, perhaps if the cargo was smelly or they had hook anchors, which were banned beyond Damme as they would pierce the puddle-clay linings of the canal. Rowed lighters and horse-drawn barges plied the route between the three centres and many vessels were under sail. Cranes stood on the wharf ready to unload. At Damme alone, it is estimated that each year 28 million herring were unloaded, principally for Hanseatic consumers. All the fish would need salting or smoking there before they were sold, and a dedicated industry grew up alongside the wharf at Damme to serve this market.

The wide range of items to be had from Flanders betokens the full reach of the Hanse through Bruges. Beer was a mainly local product, from Flanders and Artois, and it was growing in reputation across England where the distinctive brownish-grey 'Raeren ware' mugs accompanied the beer in large numbers. With their upright rims, globular bodies and flared, thumbed pedestal bases they are very common in the urban archaeological record of the late fifteenth and early sixteenth centuries. Theirs is the form seen in paintings by Peter Breughel the Elder such as *The Peasant Wedding*, which now hangs in Vienna. They were much copied by potters in Cologne, Siegburg and other German towns as export items for an England that was increasingly thirsty for beer, while Swedish iron ingots with the distinctive name 'osmund' – which appears frequently in port books such as Boston's from the 1390s – could be had direct from Sigtuna and Gotland. But for an English trader there was considerably less risk to shipping at Bruges, providing Hanseatic prices were not too high after commodities had changed hands several times.

Copper was always in demand, and most of it came to the English market all the way from eastern Europe. In all, 60 per cent of the copper in medieval Europe came from the Tatra mountains, travelling down the Vistula to the coast, where Danzig (now Gdansk, Poland), a Hanseatic partner city with strong ties to English commerce at Lynn, maintained a high stake in the trade.[6] On occasion, with such a long supply route there was a dearth of copper available and in the archaeological record it is not uncommon to find numerous pieces of broken copper alloy vessels and utensils gathered together in a bronze-caster's 'hoard', such as beneath the floor of a house in Derby Lane, Coventry, ready for smelting and re-casting, much of it for trinkets, badges and buckles. Fundurs (foundrymen) lived nearby. It was said that

'Cherysshe Marchandyse'

Danzig owed all its splendour to its English trade, and copper was no small part of that, along with wax, building and shipbuilding timber ('borde', above) and bowstaves.[7]

Danzig was the Hanseatic port for much of the wax imported into England and also on the Bruges list, above. Although it leaves no evidence in the archaeological record, wax provided better-quality candles which illuminated ten thousand churches and hundreds of monasteries and nunneries of a dozen orders across England and Wales. Tallow (animal fat) might be used by the ordinary householder, but it was smoky, smelly and left a sooty mess. Wax was always preferred. Even as early as the first decade of the fourteenth century, England imported 665 kilograms of wax – a great deal considering its lightness! Sudden shortages in England gave rise to accusations that the Hanse was holding back supplies to drive up the price. The merchants were acquitted, but barely.[8]

From the Carpathians, even further away, came bowstaves in large numbers, for both longbows and crossbows. The old idea of English bowmen using English yew bows is largely a fallacy. Across England there were simply not enough of the painfully slow-growing yew trees available for cutting for our many armies. Carpathian yew bows became particularly common a hundred years after the *Libelle*, when Henry VIII, in an age of compulsory archery practice for young men, and building up his army against the French, sought them as a named subsidiary cargo alongside wines in Venetian galley holds. They were shipped in barrels and crates, and their careful freightage is always mentioned since they might easily be damaged by rough handling and exposure to the sea.

Steel from Germany and Spain was of the highest quality and represented the best of the steelworker's art, being reserved mainly for armour and weapons. Smaller items were imported as well, usually to order from continental makers. From Kingswell Street, Northampton

Spanish silver-inlaid steel rowel spur from Kingswell St, Northampton. Scale 2 cm. Photo courtesy of Museum of London, Northampton.

comes an exquisite rowel spur of steel inlaid with silver skulls and skeletal figures lined up head to foot. Judging from its size it was a lady's spur, from a small boot, and its loss must have been dispiriting to its wearer. It is probably Spanish in origin but is just as likely to have been bought at Bruges or another market in the Low Countries.

Portugal

Throughout the fifteenth century the Portuguese played a small but not insignificant role in supplying England, mainly with fruit and wine.[9] In the first year of his reign (1400), and just in time for Christmas, Henry IV indicated his liking for Portuguese wines when he paid the merchant Oliver Martin for ninety-six pipes of Algarve wine, specifically set down as 'for the king's use'.[10] Political relations with Portugal were particularly close at the start of the fifteenth century, if not always smooth, and for the most part they only improved, commensurate with the range of goods and foodstuffs Portugal had to offer – and in return, of course, that country's need for English wool and tin. Long before Portugal piqued European interest in the late sixteenth century with sugar and slaves, it had a flourishing trade with England in which 200 to 500 tuns (1 tun = 256 gallons) of Portuguese wine passed through Bristol annually, and in some years London and Southampton took the same amount. Some 85 per cent of Portuguese ships in English harbours were out of either Lisbon or Oporto.

Like all our partners, Portugal's trade was influenced by English politics, be it Anglo-French, Anglo-Castilian or Anglo-Burgundian. To some extent its shipping could stay out of northern troubles since almost direct routes steered her well west, taking in Ushant, the Scilly Isles, Cape Clear in Ireland and Cape Ortegal or Finisterre in Spain. These direct routes largely avoided the storms of Biscay, the rocky coast of western Brittany and the pirates who frequented the inshore waters and plagued all shipping, let alone the Crown-sanctioned and violent maritime exercises in which England took part. The Portuguese also traded in Ireland, often via Bristol, and their royalty married into the ducal house of Burgundy in 1429, encouraging trade with Bruges and the Low Countries. However, it was Burgundian embargoes on English cloth which gave rise to the parlous situation in 1436–39 when the *Libelle* was written.

The author of the *Libelle*, notes Warner,[11] writes of Portuguese imports around 1436:

> They bene oure frendes wyth there commoditez, Here lande hathe oyle, wyne, osey, wex and grayne, Fygues, reysyns, hony and cordeweyne, dates and salt hydes and such merchaundy.

Childs notes[12] a near-contemporary document in the British Library which greatly expands upon this list:

> Also in Portyngale the cheffe merchaunyse is swette wyne that growe within the land, that is to say bastard, capryke

osey, raspey, reputage, and land wyne; there is also oyle olyffe growing whiche is most holsumyst for mann ys mete and medicus, and wher ytt is old yt is good woll oyll; ther is also wax, hony, datys and figs, poundgarnett, oryngys, lytomse powyders; there is a mountayne that is called Rock Seyntoure [Mt Cintra] and there on growth grete plente of the beste grayne that is to grayne cloth with; ther is also grete salt.

With this list in mind, it is worth noting that research shows sailings took place all year round but that summer sailings tended to predominate. There was also a flurry of Portuguese arrivals in English ports each December as mountains of fruit and sweet wines were brought in for the Christmas season.

To some extent the frequency of Portuguese shipping in English ports decreased during the middle decades of the fifteenth century, largely because of volatile political situations and England's frequently hostile dealings with other neighbours, and sometimes suppliers too. Despite a strong three-way trade between Portugal, England and Burgundy (via Flanders), the Burgundian embargo on English cloth forced the Portuguese to pick a side.

The tide turned once more from around 1470, partly due to a better political situation but surely also as the changing market accounted for other carriers of similar produce, such as Florence, whose journey was always that much longer and fraught with difficulty.

By the end of the century the list of goods had lengthened still. Oranges at this time may have begun England's enduring love affair with marmalade, perhaps at that stage little more than a useful and enticing way of preserving that fruit which might otherwise not survive a long, rough sea passage before being distributed inland from Bristol, Dartmouth, Southampton and London, the favoured ports of the Portuguese. Others took Portuguese produce direct, right around to East Anglia, but Southampton was their favourite. In the 1490s their trade surged with Portuguese shipping, by which time Portugal was the principal supplier of sugar, rather than any north Italian state. Bristol too relished what Portugal sent and its need for the shipping was great compared with London; the city took almost a fifth of its wine from Portugal, whose vineyards supplied 600–700 tuns annually at that stage.

Until the 1480s Portugal rarely carried goods for anyone else, something which is usually noted of Basque ships from either Spain or south-western France, but they were not closed to possibilities and in that year the Portuguese did carry alum for Genoese merchants, at a time when the supply of that material was woefully unreliable and the Genoese star was waning.

It was, however, at the very end of the fifteenth century that Portuguese influence in international shipping to northern Europe suddenly made a huge difference, for they were the ones who single-handedly dealt a massive blow to Venetian trade with Flanders and England.

From the 1470s, little by little, the Portuguese had been sending exploratory fleets south down the coast of west Africa in search of gold. Eventually they rounded the Cape and began settling trading posts up the east African coast; some later became colonies, including what is now Mozambique. The explorers gradually struck north and east until they forced a sea passage to India in the 1490s, also settling traders in Ethiopia along the way. The result was to break Venice's centuries-old overland spice trade. Cairo, Alexandria and the Middle Eastern land routes were bypassed completely, and the Portuguese position was initially weakened by the indignant sultan building ships at Suez specifically to attack these new upstarts.[13]

In March 1504, the flustered Venetian ambassador in England announced that five Portuguese barques had arrived at Falmouth with 380 tons of spices from Colocot (India).[14] By the following

August, Venetians in Southampton and London were complaining that their spices were now worthless at Antwerp by reason of the Colocot glut. Only one year after that, at the beginning of 1506, Venetian spies reported that some very big Portuguese ships were anchored in the Netherlands: 'Three very fine ships belonging to the King of Portugal, lately built in Holland for the Calicut voyage, are now in the port of Middelburg, of 1000-, 700- and 300-tons burden. They are to join 40 Spanish ships of 150–400 tons, fully provisioned. Many noble guests are aboard, plus 200 German troops, well-armed.'[15]

This was clearly no half-hearted measure, and it is clear that the Spanish, too, had realised they could get favourable trade in India despite the Colocot voyages being long, expensive and very dangerous; hence the presence of heavily armed German mercenaries, who were probably protecting Hanseatic interests in the cargo. Around this time, it was reported that 104 ships had embarked on such voyages and only seventy-two had returned. Nineteen were known to have sunk; of the rest there was no news, and they were presumed lost, sinking somewhere quietly out of sight of their compatriots, prey to pirates or the victims of storms.[16]

The Portuguese had invested too much effort to give up their newfound advantage. The crestfallen Venetian ambassador in London wrote in April 1514, 'Two Caravels. Each of 550 tons burden, arrived London from Calicut. Carrying mostly pepper, ginger and sandalwood, but had not a single pound of cloves, nor was there an ounce of cloves in all Lisbon.'[17] It seems he had still room to berate his competitors for neglecting to ship cloves, but it was hollow gloating as the damage was done. In a few short years the Portuguese had all but ruined Venice's previously unchallenged monopoly on spices, and they began the sixteenth century as one of Europe's growing maritime powers, largely at Venetian expense.

Brittany

During the fifteenth century Brittany remained independent of France, and perhaps partly as a result it attracted the separate and carefully directed ire of the writer of the *Libelle*. It was not until 1514 that Brittany merged with France when Anne, Duchess of Brittany married King Francis I of France.

Listed in the *Libelle* are the principal exports of Brittany to England: 'Salt, wynes, crestclothe and canvasse.' That may seem matter of fact, but the writer had little good to say of Bretons, who were, it relates, 'gretteste rovers and the gretteste thevys',[18] adding that 'Brytayne is of easy reputasyone and Seynt Malouse turneth hem to rebrobacione'.[19]

Clearly no love was lost between English merchants and their Breton counterparts, with the men of St Malo regarded by the English as being of the lowest calibre. Relations were certainly not helped by a sudden and very destructive raid in which the Bretons torched Plymouth and Dartmouth in 1403. English reprisals were swift, however, one William Wilforth seizing forty ships of all sizes with their cargoes of iron, oil, tallow and 1,000 tuns of wine out of La Rochelle. The stricken Breton ships were set alight and the land for many miles around Penmarc'h and St Mathieu was plundered.[20] It may have been Bretons who then plundered Portland in 1404 and 1405, although many reports simply refer to 'French' attackers, making little distinction.

It is a shame Brittany had such a reputation by the 1430s, for it was this duchy that would become the unwitting saviour of the English Crown before the end of the fifteenth century. Although it was the place of young Henry Tudor's incarceration, it was also a safe haven for the fugitive claimant as he waited out the last years of Yorkist rule in preparation for ending the Wars of the Roses, whereupon he would ascend the English throne as Henry VII in 1485. He and his closest companions were moved around and variously held securely as hostages in Vannes on the south coast and at the castles of Largoët and Josselin for some years.[21] Despite

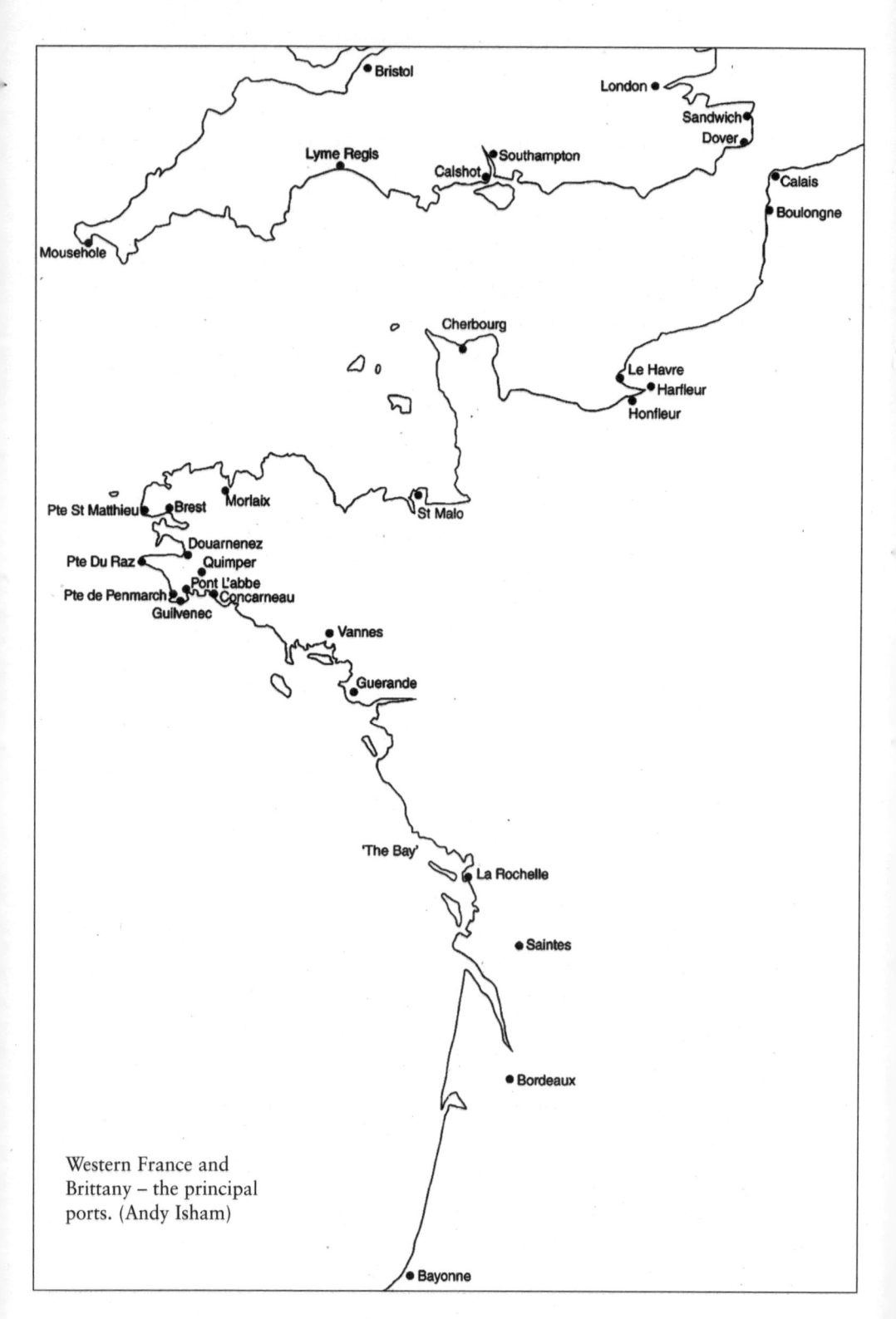

Western France and Brittany – the principal ports. (Andy Isham)

the privations of life in exile, Henry and his followers were initially welcomed and did nevertheless form a personal attachment to people and places in Brittany which transcended politics.

Imports from Brittany may have been relatively few, but they were very important. Wine is not an obvious product of that area today but it is mentioned in a number of places, such as in respect of Abbot Thomas Pennant who, at Basingwerk Abbey, a Cistercian house in North Wales, kept a sumptuous table, serving wines from Aragon, Castille and Brittany, presumably catering for the stream of pilgrims to nearby Holywell and across to Bardsey Island and back.[22]

Salt was a different matter. It was needed for every kitchen in every city, town and village market that was more than a few hours from the coast. It was the bulk necessity of all food preservation, notably meat and fish, and huge quantities came out of the Breton *marais*, a salt marsh converted into many hectares of shallow foreshore brine-pans, and then through Brittany's south-eastern port-market at Guerande, still a magnificently walled and moated medieval town today, its defences both proclaiming and protecting its salty fare. Often the salt was taken on board as a secondary cargo, originating in coastal areas largely unaffected by the armies of the Hundred Years War, although some did travel to the Ile d'Oléron and Poitou for salt alone. This was a route which might keep the wine supply flowing when England and France were at loggerheads, as they so often were. Sailcloth and canvas were provided from towns in the interior, such as Locronan. Brittany's thriving sailcloth industry went on to equip the French Napoleonic navy at the turn of the nineteenth century.

England had its own coastal salt production, particularly in Essex and Hampshire, but it is thought that it was affected, particularly after the Black Death, by workers drifting away to more lucrative industries in the cities, particularly the cloth trade.[23] English salt had also been produced for centuries in pans across Cheshire and Worcestershire. However, there was never enough to supply the country's needs. Scarborough, Hull and Lynn were the main import points to start with, but by 1450 some 70 per cent came in through London, where Billingsgate took in mountains of salt. During the fifteenth century more than 200 English merchants were solely engaged in the Biscayan salt trade.

Breton salt was of course hugely attractive to others, including the Hanseatic League, who maintained an entire salt fleet in Brittany – the so-called 'Bay Fleet' – which took advantage of the duchy's many small south-coast port inlets and creek anchorages, such as Concarneau, Pont l'Abbé, Guilvinec and the bay anchorage and gentle landing beach at St Gildas-de-Rhuys. However, along with Guerande it was the town at Vannes on the Gulf of Morbihan which commanded most regular traffic. On the north coast, St Malo (mentioned by the *Libelle*), Dinan, St Brieuc, Paimpol and Morlaix had greater local control.

The Atlantic-facing Breton coast is wild and windswept, with some of the most treacherous rocks and mountainous seas to be tackled anywhere on the northern passage from Biscay or the Mediterranean. It is the western extremity of the basin which takes in the north Breton coast, the west coast of the Cotentin peninsula, the Channel Islands and some of the south coast of England. Together, due to the Coriolis effect, it boasts the second-highest tidal range in the world, up to 10 metres. At Guilvinec a graveyard of small ships from the intervening centuries attests the ongoing temper of this rocky maelstrom. Small Breton coastal churches wear the badge of their mariner congregations – small but intricately carved ships in relief – on their wind-eroded architecture, as at St Nonna, Penmarc'h. Out at the Pointe de St-Mathieu, at the extreme tip of Brittany's three Atlantic-facing fingers, still stands the medieval monastic 'lighthouse' of the same name, the first of three to stand there, originally manned by the monks from the Benedictine priory of St Mathieu, who perhaps occasionally might act not as saviours but wreckers if wider Breton sensibilities had been sufficiently

Fifteenth-century great ship, one of a number carved in relief on the granite churches in and around the port of Guilvinec, Brittany. Here St Nonna, Penmarc'h, Finisterre (29), France (2010).

affronted. No stretch of the Breton coast was safe unless guided kindly by those who knew it.

When in 1449 the English seized the entire Hanseatic Bay Fleet at sea, with its cargoes fully loaded, the loudest protests came from the Hanse; the Bretons were quiet as they had already been paid for this massive annual consignment, which would have been headed north towards the Zwin inlet near Sluys and the herring market at Damme, just down the canal from Bruges.

Scotland and Ireland

'Felles, hydes and of wolle the fleese' are described by the *Libelle* as deriving from Scotland. This list draws no further comment from the author, for none might be considered luxuries or fripperies. They are very much of the ilk that England too provided to its neighbours, including Scotland, suggesting a trade of convenience as regional demand dictated. Such trade was undoubtedly impeded by the incessant warring between the two kingdoms.

Ireland is not specifically lambasted for its trade with England, possibly since it was considered an extension of the English Crown's dominions, with all the problems that entailed. Nevertheless, Ireland's trade with England was notable and there was much interchange between the Irish and the merchants of Bristol and, to a lesser extent, Chester, Liverpool and North Wales. Many English monastic houses had lands in Ireland, not least St Augustine's Abbey, Bristol, whose abbots with their stewards made regular journeys there and back.[24]

Coventry's Holy Trinity Guild registers record those Irish goods which specifically reached them in the sixteenth century, when they were first compiled: fish, hides, timber and rough cloth.[25] In fact fish had been the principal Irish export to England, mostly into Bristol, and this continued through the fifteenth century until a greater emphasis was placed upon cloth exports in the sixteenth century. In 1516 it is calculated that the Irish fleet active in Bristol amounted to forty-two different vessels, sailing mainly out of Waterford.[26] By around 1540 more than half of all Irish exports into England were of cloth, a fivefold increase from the start of the century. At least some of this was probably related to the growth of Liverpool and boats coming in via Anglesey and North Wales.

Ireland also provided an early pool of labour in England, as it still does in the twenty-first century. This was at times the cause of resentment, and in 1394 relations with Ireland had reached a nadir when Richard II's government ordered all resident Irish to return there, which naturally led to a dramatic drop in revenues from the island. The nuns of Grace Dieu Augustinian nunnery in Leicestershire recorded that each year their annual harvest was brought in by itinerant Irish workers and a single Welshman (possibly their middleman).[27] They might also have been employed elsewhere, although it is not possible to say where, other than to speculate that it must have been not far from Grace Dieu as most harvests would have been within days or weeks of each other, before the rain came and the operation on a wider scale would have needed more men, not more time. A similar input of manpower would have been needed for every nunnery of every order as their gender alone entailed restrictions in the church's eyes as to what they could and could not do. It is tempting to ask how many looked to Ireland for seasonal labour. In the 1540s John Leland noted that Minehead in Somerset was exceedingly full of Irishmen. So much for labour restrictions!

Wales

The single Welshman helping the Irish bring in the Grace Dieu nunnery harvest in Leicestershire is far from alone. Internal trade with Wales is not specifically mentioned in the *Libelle*, since by the fifteenth century Wales was joined to England's crown by the gift of the Principality to the heir to the English throne when each monarch ascended in his turn. However, cattle were regularly imported into England along the drove-roads from Wales, often called 'Welsh-roads', well into the Midlands. In the fifteenth century, fields on the north-west side of Coventry were turned over to grazing for the hundreds of such animals that regularly arrived in herds driven from Wales and put to grass before they were either sent to market for the city's own meat or for selling on. Nearby on Hill Street, close to the end of an extramural suburb that fronted that same grazing land, stood 'the Welsh House', specifically a pageant-house for those itinerant Welshmen regularly engaged in the droving and selling of cattle. The livestock market there was the largest in a wide area and Cistercian nuns from Catesby near Daventry (25 miles) and Benedictine monks from as far as Peterborough (50 miles) were sent there to buy Welsh cattle.

Similarly, while staples such as cows for beef and milk were brought into the Midlands from Wales, so too was Welsh labour.

Just as for the Irish harvesters in Leicestershire, so too there is indication of Wales providing specialist groundworkers for the English market. One travelling group, mainly 'ditchers and dykers', in the early 1480s found themselves helping to build Kirby Muxloe Castle in Leicestershire for Lord Hastings, a programme which lasted four years. Their surnames are unmistakeably Welsh: Morris ap Price, Davy Jonson, Ellis Gough, John Davy, Pritchard, John and Hugh Powell, William and John ap Gryffyth, John Hughes and Lewis Williams.[28] Travelling together, they probably accounted before and after for numerous English groundworks programmes.

William Worcestre, writing in 1480, noted that at Bristol there was a specific quay called 'the Back', where Welsh ships docked to unload their produce from Tenby, Milford Haven, Haverfordwest, Laugharne Haven, Llansteffan Haven, Kidwelly Haven, Swansea Haven, Neath Haven, Cardiff Haven, Usk Haven, Caerleon Haven, Tintern Abbey on the River Wye, Chepstow Haven and Betysley Water (possibly Beachley) on the River Wye. Clearly there was a considerable market for southern Welsh coastal villages to sell homemade produce into Bristol, the nearest major English population centre. Some, of course, may have been 'coasting', or re-exporting their own imports, perhaps even from further up the Welsh coast or even from Ireland, at a profit.[29]

Brabant, Zeeland and Hainault

The *Libelle* lists 'madder, woad, garlike, onions [and] saltfysshe' as being imported from these north-west European duchies and geographical areas, which included the Dutch ports of Haarlem, Dordrecht and Middelburg, their boats crossing regularly to England, along with Belgian centres like 'Ieper and Kortrijk' (Ypres and Courtrai), which made acres of cloth from English wool and sold it through Bruges and Antwerp. Some of these districts fell under the sway of the Duke of Burgundy so were not always strictly independent. However, the products were also found in other markets in large quantities so it is likely that much of it was moved around inland or by coaster from other continental ports, being re-sold to English or foreign carriers. There was nothing here that was not also in Bruges and its satellite towns, such as saltfish bought at Damme and re-sold. None of the products the *Libelle* lists necessarily have to originate from Brabant, Zeeland or Hainault; they are as much the produce of otherwise wider markets as the competing ports of foreign nationals.

Iceland

Reckoning Iceland's contribution to English trade to be minuscule (which it was in 1435, compared to later in the century), the *Libelle* notes the following: 'Of Yceland to wryte is lytille need some of stockfisshe; yit for soothe in dede out of Bristow and costys may one men have practiced by needle and by stone.'[30]

The isolation of Iceland from mainland Europe and England made for difficult trading, but the dismissal by the *Libelle* is far too simplistic. The author's allusion to using the semi-fabulous lodestone (needle and stone) to navigate the open waters of the Atlantic to make a route from Bristol to Iceland placed it in the realms of the almost mythical, although there was nothing mythical about the mountainous, freezing seas this far north.[31] The use of the Viking lodestone, which allowed navigation through cloud and sea fog to maintain a heading before the proper compass was invented, made the short cod fishing season just about viable, although there must have been considerable loss of ships and many lives.

As ever, politics was present even in respect of this isolated island. There was protracted antagonism between England and Denmark, ruler of Iceland, which made trading difficult (sometimes impossible), but ironically for many years a trade flourished, mostly when international agreement was in place to limit it.

An early turning point was reached in 1427 when the Danish synod of the Catholic church appointed two English bishops to

Iceland. It was to supply these bishoprics that the first licensed English trade to Iceland began in that year, with Bristol able to provide much of what the exceedingly barren island craved of Europe's produce. It may be that this trade was barely into its stride by the time of the compilation of the *Libelle*, at least in the hearing of its embittered poet. The murder of Iceland's Danish governor by men of Bristol and Lynn in 1467 brought half a century of growing relations to a low point, and the trade from then on was much diminished, quantities being carried in foreign vessels or diverted via Bergen which, packed with ships that left it too late to depart, had a reputation as a 'wild-west town' during the long Norwegian winter.

Writing in an account of 1477, Christopher Columbus, who knew England and its seafarers well, noted in relation to Iceland how 'the English came with their merchandise, especially those of Bristol'. However, what of Icelandic imports into England? Records show that although Bristol was the paramount trading partner during the fifteenth century, it was far from alone. Ships from Bristol were joined in Icelandic waters by those of Lynn, Hull, Scarborough, Newcastle upon Tyne, Orwell, Whitby, Grimsby, Dunwich, Walberswick and Southwold.

To underline the importance of deep-sea fishing around Iceland, it is worth noting that Coventry, like many cities, sought marine fish from Iceland, especially stockfish (air-dried cod); Coventry fishmongers maintained their own ship at Lynn expressly for the Iceland run while also chartering ships at Sandwich. As centres of fishing, Lynn and Great Yarmouth (hereafter Yarmouth) were in the first rank and alongside Coventry's own ships berthed the monastic boats of Beaulieu Abbey as early as the thirteenth century, their cargo then handed on from Norfolk, probably by coaster.[32] The fish that Beaulieu bought was salted using both locally bought and imported salt from Poitou.[33] Fish from Iceland and salt from Poitou constitute a politically precarious pair of imports indeed.

An English ship in some startling difficulty south-east of Iceland, in Olaus Magnus' 1539 *Carta Marina*. Thanks to Uppsala University Library for permission to use this detail.

Many excavations at urban sites and medieval religious houses have shown that, even in comparison to riverine species and those reared in monastic fishponds and *vivaria*, it is the bones of marine fish species which so often predominate in the archaeological record. Lying as it does – as far inland from the sea as it is possible to get in any direction –Coventry is a stark indicator of the urban desire for marine fish on the table. Even as the city's fortunes struggled terribly in the last quarter of the fifteenth century, with further setbacks in the early sixteenth, consumption of the fruits of the sea remained great. The city's Benedictine cathedral priory maintained its own salt-pans at Droitwich for preserving purposes, alongside the city's saltfish imports through Yarmouth and Lynn. Northampton too, equally landlocked and well past its thirteenth-century heyday, but much-excavated since the 1970s, was equally reliant upon the supply of marine fish for the table through the 1400s in a variety which marks out an ever-aspirant and well-fed urban population.

Not all fish stocks from the northern seas that were landed at northern, eastern and western ports can be said to derive from Icelandic waters, if expanses of sea at that time can even be described in such nationalistic terms. Ships were sent to follow migratory herring around the north all the way across to Norway and Denmark and down the North Sea. Much further south, consumers took their fish from elsewhere, all seeking the same migratory shoals as the year progressed and rival fleets were seen off neighbours' coasts, to the chagrin of local fishermen, who were often provoked to violence.

Around the country, records indicate the massive shopping lists of monastic communities seeking marine fish all year round. In 1307–08 the cellarer at Durham Cathedral's Benedictine abbey bought somewhere between 200,000 and 264,000 herring, while the kitchen bill for Winchester Cathedral's Benedictine abbey included over 53,000 herring, to which they added salt salmon, cod, ling, hake, mackerel and conger eel, albeit these were bought at Portsmouth so probably from southern waters. The end of such monastic purchases in the Dissolution of the Monasteries beginning in 1536 could seriously disadvantage local fishing fleets and the small ports they used. Indeed, John Leland noted around 1546 that Portsmouth was almost deserted except for the navy presence (see below). In 1416–17, the Benedictine abbey at Selby bought 40,000 herring at York market (via Hull) while excavations at Leicester's Austin Friary recovered cod, haddock, ling and plaice. Again and again, marine species predominate at an array of monastic tables.[34] They were also dominant in a drain assemblage from Barnard Castle in County Durham, the product of some fine dining in the great hall in the fifteenth century. Of twelve species present, herring predominated but only one type – pike – was exclusively a freshwater fish.[35] However, little can be said of the porpoise meat recorded as being on sale at Coventry market – that was presumably a very occasional and happenstance delicacy.[36]

Fishing boats at this time could not be out of port for very long, although they did fish in fleets to keep an eye out for each other. In the many centuries before refrigeration, any voyage was limited by the 'shelf-life' of the fish as fresh produce. Out of Bristol, Iceland could be reached in about a week. Some fish might be salted on board, but the greater majority and any smoking had to be left until the catch was landed. The fish were then bought and moved by the 'last' or barrel load, either direct to the customer or via the marketplace – to the Midlands this was an inland journey of more than 100 miles from Lynn. Monastic consumers might make separate arrangements of their own along their preferred trade routes by road or riverboat; the Cistercian Combe Abbey in Warwickshire maintained its own *staithe* (wharf) on the River Wensum at Norwich, which would necessitate a road journey of some 135 miles but which met open waters at Yarmouth, where its fellow Cistercians of Beaulieu Abbey also fished.[37]

There is no doubt that while the author of the *Libelle* had no gripes with those who imported from Iceland, this may have been because the goods brought in were so much staple fare, in no way luxury. Indeed, stockfish was a particular Lenten fare, church approved. It is also of note that bone evidence of marine fish is common on many archaeological sites, especially where a sieving programme is in place for their recovery, enabling a good overview. The list of northern, eastern and western ports which sent ships as far north as Iceland is a long one, and while archaeological fish bones do not normally betray an exact origin, all who bought stocks landed at one of these ports would undoubtedly be consuming some 'Icelandic' fish.

Amongst the regular catches and imported stockfish was the occasional whale from deeper waters, although these are perhaps as likely to have come from butchery of happenstance beach-strandings. Whales had certainly been exploited in England since at least Anglo-Saxon times[38] and what may pass as an improbably slender medieval harpoon found off the Sussex coast might suggest there may have been some rudimentary hunting.[39] Excavations at inland sites have recovered whalebone chopping boards (made from whale vertebrae) and other artefacts from as varied origins as Lincolnshire, the Isle of Wight, Cornwall and Yorkshire.[40]

The Italian City-states

Arguably the bitterest bile encountered in the *Libelle* is reserved for the Italians.

Tuscan firms had been established in England since the 1270s. The Genoese came soon with alum, making their first confirmed voyage with that cargo in 1278.[41] Although continuously documented trade with Venice went back at least to 1202, the first Venetian state-sponsored fleet arrived in England in 1319. However, there was an inauspicious start to the relationship when a fracas in Southampton prompted a swift, if temporary, reversal of state-sponsored ventures.[42] For the fifteenth century, most exotic imports, whether bulky or not, came in through London or Southampton or, to a lesser extent, Sandwich. Venetians and Florentines sold little in Southampton beyond sweet wine and black soap. The exotics passed through as shipments by road, still in the name of Italian shippers and agents, often based elsewhere, but usually living in London.

Genoa

Of the Genoese, or 'Januays', the writer of the *Libelle* noted: 'In grete karrackis arrayed withouten lake wyth clothes of golde silke and pepir blacke, they bringe wyth hem and of wood grete plente woll-oyle wood aschen by vessel in the see coton, roche-alum and gode golde of Jine.'[43] His acceptance of Genoese trade is grudging.

Competition between Genoa and Venice was long-standing, leading to regular flashpoints. Neither gained an upper hand for long, until in 1380 the two sides clashed at Chioggia on the Venetian Lagoon. The Genoese lost badly, and from then on the Venetians put clear water between themselves and their western Mediterranean neighbours.

In 1424 the Genoese could boast over sixty large ships (carracks, not galleys) on their books, but within fifty years this had dwindled to little more than twenty. Until the middle of the century they had been instrumental in the eastern slave trade, through Caffa on the Black Sea, supplying slaves from eastern Europe and the Steppe, mainly to the Mamluk sultans of Egypt.[44] It was a lucrative trade and, augmented by Russian furs, they made great profits.

For the first half of the fifteenth century, it was woad and alum that provided the Genoese with their principal cargoes into England, mostly through Southampton. So great was their involvement that at Romsey in Hampshire they controlled the textile industry, employing local craftsmen to full, dye and mend or finish cloths previously bought at far-flung inland markets or imported on Genoese vessels from Flanders.[45] This trade they pursued as far inland as Warwickshire, supplying most of Coventry's woad and all its alum for its famed and much-sought-after sky-blue woollen cloth. It was an inherently vulnerable trade that relied on distant suppliers.

When Black Sea ports were overrun by the Turks, their trade routes became harassed in the extreme and the Genoese were forced to operate almost entirely out of the Aegean island of Chios, where they already controlled the supply of alum out of the mines of Phocaea, a Genoese colony now in western Turkey. For a time, when alum was in short supply, the Genoese simply shipped more woad[46] even though the resultant blue dye the woad helped create might not be as fast as anticipated without the usual recourse to alum as the mordant. They also brought in large cargoes of fruit and wine from the Mediterranean, together with hugely expensive paper, which was of course handmade. Their cargoes contained few spices, which were the monopoly of the Venetians at the time.

However, the Turks were completely in the ascendant. Constantinople fell to them in 1453, but for the Genoese it was when they overran the alum mines in Phocaea that they felt it most, losing their principal eastern marketplace and their suppliers at source. England already sought huge amounts of alum from these Genoese carriers. In 1447–48 alone 175 tons came through Southampton, destined overland for London.[47] Realising the value of his newly won trade, the Ottoman sultan began to levy unreasonable tribute and the alum supply to the west swiftly began to dry up from 1458, briefly depriving (among others) a dozen English cities from Shrewsbury to Winchester of the mordant that fixed their famed dyes and gave their woollen cloth an edge in the international marketplace.

The situation was clearly dire for the Genoese, such that when a Genoa-born pirate captured some English ships off Malta in 1458, the Genoese were blamed and the Crown seized all Genoese merchants in England. Genoa meekly protested, unwilling to sever diplomatic links.[48] They clearly badly needed the alum trade to England restored, and quickly.

Merchants scoured Europe for alum, leading to the discovery in 1462 of a source at Tolfa, north of Rome, in the Papal States of Italy.[49] Thereupon Pope Pius II banned the use of Turkish alum and funelled the profits of Tolfa towards potential crusades, and his successor Paul II issued a faculty for a negotiated national price for the alum with the court of Edward IV and another for the Duke of Burgundy.[50] Within a short time, the Tolfa mines were employing 8,000 men. This might have been to western benefit generally, and certainly to England's cloth dyers specifically, but the exclusive contract to haul the alum out of the port at Civitavecchia was awarded not to Genoa but to Florence and the Medici family, who quickly cornered the market, to Genoa's urgent distress.

From that moment on, the Genoese were at a trading disadvantage. They never recovered to any great extent; without a strong eastern connection Genoa's trade to distant England was insufficient to survive on its own, and it quickly lost ground. It went into catastrophic decline during the reign of Edward IV, hastened by the loss of the alum trade to Florence. As will be seen, the Florentine understanding of their business was such that English dyers were not top of their list of clients. The old Genoese standard of alum supply could not be relied upon if it was monopolised in Florentine hands.

Florence
The ire which the *Libelle* reserved for the Florentines is shared with Venice,[51] perhaps because when it was composed the Florentines had barely had a decade to make their presence felt independent of their Adriatic neighbour (see below). Their growing strength, however, could be gauged by the fact that in 1422 their wealth and influence enabled them to circulate 2 million of their own florins.[52]

Through the 1420s Florence was working hard to become a maritime power. It was a struggle for the landlocked city-state, not least because it spent much of a decade at war with its neighbours Genoa and Milan, but the acquisition of Porto Pisano and Leghorn (Livorno) finally gave it a gateway to the seas via Pisa and the River Arno. Although these were very much imperfect anchorages, they at least gave the Florentines what they needed to trade overseas under their own power, and they set about creating new routes from scratch in all directions across the Mediterranean.[53]

The Florentines made their first state trading visit to Southampton and London when they sent a galley fleet in 1425. They were already involved in a private capacity in shipping wine to England from Bordeaux, although they had often used Genoese or Catalan shipping.[54] However, this was increasingly not a trade in which they could garner great profits as it was heavily oversubscribed with carriers. By 1429–30 they had sent four state galley fleets, principally for English wool and usually to Southampton, this last being a voyage from which we are fortunate to have the surviving diary of its forty-seven-year-old captain, Luca di Maso degli Albizzi (1382–1458).[55] The journey was designed to last as long as seven months; sometimes it took much longer, and the same journey taking eleven months is not unheard of, with the galleys mostly unable to be at sea for more than a week before they needed to reprovision, regardless of the weather. The galleys usually spent two months at Southampton and Sandwich, unloading and loading.

Their regular route on leaving Porto Pisano involved stops at Marseilles, Port-de-Bouc, Aigues-Mortes, Cadaqués, Barcelona, Mallorca, Valencia, Deira, Javea, Benidorm, Villajoyosa, Alicante, Almeria, Malaga, Gibraltar, Cadiz, Lisbon, Pontevedra, Ribadeo and then north across the Bay of Biscay, avoiding the treacherous Breton coast. Albizzi's diary records that on this last leg[56] the fleet of 1429–30 sailed a long way further north than they had perhaps intended, accompanied by a flotilla of Portuguese ships, before turning east towards Southampton since they found themselves far west of their destination in the *Golfo di Musuofulo* (Mousehole Bay), curiously (if erroneously) described by Albizzi as being in the Bristol Channel. There they began to navigate along the coastal seamarks of their Portolan charts: *Capo di Gomestri* (Cape Goodstart), *l'Isola verde* (a green island – possibly Looe Island), *Palamua* (Plymouth), *Artemua* (Dartmouth) and *Antone* (Southampton itself). Some Florentine galleys also called at Sandwich in Kent. Upon leaving, Albizzi's diary mentions passing the *Isola di Vicche* (Isle of Wight), *Calzadores* (Calshot Spit), *Capo di Belcheppo* (Beachy Head) and *Capo Dobla*

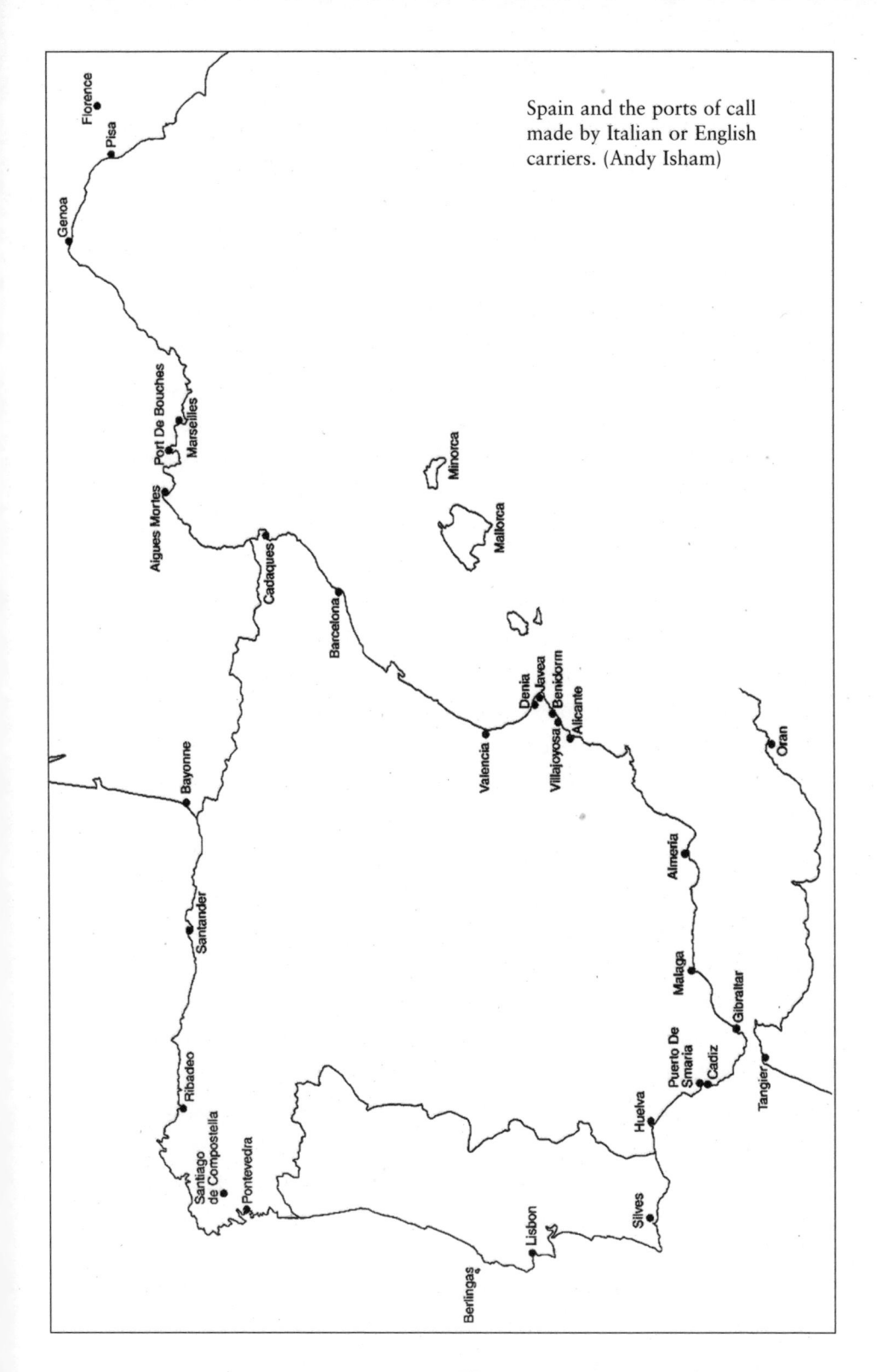

Spain and the ports of call made by Italian or English carriers. (Andy Isham)

(the white cliffs of Dover). With a fair wind, it was then open sea to Ostend and on to Sluys, the port of Bruges – in all, a journey of eighty-four days.

The return leg of the journey was faster. After a second visit to Southampton, when they had forty-five days allotted for unloading and loading, they crossed Biscay once more to Lisbon, and on to Silves, Cadiz, Gibraltar, Malaga, Almeria, Javea, Majorca, Minorca, Gorgona, making port at Porto Pisano. The return leg on that occasion took thirty-three days. It is interesting to note the two itineraries, comparing them with what was set down for the Venetians slightly later (see below). While there are some similarities, there are also very different ports in their comparative lists.

Albizzi's galley complement was 130 oarsmen and twenty-five marines and senior sailors. He also notes that his ideal complement was 160 oarsmen and fifty others. From elsewhere we know that it was common to have more than 200 crewmen.

Albizzi himself was frugal in what he carried. He had his clothes and armour, eight crossbows and lots of bedding, his personal pennant and flag, a copy of the letters of St Paul (he was clearly fully literate) and a pair of slippers. He must have taken his standing in port very seriously since he paid 28 florins to have a new flag made for the journey, perhaps fearing that a new ship might need additional recognition signals. In Majorca he bought six small baskets; in Cadiz silk handkerchiefs; in Bruges and Southampton he bought lots of cloth of all types, candlesticks, brass bowls and jugs, and birettas for ecclesiastics back home. He transgressed into the frivolous when he bought a monkey, but as a more sober gift for his wife he bought hairnets.

In terms of their cargo, these galleys were loading at successive ports in the Mediterranean, and when they first left Porto Pisano they were three-quarters empty, loading 200 tons of cargo at Barcelona and 40 to 50 tons at Villajoyosa, which was destined for places other than England, probably mainly Sluys for Bruges. England may have seemed a difficult prospect, since in the Florentine statutes at Bruges as early as 1426 there is a sanction for ships calling at England to offer or take bribes, potentially backing up some of the charges of the *Libelle* in which many are accused of this.[57] Cargoes for England came to include madder (for dyeing), almonds, dates, raisins, rice, wax, silk, cochineal (for dyeing) and saffron, none of them being of themselves voluminous.

By the time they reached Southampton, the Florentine and other Italian merchants there unloaded their orders from Albizzi's galley for the English market, namely: twenty-two bales of dates; thirty-three bales of aniseed; eight bales of cochineal; thirteen barrels of oil; two boxes of preserved fruit; ninety-eight small baskets of raisins; nine barrels of sweetmeats; four cases of silk cloth; eight quarters of figs. Weighing perhaps 20 tons in all, this constituted a small proportion of the whole cargo. It is perhaps little wonder that in these early days a Venetian chronicler, Morosini, commented on the (in Venetian terms) poor cargoes carried by the Florentine galleys leaving Porto Pisano for the far north.[58] Unlike their counterparts in Venice, the Florentines were never interested in establishing a market for spices, but rather wished to sell cloth in the Eastern Mediterranean, good cloth they could get only in England and in Flanders, where most of the cloth was also English.

While his crew stayed in and around Southampton, Albizzi went on a number of inland excursions, visiting Farnham, Guildford (perhaps to buy Guildford woollens) and Kingston upon Thames, for all of which he notes the distance from London.

For most of its northern trade, Florence never sent more than a fleet of three galleys, often just two, and the regularity of these state fleets was susceptible, as was everyone, to bad weather (one of the galleys was lost at sea in 1463), politics and piracy. One fleet in 1465 even contended with plague on board. But unlike Venetian fleets, which could number ten to twelve ships on occasion, the

Florentines always lacked the numbers which offered a measure of safety on these long journeys. They often fell in with rivals to make up convoys for mutual protection.

Crisis beset the city in the years 1431–34, and in 1432 they suspended sailings completely. The period 1448–50 saw the sailing schedules break down throughout the western Mediterranean, even as they operated other long galleys as a protective screen against pirates, and during the 1450s the rhythm of their northern sailings was frequently disrupted. It was not entirely their fault as this was a time of international crises affecting all carriers, not least anti-Italian feeling in England, which helped ensure no Florentine state fleets were sent between 1448 and 1455, nor in 1457. The political tide was for the moment running against them. Even the well-prepared and grounded Venetians struggled at this time. Mallett was particularly perspicacious when he said, 'The possibility of handling almost unlimited quantities of alum had a considerable effect on the history of the Florentine galleys.'[59] It would, however, be only a brief period of prosperity.

The Florentine attitude to the north certainly changed with the award of the Tolfa alum contract by Pope Pius II, but in this lay an inherent danger – that their entire northern trade was dangerously susceptible to politics. However, when they could, they made hay. In 1466–67 the Florentines carried almost 200 tons of alum for England, without any recourse to Flanders at all. The Medici galleys, in a private (if high-profile) venture from Florence in 1470, loaded 300 tons alone for England, although Southampton records show only half that was unloaded there, the rest being perhaps unloaded in Sandwich or, more likely, London. In 1473 the same galley was carrying a large cargo of alum when it was captured, while another Florentine galley unloaded 250 tons at Southampton.

Well into the 1470s there was still considerable demand for alum. In 1472 a Medici-owned Florentine galley left Porto

Pisano so heavily laden that 1,100 sacks of alum had to be left behind, and more alum was unloaded onto a Portuguese ship in Cadiz. However, organising the galley fleets became increasingly difficult during the 1460s and 1470s. By then it was not merely the Venetians and the Florentines who were doing maritime trade between northern lands and the Mediterranean – even the English were doing so in increasing numbers. Florence no longer needed to do the unpalatable and depend upon the fleets of economic rivals and its political enemies if its own galleys were mothballed. Ships of numerous seagoing nations along its western sea lanes, including England, were increasingly available for hire, and were offering commercial terms better than its own ships could exact at the end of their long voyages. In 1477 the last Florentine communal fleet left for England and Bruges, and within a year Florentine state shipping had disappeared from English waters.[60]

Venice
The author of the *Libelle* was equally vociferous towards both Venice and Florence.[61] It is, however, Venetian merchants who, time and again, came in for criticism: 'The grete galees of Venees and Florence be wel ladene wyth thynges of complacence. All spicerye and other grocers ware, with swete wynes, all maner of chaffare, apes and japes and marmousettes taylede. Nifles and trifles, that littell have availed and thynges wyth whiche they fetely blere are eye wyth thynges not enduring that we bye.'

'Things of complacence', 'nifles and trifles' – fripperies – had always roused the indignance of those less inclined to luxury in many cultures. Those whose heads were turned by trinkets, luxuries and indulgences have often been considered flawed and lacking in character, and such characteristics were associated with the east. Even as far back as the eighth century BC, Homer had noted disdainfully of eastern trading visitors: 'To this place came

Pet 'Apes and Japes and marmousettes tayled' were particularly reviled in the *Libelle*. Here a captive monkey is urinating into a jug, on a fifteenth-century misericord from Holy Trinity, Stratford-Upon-Avon, Warwickshire (2013). This is the parish church of William Shakespeare (1564–1616), who is buried here.

Phoenicians, well known for their seamanship, but greedy men, bringing countless fripperies stowed aboard their black ship.'[62]

Among the luxuries England imported, almost certainly the most expensive were spices, most of them destined for the tables of noble country landowners. A small number of importers fought hard to maintain control of this trade, which involved the tortuous and difficult Middle Eastern trade through Islamic lands, as far east as India and south to Arabia and into the African interior.

Old Cairo (often called Fustat) – and then out from the port of Alexandria – was the main market for most of the medieval period, with considerable quantities of spices also coming via Beirut, Lebanon and Damascus, Syria. It was the Venetians whose merchants, based in these great and ancient cities, carried on most of the trade, paying ever higher prices which funded the extravagant lifestyles and sometimes oppressive regimes of the Mamluk sultans, who also had a liking for English woollen cloth, coloured with dyestuffs the Italians themselves had carried to Southampton and Sandwich. For a couple of centuries, it seemed the Italian trade was unassailable although, as will be seen, it was under constant pressure. Even the practised Venetians could come a cropper; almost at a whim the sultan in Alexandria could have all sails and rudders confiscated until port dues were paid, and that was even before the marketplace at Cairo was reached.[63]

The first Venetian state fleet had come to England in 1319. Starting as it meant to go on, its cargo was well suited to an English sweet tooth and comprised roughly 10,000 lbs of sugar and 1,000 lbs of candy. They carried 3,580 measures of other goods, so it was far from a drop in the ocean. They unloaded at London and went on to Boston, Lincolnshire, where they bought wool and loaded for Flanders. In a nasty downturn to the new trade, they were set upon by English pirates and the merchant in charge, the man behind the financial venture, was murdered.[64]

The Arsenale, Venice – construction sheds of the state galleys. Photo courtesy of Steve Parry.

Within little more than a decade there was a flourishing return trade, however, and the Venetian authorities (the Signory) decreed that the sailing calendar should coordinate with their overland merchants to avoid a glut of (English) woollen cloth arriving at Venice by two means and causing the market price to plummet. By the early fifteenth century this was tightened up and two months had to be allowed after the return of the Flanders galleys before overland freight was admitted.[65] In reality the maritime route was infinitely preferable; although the average overland journey from Venice to Bruges only took twenty to twenty-nine days, the roads were poorly maintained and dangerous, and it took as many as seventy draught animals to pull a load equivalent to that of a single modern articulated lorry. A mounted convoy might be expected to cover no more than 25 miles per day, which amounts to a great deal of stabling reserved and fodder consumed.[66] It was not very profitable. Venice bolstered its own chances of cornering north-Italian markets with an expansionist and acquisitive political policy among its neighbours in the decades following the Black Death, overcoming on land Treviso (1387), Verona and Padua (1405), Udine (1420) and Bergamo (1428), inheriting Ravenna (1441) and finally acquiring Cremona (1499).[67] It was fully in control of a notable hinterland by the middle of the fifteenth century when it was still growing.

For the Venetians coming to England, the fifteenth century opened with a personal privilege extended by the English Crown which must have had the entrepreneurs among the crews cock-a-hoop with delight: Richard II, in his final regnal year, gave royal assent for passengers on the Venetian state galleys to sell their 'small wares', namely glass vessels and earthenware plates, on the decks duty free (no mention of monkeys), and further allowed each passenger to dispose of one barrel of wine of not more than 10 gallons.[68] Not only did this 'seaman's portion' make an impromptu market of the deck and the docksides at London,

Sandwich and Southampton during loading and unloading, it did so while allowing individuals in Venetian state pay to make a personal profit. Throughout the fifteenth and into the sixteenth centuries, when word went ahead to London that the Venetian state fleet had been spotted off the Downs (Kent), a crowd would begin to assemble on the dockside at Rotherhithe to eagerly await the long sleek craft, its sails furled, stroking its way up the Thames to Southwark. Equally it must have been an anti-climax if the fleet decided instead to transfer its inbound cargo to lighters as far out as Gravesend, which it sometimes did!

This welcomed northern trade was sufficiently established and lucrative that in 1400 the Venetians elected two permanent paid ambassadors to England, each to have a small embassy in tow comprising three squires each, a secretary, servant, understudy, steward, cook and three packhorses, although they had to find their own grooms and carriage of freight. The cost to Venice was to be defrayed by a 1/200th levy on all their shipping in and out of London.[69] This might seem a tiny levy and suggest an embassy on a shoestring budget, but in must be borne in mind that at that time Venice owned some 3,300 ships and managed some 36,000 employees, testament to their unassailable hold on Mediterranean trade routes.[70] It was 1/200th of a very large turnover.

Most people who knew Venice were in awe of it. In 1483, the Dominican Friar Brother Felix Fabri arrived there on his second pilgrimage to the Holy Land. He had visited before, but he could not resist writing of its delightful charms: 'As we sailed further on, we found before our eyes the famous, great, wealthy and noble city of Venice, the mistress of the Mediterranean, standing in wondrous fashion in the midst of the waters, with lofty towers, great churches, splendid houses and palaces.' Awe indeed – and Brother Felix was a well-travelled man.

The year 1408 brought a flurry of new directives. In January it was stipulated that the captain of the Flanders galleys was to remain in London for fifty days, while the timing of freight to and from London and Flanders was further refined to ensure prices remained buoyant and a glut was avoided. The value of London's share was highlighted when any shortfalls on loads from Flanders were allowed to be made up by a greater share being redirected from England, so long as safe passage from Sandwich could be guaranteed.[71] It was a style of opportunistic search for the right marketplace at just the right time which became a hallmark of Venetian trade policy.

A month later the Signory agreed rates for redeeming their crews in England. This seems to have become a problem during longer stopovers for unloading and loading, when crewmen would melt away into the taverns and fleshpots of London, often getting drunk, running out of money and having to work for their supper.[72] At Bruges such problems of destitution might be kept out of the city thanks to the stockade or basin at Sluys, which permitted only the landing of high-value, high-quality commodities. Any carrying super-abundant freight were to unload outside the stockade.

Later in that year Venetian galleys were found to be carrying contraband, outside London byelaws and regulations, although keeping up with all blacklisted commodities was often difficult since these might change with bewildering speed. It was resolved to send churchmen into the equation, rather than eminent Venetians, so that both fair dealing and personal safety could be guaranteed. In practical terms, when routine customs searches saw bales and crates opened and examined, the discovery of contraband aboard meant that goods were seized and declared forfeit, since the quality – and therefore the duty – might be greater than the manifest suggested. Thus, the Venetians might be accused of underpaying the exchequer on their imports.[73] In the following year, the Venetians made pointed reference to the losses they incurred due to these unscrupulous traders, who had pocketed the difference. As a result, back at Venice, their goods were to be forfeit in any further situations of this kind.[74]

At the height of England's war with France, the Venetians were inexorably drawn into the struggle. England's invasion fleet was drawn almost exclusively from the Easterling merchant fleet of Netherlands ports – as a long contemporary list of ships by name, type and home port attests, singling out Haarlem, Dordrecht and Middelburg – setting the Easterlings against France.[75] No regular visitors to either English or French waters could escape the effects of war between two such close neighbours and trading partners. Thus France, by hiring Genoese vessels against the English, was harming Venice, which also had three cogs impounded by the English. Venice was powerless in such circumstances and made a rather lame protest, only securing the release of their ships by the issue of royal safe-conduct passes when they satisfied the Crown they were merchant vessels and not rigged for war.[76]

Regular trade resumed as military activity waned. By the middle of the century, the Venetian galleys called regularly and profitably at Southampton, Sandwich or London, in some cases more than one, sometimes before proceeding to Flanders, sometimes after a visit there and sometimes with the fleet split to get the best of both worlds. Much effort was expended during these middle years on ensuring a strict hierarchy of duties was in place to ensure that the correct duty was paid on cloth of different qualities. There was even a scandal concerning what was described as 'counterfeit cloth' from England and Flanders, made in the Florentine fashion, and on which an exponential scale of duty was imposed in 1457–58 to discourage its purchase in case an immediate prohibition on its import proved ineffective.[77]

While Venice traded far westwards to England and Flanders, it also traded eastwards and southwards to 'Barbary'. The main ports were their own dominions at Naupactus (Greece), Candia (Crete) and Rhodes, and there were permanent berths with trading legations and privileges in Muslim lands at Beirut and Alexandria, with southerly Mediterranean ports including Oran. There they dealt directly with the Muslim sultans in Damascus, Jerusalem and Cairo, and tapped into the spice route from India and Africa and the even longer silk road from Cathay (China). By the mid-fifteenth century, these trade routes were some 300 to 400 years old and well-established, as was Venetian supremacy in their use. By the mid-fifteenth century there were usually numerous Venetian ships at Alexandria and Beirut at any one time.

This route began to fall apart as the Turks increasingly spread their military influence and empire, driving their southern neighbours out of Cairo and the Holy Land. Just as alum supplies dwindled for the Genoese fleet after 1458, so too the Venetian free movement in the Eastern Mediterranean became nearly impossible from 1465 amid internecine warfare among Muslim lands. On numerous occasions Venetians were captured and held to ransom. What eased the situation was a Venetian edict giving greater market for northern cloths in Barbary ports before the Flanders galleys returned to Venice, since the Muslim hunger for these high quality bolts of cloth remained just as high if not higher.[78] Only if the Flanders galleys were loaded with copper or tin were they to proceed straight to Venice, since from 1430 a dispute between Venice and the Mamluk sultan Barsbay (r.1422–37), who tried to break their monopoly on the spice trade, resulted in Venice's tit-for-tat refusal to land coin, bullion and raw materials.[79] Venice had enjoyed trading privileges in Alexandria since 1238, only twenty years after the Sixth Crusade, so its bargaining power was considerable.

In 1433 the fleet which left for Beirut and Alexandria carried 150 merchants, a million ducats of oil, honey and fruit, and about half as much in cash to spend in their spice markets. This money bought carefully collected and mixed Egyptian potash, which would go into Venice's exquisite glass, famed across northern Europe.[80] Venetian trade supplied Egypt's lifeblood and fed the spice and silk caravans which wound their way across from Fustat to Baghdad and Pumbeditha (now Fallujah) and all the way across to China and the Malabar coast of India. That trade, essential to both parties, is best exemplified by the exceptional body of written letters and accounts in Hebrew, Greek and Judaeo-Arabic, saved from the destruction of the Cairo Genizah in the early twentieth century and more recently conserved and translated by scholars.[81]

Relations with the Mamluk sultans were always hugely political, even though they were conducted through Jewish middlemen, and by the early sixteenth century Venice was actively preventing iron being sold to lands of 'the infidel' since it could be, and often was, used to make munitions deployed against Christian armies. Trade between Venice and its Islamic neighbours would become pivotal in the second half of the sixteenth century, and the republic would suffer badly in what became an unequal struggle.

In England, war within and without was causing difficulties through the middle decades of the fifteenth century, but trade did continue, if occasionally interrupted or disjointed. The Flanders galleys always had the option to miss out Southampton, Sandwich or London and head straight for Sluys and Bruges instead; as it was, they often split up and went to each of the accustomed ports. When Edward IV was forced to flee into the arms of his brother-in-law the Duke of Burgundy in Bruges for a few months in 1471, Flanders did continue to trade with England, but under the awkward cloud of knowing it harboured the ousted claimant to the English throne.[82] During that time the Flanders galleys could get no English escort through the Channel and had to convoy beyond the Isle of Wight with whoever they could find to join them for mutual protection.

Even as the Wars of the Roses were ending, there is a particularly detailed notice of a Venetian state fleet sailing to England in 1485. Two were London-bound, while two were to go to Bruges. Each had a notable complement costing a total salary of 600 ducats, and their number included thirty good arbalist men (crossbowmen or riflemen) aged twenty to fifty, each on a monthly salary of £19. Among this armed complement, which reflected the increasingly difficult problem of pirates, were to be four noble youths in each galley, presumably learning to become good citizens and servants of the Signory. Each galley could supplement one specialist advisor in lieu of an arbalist.[83]

For the return each galley was encouraged to load 120,000 lbs (roughly 60 tons) of light goods (not wool), plus 80,000 lbs weight of copper and tin, but no more, presumably because the burden would be too great for the rowers if a turn of speed was needed; each already carried some 20,000 lbs of ballast. The galleys were asked to purchase four pieces of artillery each at their destinations, which on return were to be given to the Arsenale; its stock as a result must have been a bewildering mix of types and calibres, each with its own shot, but this catalogue of the latest ballistic advances across Europe must have been second to none, keeping Venice at the forefront of artillery development! As to their route, the galleys were given leave to call at Palermo and Messina outbound, to dock at either Southampton or Sandwich, and on the return leg were allowed to call at Antwerp and Middelburg, Alicante, Pisa and Talamone.

Furthermore, if ice detained them at Sluys, the overstay was to be deducted from time at Southampton – perhaps reflecting the struggling English economy at that time – but in recompense they could add stopovers at Malaga and Almeira. Thereafter one of the galleys was to go via the ports of One, Oran and Tunis in North Africa and then strike north to Syracuse. This was Venice at its best, making the most of trading opportunities to seek the best market as fortunes fluctuated.

Of particular interest was their intended outward cargo manifest: small spice, Levantine sugar, raw and spun cotton, currants, lambskins, dressed and undressed hides, wax, paper (in bales of twelve reams), silks, fustians, cloths, household utensils. There was a warning not to try to smuggle raw silk or silk cloth by passing them off as spices. This suggests not only that such practices were still prevalent, to the detriment of the Signory's reputation, but that customs inspections were often not particularly detailed. The stakes seem to have been high nevertheless, since in addition to their salary each captain was to be awarded a bounty of 3,500 ducats.

The end of the Wars of the Roses in England should have left Venetian trade in England unassailable, especially since the preceding decades had been so unkind to their nearest rivals, Genoa and Florence, but it was not to be. Venice was under fire on all sides, and although Florence and Genoa had fallen by the wayside, the financial situation in Venice was worsened by its disastrous wars in the Mediterranean against encroaching Islamic forces which both threatened its supplies there but also destroyed its eastern markets for northern European products in the opposite direction. In 1465 the Venetians were forced to cease their annual Barbary galleys, with their merchants held to ransom.[84] This dire situation of fast-disappearing markets and newly hostile suppliers had begun to make its mark on the northern voyages by 1480, when it was noted that the London factory was bearing the burden of the whole annual Flanders voyages, but to its own detriment – it was said to be almost bankrupt. Debtors were reneging on their dues and there was a need to shut their warehouse to all customers to prevent them from removing their goods until accounts could be prepared.[85]

The last years of the fifteenth century and the early decades of the sixteenth would see no let-up in these pressures on their trade. Between 1488 and 1492, returns to the Signory noted that their trade into England of sweet wine (Malmsey/Candia) was being harmed by their rivals, who brought bulk wine cargoes from Candia, obtaining better trading privileges at the ports than the Venetians with their mixed cargoes. It stood to put the entire

Flanders voyages in peril.[86] However, in that latter year Henry VII refused to alter the duty on Malmseys, which might have solved the problem.[87] He further exasperated the Venetians when in the same year he seized the Flanders galleys for use in his own military expedition against France. Helmed by English captains unschooled in handling oceangoing, oared galleys, and perhaps propelled by their usual complement of rowers, they were either crashed or were rammed into the harbour works on entry into Calais, seriously damaging them.[88] Three years later two of the four Flanders galleys were lost in a Biscayan storm, including the flagship.[89] Ironically, the English soon after complained that the Flanders galleys no longer came to England 'on account of the wars'.[90] It was hardly surprising, although a personal appeal was nonetheless made by Henry VII, who surely had not helped his cause by his actions.

In official returns to the Signory in 1497, Venetian traders noted that England was 'very much at peace' (although at that moment they were presumably unaware of a major uprising in the tin-mining communities of the south-west), and expressed their approval that Henry VII had sent a Venetian, the hand-picked John Cabot, on a voyage of discovery south and west into the Atlantic, noting new fertile islands and the aforementioned seven cities 400 leagues from England on 'the western passage'.[91]

Venice jealously guarded its now dwindling trade against any and all comers. In 1490 news reached the Doge and Senate that Florence was agitating for England to set up a wool-staple at Pisa. Their reaction was to instruct their ambassador to leave no stone unturned, and they too wrote to Henry VII, expressing their dismay and noting that if this happened they would have no further reason to send their fleet to England, which would see the country's supply of 'spices, wine, and other commodities' simply dry up. It was a threat without doubt, and perhaps they were unaware of how much came in with other carriers, including increasingly

'Cherysshe Marchandyse'

English ships, but their position was already weakening and they keenly felt even potential blows.[92]

The returns of the Flanders galleys in the early sixteenth century demonstrate the increasing pressure under which Venetian trade was operating. By 1517 the Flanders galleys contract ran to 266 clauses to try to address every eventuality.[93] Some size of the galleys can also be gauged since that contract specified that each should carry 20,000 lbs of ballast even before they began loading, although it does not specify what that ballast should comprise.

The issue of Venice losing out to rivals carrying sweet wine to England was solved for the moment by the newly crowned Henry VIII, whose fondness for wine and war coincided. In 1511 he undertook a private contract for a Venetian merchant to send him 'a large number' of Venetian bows in privately registered ships which should carry 500 butts of Candia wine as their principal cargo.[94] The sole freight of bows was not allowed. Again in 1514 the Flanders galleys carried Malmsey and ten bows for each butt of wine.[95]

The following year it was noted to the Signory that the Portuguese had imported 400 pieces of tin (presumably ingots) into Lisbon from India, part of their growing trade around Africa's cape. They noted that the Portuguese were boasting they could get as much as they wanted, which would be to the detriment of the English.[96] England's tin mines were already suffering after Henry VII's punishment of the restive Devonian and Cornish miners who had marched on London in 1497, culminating in the Battle of Blackheath at which their 'rebellion' was brutally put down.

New markets were to some extent opening for Venice but not necessarily for its own ships. By 1508 pearls from the pearl fisheries of Cubagna (the recently discovered Hispaniola and Cuba) were worth an annual 75,000 ducats at Seville.[97]

Venetian prospects and English trade were sufficiently in the doldrums in 1510 for a clause in a peace treaty between England

and France to specifically call for all molestation of merchantmen, *even* Venetian, Genoese and Florentines, to cease. The Venetians were to have access to English ports alone (and by now they had switched from London to Southampton as their preferred port), the Genoese and Florentines to both French and English ports alike.[98] It came too late for Venice, which paused its state fleet to English waters in the years 1509–15, only resuming in 1516.

Venice had been further hobbled in 1514 when a huge fire destroyed much of its financial district (the Rialto). All the while, piracy and the expansion of a hostile Islam continued to take their toll everywhere. In 1517 it was stipulated that even in the Adriatic, Venice's own backyard, navigation between Ragusa (now Dubrovnik) and Istria was to be done only by night. And on the way across Biscay there was to be no call at Santiago de Compostela, presumably lest they lose overzealous crew to the religious shrine there, and so time on passage.

That year the Flanders galleys contract once again set down the required crew, including great consideration for defence.[99] Four galleys, each to be crewed by a master (captain), his servant, mate, advisor, thirty bowmen (including four young noblemen as before), sailing master, state-sponsored assayer, eight pilots (with instructions as to where to board them), two scribes, a caulker, carpenter, cook, cellarer (clearly the galleys carried wine in their cargo), oar-maker, footmen and 171 oarsmen. Numbers going ashore at any one time were to be restricted (presumably to defray trouble and minimise desertions). The contract further stipulated that the merchandise was to be stowed below deck, but not below the waterline, to prevent spoiling.

At about this time (1520), the typical itinerary for a four-ship fleet took in Messina (four days' stay), Cadiz (six days' stay to purchase hatch covers, hoist the barge and cockboat prior to going into the Atlantic and to take on additional rowers – the crew usually went ashore here) and Otranto (a brief stop at the captain's discretion). After Southampton, two ships would go on to Sluys (twenty-five days' stay) then return via Arnemuiden, or go to Sandwich, where they would stay for sixty days, being strictly ordered to drive their own new mooring piles so as not to leave their ropes trailing and rotting in the mud. Pilots were taken on for the Gulf of Lyons, suggesting other stops on the southern French coast, and for the Bay of Biscay, suggesting the galleys hugged the coast before striking north from the western tip of Brittany. The return leg was then via Cadiz (four days), Mallorca (four days), Palermo (twelve days) and Messina (eight days). They would then go on an eastern leg to Dalmatia.[100]

As if trade was not already bad enough, a period of poor weather without recent precedent took an unusual toll on the Venetian fleets and prepared itineraries were liable to be changed without notice. In 1519 they were forced to anchor and ride out a storm at 'Porto Camera' (Camber, next to Rye and Winchelsea) since the weather prevented passage onward.[101]

In late 1520 the weather was particularly stormy in the Bristol Channel and shortly after a huge storm shifted thousands of tons of sand and mud, blocking the approach to Sluys in the Zwin inlet, dealing a dreadful blow to the economic life of Bruges and forcing loyal merchants to begin wholesale moves to Antwerp, which was already on the up. Throughout the 1520s Henry VIII also waged war against Flanders, making consecutive stops in England and Flanders very problematic. In 1522 he seized the Flanders galleys and did not release them until summer the following year, by which time many of the bored, unpaid crews had departed or deserted and the galleys needed repair. By 1525, Henry was wholly concentrating on preparations for a new war with France. This left the Venetians crossing hostile waters, at every pull of their oars 'exposed and having to pass French towns and harbours' and needing to trade in the strictest secrecy – surely a *non sequitur* for the flamboyant Venetian spies and secretaries, whose correspondence was prolific.[102]

Utterly deterred by now, Venice paused its sailings to England completely and no state fleet sailed until 1530. More enterprising Venetian merchants continued to use other carriers; a Ragusan vessel moored on the Thames in 1525, although four French vessels harried it into abandoning its voyage and turning back.[103] The pause had been too much for Venice, and any real sustained resurgence was just too expensive. The last Venetian state fleet left English ports in 1533, bidding adieu to an England on the verge of great change as its traditional European links were finally severed by Henry VIII's own brand of reform. A chain of new coastal artillery forts would be built in the 1540s to protect the principal deep harbours and anchorages, but they were too little, too late.

The Baltic

All Scandinavian trade with England is tied closely with wider trade with the Hanse, who maintained strong links and rivalries this far north. At Bergen stood a Hanseatic *kontor*, and while much of Norway's exports comprised fish stocks from off its coasts every bit as extensive as those of Iceland, the archaeological evidence speaks of smaller commodities which may or may not have come in as finished products. Neither country in the fifteenth century lay within its modern borders, and Scandinavian politics was most unlike its modern counterpart. The *Libelle* makes no specific mention of either, but this may be because the writer could not discern the products of either once they became lost in the melting pot of the English marketplace.

Iron for onward smelting came from Örebro and Österbybrük in the Uppland region of Sweden, sometimes as much as 300 tons per annum, and was specifically known to the English as osmund, while through Trelleborg in southern Sweden came sharpening stones, which are found all over the landlocked Midlands in both urban and rural contexts, such as at Burton Dassett, Warwickshire. Both could be imported as ships' ballast, to be prepared totally in

England, although the tendency is for the latter to be considered by archaeologists as fully Scandinavian creations. Although in modern Sweden, the coastal trading town of Trelleborg was owned by Denmark throughout most of the medieval period and was subject to the vagaries of England's dealings with the Hanseatic League. Other, Norwegian sources were also Hanse-controlled.

Furs from the far north were a regular import, out of places such as Sigtuna, Sweden, where the late medieval town plan is still preserved and excavations have shown a thriving port, dealing all across the Baltic and beyond into Russia and what is now Poland, through Gdansk and down into the Carpathians. Fur was also traded out of Novgorod in Russia, where the Hanse had one of their four *kontors* (the others being at Bergen, Bruges and London).

When the French king Jean II was a captive in England (1356–60, 1363), he was a prodigious consumer of miniver (squirrel fur), also known as strenling or stralling, and many hundreds of such pelts were needed just to make a single cloak or coat, his outfits containing up to 2,500 a time.[104] Clearly not all English consumers knew their furs, since it became a jibe on the continent among Hanseatic merchants, who said, 'We buy fox skins from the English for a groat and re-sell them the foxes' tails for a guilder.'[105] Both the real and perceived value of miniver was such that it remained subject to sumptuary laws for most of the medieval period, restricting its use to the upper echelons of society. Bones from European squirrel have been excavated in medieval York, confirming in archaeological material the link with the sparsely inhabited far north along distant wintry trade routes, largely unobserved.

More recently, excavations in Parkside, Coventry in 2010 recovered the contents of an urban rubbish pit in which lay the remains of numerous squirrel pelts, the detritus of a late medieval skinner, working in the 1520s and perhaps supplying furred garments to consumers at a time when sumptuary laws were being relaxed.[106] The presence of multiples of foot bones is indicative of the deposition of pelt offcuts. The skinner's neighbour was a pinner, again heavily involved in the processes of making clothes for the city's discerning elite.

The Hanseatic League

The area today encompassing Germany, the northern/eastern Netherlands, parts of Poland, the Czech Republic and Slovakia, and almost the entire Baltic Sea littoral right up to Russia and the Gulf of Bothnia was in the fifteenth and early sixteenth century the preserve of the trading association known as the Hanse or Hansa, or Hanseatic League, based in Lübeck and, to our modern eyes, predominantly German in tone and influence. It existed so that its members could trade on beneficial terms, their combined purchasing power being greater than anything the cities and states could wield alone.

By 1400, Hanseatic dealings in England went back a long way. German merchants had been in England since at least the reign of Henry II. Richard the Lionheart gave considerable gifts to the men of Cologne for their help in raising his ransom and freeing him from exiled captivity in 1194. By the late thirteenth century, the Hanseatic Rothschilds were funding the wars of Edward I against Scotland and Wales. During the fourteenth century the crown jewels of Edward III were retained in Cologne and pawned for loans because Edward owed a million gold guilders to the Florentine banking house of Bardi. When the time came to redeem the crown jewels, the king could not pay; it was the London Steelyard which put up the money to redeem them, and in return they accepted new trading privileges. At around the same time the Cornish tin mines owned by the Black Prince were let out to Hanseatic merchants. Sadly, in the Peasants' Revolt of 1381 many Hanse merchants were beaten up, some murdered, having been tested as to whether they could pronounce English words without an accent, particularly 'bread and cheese'.[107] During the fifteenth century a weakened England's distraction with the Wars of the Roses was generally to the benefit of the Hanse, but interactions were complicated at this time by shifting political fortunes.

The Hanseatic League guarded its hard-won trading privileges jealously, fighting tooth and nail to preserve them; they even went so far as to sanction their own member towns when they stepped out of line or appeared ready to break ranks and ply their own trade independently. It may be said that the league was a worthy forerunner to the European Union; and indeed, there are echoes of the Hanse in modern practices, but with 500 years between them the comparisons can only be fleeting and essentially cosmetic. Certainly, the Hanse could exert great power to keep its member states and merchants in line, and certainly they needed to on numerous occasions, since individual elements did try to go their own way – sometimes successfully.

Although it was the originator of the London operation, Cologne was a regular backslider and sided with England during the fifteenth century, straining the Hanse. In the sixteenth century it was the main cause of disharmony between England and the Hanse, although it may be said that England was always needling for trade privileges which split off individual traders from the Hanse. Cologne has been described as often acting as a 'sole trader', a particularly apt term.[108]

Prussia was England's preferred partner trading across the Baltic for most of the fifteenth century. Its politics meant it could be separated from the body of the Hanse and private deals could be done. It had a poor reputation for solidarity with its Hanseatic partners, although when working alone the Prussians would give the Hanse assurances to the contrary.[109] The criss-cross of trading that the Hanse controlled spun a web across the Baltic for its own benefit. From Blankenberge came granite, from Gotland and Bornholm came limestone for Germany and for the Netherlands came Baltic grain.[110]

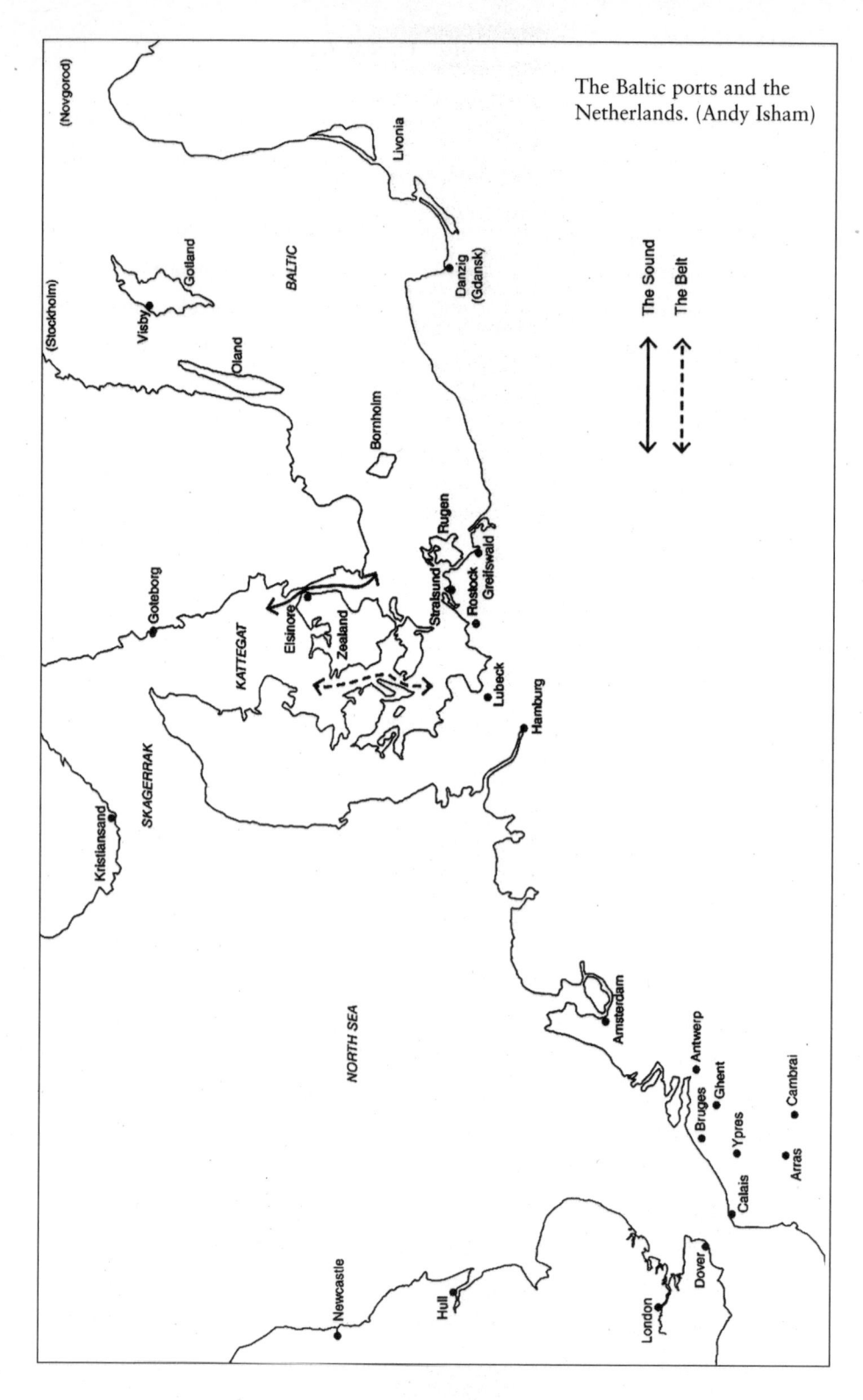

The Baltic ports and the Netherlands. (Andy Isham)

'Cherysshe Marchandyse'

That net spread much wider for the most specific materials and commodities: for instance, English bowmen received most of the yew for their bows from Austria and the Carpathians by way of Danzig.

The Rhineland towns, geographically closest to England itself, dominated trade with the English and it is recognised that by the early sixteenth century Rhenish stoneware mugs found their way into most towns and cities across England as the fashion for consuming continental-style beer spread rapidly.

By the fifteenth century the Hanse had set up four principal *kontors*, as their overseas trading hubs were called, at Bruges (later moved to Antwerp), Bergen, Novgorod (closed in 1494, reopened in 1514) and London. From here they ran their affairs efficiently and to some extent secretly across the entire North Sea and Baltic littoral. The presence of the *kontors* reduced competition between Hanseatics, and most regulations included measures designed to level the playing field between them while dictating the minimum required profit margins and managing financial risk.[111]

For the London *kontor*, the Hanse set up their cloistered base of operations at the Stahlhof or Steelyard on the north bank of the Thames, which enjoyed direct private access to a wharf on the Thames. It was also sometimes called the Easterling Hall, which simply meant 'The hall of the eastern merchants'. Today, the UK still derives the full name of its currency, pounds sterling, from pounds *easterling*, testimony to the reliability and stability of their trade and exchange. Zimmern[112] relates that the Steelyard stood on Thames Street close to Dowgate just above London Bridge, once the only city gate that led directly to the water. The whole length of the street leading to the postern gate was lined with the wharves, warehouses and houses of the Hanseatic staff. The imposing north front was of several storeys. It included their great hall, the gabled roof of which was surmounted by the double-headed eagle. Here they met and ate in sumptuous surroundings, reputedly decorated in the 1530s by Hans Holbein the Younger. Its walls survived until 1851.

Close to the river lived the housemaster, whose house was served by a fine kitchen producing Germanic delicacies and Rhenish wine at a discount. Between the two was a garden planted with a mix of fruit trees and a vineyard and which also served as an enclosed place of discreet recreation. The merchants used German as their common language, from which they derived a sense of security in trying times, though this might have alienated locals at times.

Around the country the league ran smaller outposts, known as *faktoreien* (factories), at York, Hull, Bristol, Boston, Lynn, Scarborough, Newcastle, Norwich, Yarmouth and Ipswich.[113] At Lynn, Hanseatic buildings still survive along the riverside. On parts of the continental coast the Hanse had further factories, such as at La Rochelle, Bourgneuf and Bordeaux, from where they could negotiate the best prices, principally for wine and salt. At London the merchants organised themselves into strong regional groups according to their origins: Rhinelanders, men from the Baltic coast and the Baltic states (Livonia) with Gotland (Sweden).[114]

Upon the accession of each English monarch, Hanseatic trading privileges had to be renewed. If the Steelyard was organised on a regional German basis, so too the factories around the country took on a more parochial air, with different groups having preferred partners for trading.[115] Thus Lübeckers preferred working through Boston, while Hamburgers were prominent at Yarmouth, Prussians at Hull, men of Cologne at Ipswich and those of Bremen at Lynn. In London itself, Rhinelanders tended to predominate. It is unclear whether or not this has resulted in any regional archaeological biases, such as the import of the variety of Flemish and German stonewares from the later fifteenth century, but Raeren wares, noted above, seem to appear everywhere in urban contexts at around the same time –*circa* 1475 – and accompanied the rise in the popularity of beer imported from the Low Countries, much of it undoubtedly though Bruges.

'Cherysshe Marchandyse'

It has often been levelled at the Hanse that they had a stranglehold on Baltic trade, but this was far from the case. Although their position was almost always strong, and by treaty England had to compromise with them in 1437, the traffic was two-way and it must be remembered that theirs was primarily a carrying trade, often in the absence of larger English ships, and whose numbers, certainly in the early days, were restricted not by Hanseatic rules but by the difficulties of the journey and a multiplicity of languages. German speakers found a resident merchant class with whom they could converse. At Lynn there was a sizeable group of German shoemakers resident by the 1420s. In the customs accounts lists for Lynn for 1503–04, incoming goods comprised furs, cloth, feather beds, lamps, copper kettles, drinking glasses, tankards (possibly Raeren wares), knives, scissors, market baskets, straw hats and musical instruments (as at Hull). Also of increasing value throughout England were cargoes of Baltic timber, particularly the Prussian specialities wainscot, barrels and bowstaves. Both the navies and the trading fleets of north-western Europe were dependent upon Baltic ship timber, as were the builders of its cathedrals and castles, even archers across half a dozen armies. Baltic wood was the basis for the infrastructure of north-western Europe.

As a byproduct of the timber trade and its waste, wood ash was produced in huge quantities. Invaluable to England's dyers, such ash might travel across England to dyeing centres, even in the Midlands. Pitch and tar too were also a byproduct. In 1464, almost 10,000 barrels of the sticky black stuff went down the Vistula to the coast.

The English were drawn to the Hanseatic towns of the western Baltic during the fourteenth century, but the lure of the eastern Baltic was stronger, especially Danzig, through which came so many raw materials much needed and desired in England.[116] It also provided a ready and thirsty market for English cloth. Merchants of Lynn especially had eyes for Danzig, and the two port towns readily hummed the same tune.

Baltic products included amber, herring, osmund and some copper from Sweden, grain from Livonia and Prussia, beer from Lübeck, Wismar and Rostock, and wax from the south, as far as Warsaw and Lviv. Along with the great deal of copper coming from the Tatra mountains and through Danzig, the Swedish town of Falun also mined copper for the Hanse, and this too found its way to Bruges and English markets along with Swedish osmund out of Sigtuna and Visby.

Hops, sugar, fish, grindstones (probably schist from Trelleborg, found on many archaeological sites), carpets, tapestries, frying pans, playing cards, paper, vinegar and mirrors were all being bought by Lynn merchants at Antwerp, as were bricks and tiles, feeding and fuelling the existing East Anglian ceramic building tradition, which it shared with the clay lands of the Netherlands and Flanders.[117] Many of these would have been sold on one of the two harbourside markets at Lynn, which had existed there for hundreds of years.[118] These were not simply luxuries; many could not be had from English suppliers and met demands for what was notably foreign. As part of a two-way trade, Lynn merchants were settled in Rostock, Wismar, Stralsund, Danzig and Scania by the early years of the fifteenth century. From 1373, after a period of more liberal widespread trading across the Baltic and Scandinavia, Lynn increasingly traded principally with Danzig, where its representatives were known as 'the English nation in Danzig'. In fact, from the 1380s the English, mainly through Lynn and principally through Danzig, controlled more than three-quarters of Anglo-Prussian trade.[119] Both sides were strong in their partners' backyard, and Prussia became the flashpoint for Anglo-Hanseatic quarrelling. However, despite their considerable presence in Prussia, the English were never able to get trading privileges.

Tensions with the Hanse were always likely to boil over. The opening of the fifteenth century saw a major dispute with its roots in a violent naval clash during the reign of Richard II, but it was characterised by financial back-and-forth, with claims and counterclaims for damages escalating each year. By 1407 the Hanse was demanding more than 25,000 nobles from England, and England in turn was claiming almost 9,000 nobles from the Hanse.[120] Matters were complicated by English seizure of three Livonian ships and the drowning of 250 sailors (a suspiciously round number), for which another £7,500 was claimed in damages. Such was the fraught relationship at times, despite apparent 'privileges' and an oft-quoted and ratified willingness to offer reciprocity of such privileges across northern Germany.[121]

England was very definitely at the root of a major fracas with the Hanse in 1449 when it captured the Hanse's entire Bay Fleet, the dedicated salt fleet operating out of the Bay of Bourgneuf, between Guerande and La Rochelle. In response, all English merchants in Prussia were thrown into prison, with the unsurprising result that trade with Germany halved overnight! In 1454 Danzig itself changed hands and became Polish, putting trade onto a different track. Three years later the city received a charter from its new masters, giving it sole control over shipping and commerce.

Although from 1457 Danzig appeared happy to continue with Lynn merchants, giving them regular safe-conduct passes, the city was now free to deny any merchant a right of abode. This had the effect of destroying the existing system of English cloth distribution, which depended upon an expat English community there. From that moment on, Danzig controlled more than half of all trade traffic with England.[122] By the 1460s English trade in the Baltic was at a very low ebb. When England and the Hanse met in open conflict between 1468 and 1474, it was as much to try to resurrect that trade as fight against its suppression. When the conflict ended in the Treaty of Utrecht in 1474, the trade did not pick up but remained constrained by ongoing Danish hostility, which made English passage into the Baltic very dangerous indeed.

In 1474 the Hanse was granted by way of the Treaty of Utrecht properties in Hull, Boston and Lynn, where they set up a new steelyard in that same year.

As time went by it became clear that, although the Hanseatic League existed to protect the interests of its members, there was insufficient agreement as to what those individual interests were and how they changed through time. Inflexibility, which once kept member states in line, might increasingly alienate those same members. Backsliding became more frequent and conflict within and without increased.

The end of the Hanseatic League was presaged by the Novgorod *kontor* being closed in 1494 by Moscow. Although it reopened in 1514 it was never the same again, and when Bruges lost its trading position after the Zwin inlet silted up in the early 1520s, the whole league was thrown into doubt.

In the early decades of the sixteenth century, as a byproduct of the discovery of America, the Newfoundland cod fisheries opened, offering an alternative to Lübeck's trade through Bergen and Hamburg's part in that of Iceland. In addition, turning Antwerp into the spice capital of northern Europe (via Portuguese suppliers) helped break the Italian spice trade. However, these new markets had the effect of shrinking the Baltic trade as a proportion of the wider trading markets. The loss of Mediterranean shipping left an ailing overland trade to increase. Thus land access to and from central and eastern Europe increased, detracting from Hanseatic seaborne trade.[123] New markets essentially changed the Hanse, and, as Jahnke has put it,[124] such exploitation 'economically rearranged the Baltic Sea area'. In the end it was not awfully difficult to do, since everything depended upon long and difficult journeys fraught with danger. These journeys never got shorter, and, without major advances in shipping and a dramatic loosening of political restrictions, they never got easier.

3

SEA LANES AND SAILING ROUTES

Whatever arts we have or fail to have;
I touch my country's mind, I come to grips
With half her purpose thinking of these ships.

John Masefield, 'Ships'

Arrivals from the South

For anyone trading out of the Mediterranean to England, the security of the European coast was key. There were many desirable ports and anchorages, and some had the materials and facilities to repair vessels damaged by storm, piracy or other unfortunate pitfalls such as accidental fires, which almost always emanated from the brick-and-tile galley hearth.

For the Venetian galleys leaving Venice and heading out on the English run – or, more properly, the Flanders run – regular ports of call usually included Palermo, Messina, Cadiz and Otranto, before striking out across Biscay to their destination, sometimes Southampton but usually London, before their final journey to Sluys, the port of Bruges. On their return leg from Flanders, they usually called at Antwerp or Middleburg in the Netherlands, then met up at sea with their compatriots who had peeled off to London, and sailed together on to Alicante, Cadiz, Malaga, Almeira, Mallorca, Pisa and Talamone. If they carried return cargo for Barbary customers, they would make for One, Oran, Tunis and then Syracuse, before navigating into the Adriatic again. They would routinely take on pilots to help them navigate across the Gulf of Lyons and across the Bay of Biscay. When they got to England, they were required to carry their own mooring stakes and cables so that they could choose their own anchorage in the Solent and so that, when a swell rose, they were not reliant upon ropes supplied by the English which were of dubious age and had dragged and rotted in the mud for who knows how long!

Venetian carriers of Mediterranean sweet wines and spices from eastern ports did not need to make for Venice first (although they often did) but could use the many Venetian strongholds in the Mediterranean and Aegean, such as Chania, Heraklion and Candia on Crete and Monemvasia in the Peloponnese. They had a strong presence at Modon and a well-protected anchorage on the north side of the Gulf of Corinth at Naupaktos, where facilities also included shipbuilding and repair.

The Florentines stayed at sea for shorter periods between each port, their time seemingly limited under normal circumstances to, at most, a week between each call. Then they were supposed to stay in each port no more than three days, except for Sluys and Southampton. This is in no way due to any reticence as seafarers, but rather a reflection of the fact that in England they merely sought English woollen cloth and did not mind what they imported into this country in return. Thus, their very numerous, rapid port visits reflected the variety and intensity of their shopping trip to supply England with what it craved or might soon crave. Their standard route likely resembled Captain Albizzi's 1429–30 journey when he called at Marseilles, Port de Bouches, Aigues-Mortes, Cadaqués, Barcelona, Mallorca, Valencia, Deira, Javea, Benidorm, Villajoyosa, Alicante, Almeria, Malaga, Gibraltar, Cadiz, Lisbon, Pontevedra and Ribadeo before inadvertently ending up a long way west at Mousehole Bay in Cornwall.

Speed was not really an issue in the way it is in the modern industrialised world. Some ships were certainly faster than others, but that was not always an advantage. A fifteenth-century cutting-edge caravel might manage 10 knots in the hands of a competent mariner, and with a favourable wind behind it. However, most managed perhaps half that, and caravels were costly to insure compared with more sedate vessels such as the old-fashioned cog.[1]

However, there was certainly rivalry to be found that could be easily inflamed. The Florentines, when they turned to their own fleet as relative newcomers (1421), quickly gained a reputation for speed and efficiency in handling their north Italian galleys, which worked on a design similar to their Roman predecessors. The Venetians, even when flexible, complained of the competition from Ragusa, Genoa and Portugal, who mostly did not sail in galleys. They have been described as 'neurotically conservative'. It is, however, true to say that most new ventures and most maritime setbacks, not least piracy, ate away at established Venetian trade, since Venice had been in the premier position for so long and was jealous of everything and everyone. Certainly the Venetians were slow to change their ways, remaining stubbornly committed to carrying luxury goods when it was a demand for cheap bulk goods that was on the rise. Northern European ships began to ply a trade in larger fleets, agreeing to fix prices and enjoying safety in numbers. While Venice stuck faithfully to its old clients, the newcomers were not choosy as to where they found return cargoes and whole new markets therefore opened to them.

By the 1460s, the hungry Florentine galley fleets routinely outstripped the Genoese carracks and rivalled the Venetians, although they never made real inroads into the Venetian spice markets in the east. They did, however, manage to export back to the east taffetas, brocades and silks that had already come west in Venetian hands. However, they failed to protect their ships from piracy and desertion of crews was common. To their credit they only resorted to convict labour to row their galleys on one occasion, in 1464–65.[2] This came at a heavy price as the latter year saw their fleet sail with the plague on board, leading to the deaths of three of their four galley captains. Whatever their impact for a generation or two, the Florentine star waxed briefly and their trade eventually collapsed, their last state galley fleet sailing to England in 1477.

The sailing books or 'portolans' of the Greek Michael of Rhodes (c. 1385–1445), who served in Venetian pay, were compiled in the years 1434–45 and contain passage notes for English seamarks and harbours with the currents along the west and south coasts. Using these and another list of places where they took soundings, we get a clearer picture of the familiarity that the Venetians built up with the English south coast and the approaches to their chosen landing places of Southampton, Sandwich and London. Their Mediterranean neighbours would have used similar portolans, and Albizzi's 1429–30 diary may be placed alongside that of Michael of Rhodes, his direct contemporary, to tease out some definite seamarks and stops they shared. That was Albizzi's first trip to England as far as we know, but by the time Michael of Rhodes began compiling his own manuscript in 1434 he was a seasoned mariner and had already served on the Flanders galley fleet seven times since 1404, initially as an oarsman but thereafter working his way up. He had also served on numerous other Venetian fleets throughout the Mediterranean and had served some of the Signory's finest

Sea Lanes and Sailing Routes

fleet commanders. By the time of his death, he had forty-four annual fleet voyages behind him. In 1438 and 1443 he was specifically on the London leg of the Flanders galley fleet.[3]

The following table contains the places in the passage notes that Michael of Rhodes and Albizzi mention, moving west to east. The American editor of the *Book of Michael of Rhodes* was unable to identify some of the places mentioned (here in *italics*), as too was the editor of Albizzi's diary.[4] I have inserted some of my own suggestions, based partly upon my research for this book, the etymology, their place in the running order and what I know happened to other galleys. For these suggestions, refer to the notes. Two are particularly interesting as they suggest the now-lost passage along the Wantsum Channel, Kent.[5] A surprise is that a northerner, Karl Koppmann, a Baltic mariner of the mid-fifteenth century, also knew and recorded many of the same places in his own sailing book, or *seebuch* in Low German.[6] These are added, as are those same places where they are labelled on a map of Europe by a Dutch cartographer, Lucas Wagenhaer, just after the end of our period of enquiry in 1585. In each case, whether the location is a hazard or a haven, the place mentioned is a permanent one, intended to be there as a permanent *aide memoire* to mariners. It is no use including shifting sands or shingle because any advice in this respect is poor – they move. If in doubt, take on a pilot!

The intrinsic value of these portolans as sailing instructions are very much questionable, as may be seen in Michael of Rhodes' instructions for sailing into the Kent port of Sandwich, well known to the Venetians but in fact the favourite port of the Florentine state fleet for a number of decades: 'To know how to enter the port of Sandwich, know when the moon is north-south, high tide. And when you are ready to enter, you will see a forest on the land between the west and the north-west. And steer for this forest keeping off the land to the port side, at two or more arrows' distance.

Seas of Plenty

Michael of Rhodes Portolan of Spain and its crossing (1434–45)	Michael of Rhodes waters, tides of Spain, soundings at: (1434–45)	Name used by Michael of Rhodes	Albizzi diary seamarks (1429)	Name used by Albizzi	Karl Koppmann's *seebuch* name (Mid C15th)	Lucas Wagenhaer 1585
Milford Haven		Mirafiurda			Milvorden/ Mylvoerde	Muijfoordt
			Bristol Channel	Golfo di Bristo		
					Kaldey (Island) for Tenby	
Lundy		Lundei			Lundi	Lundij
Mumbles Head		Ulmi				
Appledore		Lubachi				
Padstow		Patristo			Padestaw	
Scilly		Sorlenga			Sorlinge Sello	
	Lands End	Longaneus			Cape Engelendsende	
Mousehole		Maxiolla	Mousehole Bay	Golfo di Musuofulo	Muschol/Musele	
Penzance					Pandany	
Falmouth	Lizard Point	Aloxert/Loxert			Lysart	Lisard
	Falmouth	Falamua			Valemude	
	Dodman Point	Godeman			Dodemanshovet	
Fowey	Fowey	Faduich/Fadoich			Vawyk	

112

Sea Lanes and Sailing Routes

	Eddystone Rock			Benedetta of Plymouth	Idensteyn	
	Cape Rame	Chavo de Rama				
Plymouth			Plymouth	Palamua	Rammeshovet	Ranoijk
		Premuda/ Premua			Pleymude	Plymous
			St Michael's Mount	Monte di Santo Michele		
			Mounts Bay in Cornwall	Monte Vai in Cornovaglia	Montsbaye	
Burgh Island	Green Island	Ixole Verde	Green Island	L'isola verde		
	Bolt Head	Chavo de Botre				
	Goodstart/Start Point	Godester	Goodstart	Capo di Gomestieri	Hoek van den Gholsterte	Goustart
	Torbay	Tores			Tursbage/ Torresbaye	Torbay
	Hope's Nose	Chavo de Toro				
Dartmouth		Altamua	Dartmouth	Artemua	Dortmude (& Sunte Patrix kerke)	Dartmosh
Portland Bill	Portland Bill	Ras de Porlan	Portland Bill	Capo di Brullano	Portlande	Poortlant
	St Aldhelm's Head/ St Alban's Head	Paraze de Sancta Telma			Sunte Andres lande	S. Andries

113

Seas of Plenty

Michael of Rhodes Portolan of Spain and its crossing (1434–45)	Michael of Rhodes waters, tides of Spain, soundings at: (1434–45)	Name used by Michael of Rhodes	Albizzi diary seamarks (1429)	Name used by Albizzi	Karl Koppmann's *seebuch* name (Mid C15th)	Lucas Wagenhaer 1585
	Poole	Pula			Pole	
The Needles	The Needles	Las Aguyas/ Agogias				
Cowes		Chavo de Cuor				
Isle of Wight		Ixola Doich	Isle of Wight	L'isola di Vicche	Eyland van Wicht	
St Helens (IoW)		Sancta Lena			Sunte Helenen	
Southampton		Antuna	Southampton	Antona	Hamton	Hamton
Calshot spit (not castle)		Chalzesores	Calshot spit	Calzadores	Kalkesort/ Kalkesorde	
	Hamble	Anbre				
Portsmouth		Portamua			Portesmude	Portmouth
Chichester	Chichester	la zitta vecchia				Tijchestre
	Seven Sisters	Sete Falage				
	Selsey Bill	Strany				
	Shoreham	Soran				
Beachy Head	Beachy Head	Chavo Belzep	Beachy Head	Capo di Belceppo	Bevesyr/ Bevesier	

Sea Lanes and Sailing Routes

St Andrew at Fairlight	Fairlight	Sanct'Andrea de Erlaga		
				Pilivirani (Pevensey)
				Verley/Virly	Fierlij
				Hovede (Hythe)
Winchelsea		Salaxeu		Winkelsee
Camber		Chamara		Kamer
Romney	Romney	Romaneo		Romenye
				Dinginisse/ Der Nysse
Dover (i.e. The Downs)	Cape of Dover	Dobla	Cape of Dover	Daveren, Dünen	Daur
St Margaret's at Cliffe		Sancta Malgaritta		Sunte Margreten
Kingsdown		Inguan		
Sandwich Haven		Sanuis		
	Dunes of Sandwich	Dones de Sanuis		
Tower on the Isle of Thanet*		Ture de Tenette		Tent
Wantsum Channel? ('wormy land')#		Terra Vermegia		

115

And bear in mind that the land of Sandwich you will see three bell towers, and you will steer for that forest as far as the small bell tower. You will discover there is a fourth. Keep this small one lined up with the third, then continue and steer for a forest, on a beach, then toward a mill, as far as the first bell tower on the south-west. Steer on a white point that is an island to starboard and go all out because of the current.'[7]

It may have been fine for someone already familiar with the approach – on a clear day or perhaps a night with a bright moon – but it left no margin of error for dark nights or fog, for new buildings to be constructed or existing ones demolished, or the potential for a forest to be felled (or its growth to obscure a building); indeed, it relied on two people agreeing on what was the average distance of a bowshot. It was fraught with difficulty, and for Sandwich in particular there was no indication that it would be almost totally silted up within thirty years of the compilation of these notes. It would be surprising if such descriptions were reliable for very long at all. It is for this reason that modern passage notes are regularly updated. Witness K. Adlard Coles' similarly intended volume on sailing the south coast harbours, which was first issued in 1939 and had run to five editions by 1973.

Even apparently straightforward sailing was a difficult proposition. Since many ships, such as the Italian state galleys, travelled in convoy, and others would readily do so out of a need for mutual protection, station-keeping was a must. For a big vessel to drop out of station was to risk one of them losing the wind to another, resulting in a dramatic loss of speed or, worse still, a collision at sea. Even under oars, to prevent oars clashing, and wakes taking another's water, a galley had to keep strict station.[8] To ensure this they devised a strict set of signals (shouts being largely inaudible or liable to misinterpretation), either by flags and banners and or by hand signals, and by night these signals extended to the use of lights, lanterns and the galley fireplace to signal sail or oar intentions.[9] There was also a strict hierarchy, with galley captains deferring to a fleet commander in the lead galley. There could be no room for misreading intentions or instructions.

Arrivals from the North

The Hanseatic League was the biggest and most influential northern trading partner with whom England dealt during the fifteenth and sixteenth centuries. Its fleet was numerous, and far bigger than the state-owned fleets of the north Italian states. However, not being a state enterprise *per se*, it did not necessarily own its ships, merely hired them on contract from its member cities and the many enterprising private shipowners who would work for it.

For a Hanseatic trading ship out of its principal Baltic ports – for instance Danzig, or Wismar or Stralsund on the north coast of the Baltic – or from the east coast of Sweden, the journey to England was a long one. We do possess a volume of sailing instructions from the north – and these are hugely helpful, as will be seen for the east coast ports (below) – in the form of the mid-fifteenth-century *seebuch* of Karl Koppmann, whose work, like that of Michael of Rhodes, was to provide an *aide memoire* for sailors as they negotiated the coasts. His work extended along the south coast and up to Wales and Ireland.[10]

The ships of the north were not the ancient form of galley still used by the Italians, but cogs, carracks and some more modern caravels, faster but less tested and not as suited to the mountainous northern seas, nor as familiar to those who serviced them at ports around the Baltic, Kattegat, Skagerrak and North Sea coasts.

In this period, ships to and from England and chartered from the Baltic were unlikely to make a return trip more than once a season or even once a year. They would leave in the spring and be home again before the end of August, when the weather became more unpredictable. It must not be forgotten that the Baltic freezes over (albeit not as often as it used to) and these were the days before icebreakers. Hanseatic cargo ships would reach England as early as May but often came in high summer, sometimes with English vessels that had waited to travel in convoy. With the ice threatening in autumn, one return journey across spring and summer was usually all that was possible.

So seriously did the Baltic cities of northern Germany (Lübeck, Wismar, Rostock and Stralsund) take their trade that the sixteenth-century Swedish cartographer Olaus Magnus tells us in the notes to his 1539 *Carta Marina et descriptio* that they kept their harbours 'permanently lit up so that the seamen can avoid running into danger through carelessness', a fact that he illustrates with little beacon-tower icons along the coast.[11]

All ships out of the Baltic had to carry papers to certify their origin, since some Hanseatic cities had negotiated toll privileges not granted to others, and to make the most of these, masters and sailors would often exchange flags by changing ships to make sure they were taking such a vessel.

Generally Baltic ships on the English run and English ships on the Baltic run seem to have been of 100 tons or more; this at a time when English vessels of more than 150 tons were relatively uncommon, with smaller vessels making up the merchant fleet for the most part. Where tolls were paid at Helsingør (or Elsinore), many were of 400 tons or more, especially Hanseatic vessels.[12]

Negotiating the Baltic coast of Germany or Sweden, and carrying Polish grain or timber, Bohemian copper and Russian furs, all loaded via the huge harbour cranes mounted on the town gate at Danzig, a Hanseatic ship might call at Stockholm or Sigtuna for Swedish osmund and sail round the southern tip of Sweden into the Kattegat, calling at Trelleborg for schist honestones, which are found all over England's archaeological sites. Alternatively, if no Swedish port was on the itinerary, ships headed for the island of Bornholm and then into The Sound between Denmark and Sweden.

Sea Lanes and Sailing Routes

Sailing with Copenhagen to port, Øresund (The Sound) narrows to a natural bottleneck between Denmark's largest island, Zealand, and the Swedish mainland. Here one encounters the home of the Danish Sound Toll from 1429, almost the only source of foreign income for Denmark in the fifteenth century. A natural pinch-point where maritime traffic backed up and ships had to wait in line to have identity papers checked, cargo manifests confirmed, values noted and tolls paid, geography here very much played into Danish hands.[13] The Sound Toll was at Helsingør throughout our period, except for the years 1519–23, when it briefly moved to Copenhagen. The incentive to pay up grew with the introduction of Danish cannon at Helsingør by 1539 (they are shown on Olaus Magnus' map) to cover The Sound, with more on the far bank at Helsingborg.

From 1429 the toll was a single gold noble (scaling incrementally for larger ships), which the English paid almost without quibble. Others haggled and spent a great deal of time and energy trying to get the best of what was actually a fair price. When Edward IV reformed England's coinage in 1463–64 he introduced the ryal, which conveniently had the ship of state on one side and covered the exact basic fare for travelling into and out of the Baltic.

Bulk perishables like salt and wine paid a levy in kind. A salt ship would pay six barrels and wine 3 per cent by volume; for the salt the value was deducted from the cargo, while for the wine there was no compensation. From 1519, there was also a small toll of one guilder for large ships and a half-guilder for small vessels to maintain buoys on nearby rocks and lights at Kullen, Skaw and Anholt; these were necessary to ensure the safety of passing ships, so congested was the waterway.

The English had a reputation for always paying the Sound Toll, so if it looked particularly congested on their approach, or the weather was bad, from 1490 English ships were allowed to navigate west of Zealand instead, through what is known as The Belt, a waterway to the west between Zealand and Funen, Denmark's smaller island. A ship exiting here into the Baltic did so nearer Lübeck and Schleswig-Holstein in Hanseatic waters. They still had to pay the same toll, however, at Nyborg or Fredericia. If bound for Danzig and the eastern Baltic, the island of Bornholm was the waystation to seek out before proceeding further.

In 1497 there were 814 passages through The Sound and 981 English ryals paid; in 1503 the figures were 1,140 passages and 1,464 ryals. Despite being devalued by Edward IV, English coin was always good currency at Helsingor.

The Danish Sound (east of Seladia – Zealand) and The Belt (west of Seladia) on Olaus Magnus' 1539 *Carta Marina*. Lübeck, Wismar, Rostock and Rügen at the bottom. Note the cannon covering the narrows. Thanks to Uppsala University Library for permission to use this detail.

Sea Lanes and Sailing Routes

Denmark was but a memory when the ships passed the seamark of St Laurence's church tower in Skägen at that country's northernmost tip. Exiting into the North Sea, Hanseatic ships bound for England were most likely to head for London, Lynn, Boston or Hull, each with their own Hanseatic presence, exchanges and warehousing. Many would hug the coast until the crossing was shortened. Poised to look across the North Sea, at the mouth of the River Elbe, Olaus Magnus in 1539 depicts a considerable three-storey 'lighthouse' or beacon covering the waters behind Heligoland. This seamark would have made a valuable sailing instruction before striking out for England, with ships perhaps first hopping along the Frisian islands north of Holland and then crossing the North Sea or coasting first to the Zwin inlet and Bruges before striking out across the sea.

The map of Dutch mariner and cartographer Lucas Wagenhaer, published in 1585, includes its own very distinctive list of ports on the east coast and north-east coasts that would have been frequented by Hanseatic ships. Moving north, it has almost as many entries as the fifteenth-century portolans of the south coast, but in each case it gives no detail whatsoever, with Boston among its notable absences. Included are London, Colcester (Colchester), Herwits (Harwich), Leijstof (Lowestoft), Iermouth (Great Yarmouth), Winterdiu (Winterton-on-Sea), Cramer (Cromer), Lijdt (King's Lynn), Den Hemmer (the Humber estuary), Hul (Hull), Flemburg (Flamborough Head), Schareburch (Scarborough), Witbuy (Whitby), Hempel (Hartlepool), Sanderla (Sunderland) and Nijcaste (Newcastle-upon-Tyne).

Safely at anchor at their English destination, a return trip was not guaranteed for these sailors, but side trips back across to Holland or Bruges were common, whether to take English cloth to market or to pick up goods to bring back to the Baltic.

Crewing and Victualling

Meticulous or not, all voyages had to be planned, and this meant more than ensuring a ship was in a satisfactory condition for the voyage ahead. The right crew was needed and adequate provisions were vital, usually simple but filling fare. Weight was an issue; after all, every pound not given over to cargo was a pound not given over to making money.

The 1429–30 diary of Luca di Maso degli Albizzi, our Florentine captain, noted that his galley complement for the journey to England comprised 130 oarsmen plus twenty-five marines and senior sailors. He also mentioned that they actually needed 160 oarsmen and fifty others. Totals exceeding 200 seem to be common.[14] This is very much in keeping with the numbers for the larger Venetian galleys in the annual Flanders galley run, which were in the region of 600 tons.

On the 1485 Venetian run to Flanders via London, the galleys were crewed for an interesting mix of diplomacy, business and pleasure. There were the captain and his servants, a clerk, a priest, a notary, an admiral, two physicians and musicians. There were also to be thirty good salaried arbalists (gunners) of fighting age, four of them noble youths, and there could be one competent adviser for each galley in lieu of an arbalist, presumably to give basic training in the use of the guns, which were effectively early muskets. The number of oarsmen is not mentioned. The curious mix might have been related to the parlous situation in which the Venetian factory in London had found itself. By September 1480 it was having to bear the whole financial burden of the Flanders voyages and it was, as a result, almost bankrupt. It was very nearly shut down.[15]

The 1517 contract for the Flanders galleys included a stipulation for thirty bowmen[16] rather than arbalesters. It may be that between 1485 and 1517 Venetian experience at sea led them to rely on crossbows rather than arbalests, which were at this stage crude and liable to misfire (or not fire at all) if they had damp powder, which was a constant problem. Given that the 1517 galleys were required to purchase four cannon at their destination to be given to the Arsenale upon their return, the crossbows could be switched for artillery during the return leg if necessary.

Since the North Italian galleys were a particular type of vessel, at the apex of their development, their crew complement cannot be taken as typical of other types, but it does give a clear idea as to the manpower needed to crew them, making them a complicated and expensive proposition, at least to begin with. However, by 1400 the Venetians in particular were adept and well versed in their deployment all over the Mediterranean and on the Flanders run. It did not take long for the Florentines, who shared their familiarity with the galley, to fall into their own similar stroke.

It is likely that the numbers alone made for some problematic episodes in port, and there are occasions when the crew were forbidden to go ashore, and whole stops (such as Santiago de Compostela) strictly off limits, since drunkenness, brawling, whoring and even religious fervour would all take their toll on the numbers fit for service. It may have been this which persuaded the Signory to require the Flanders galleys, if detained by ice at Sluys, to deduct the overstay from time normally allotted to calling at Southampton, thus minimising urban distractions.

The stores needed to put to sea were considerable. The 1517 Flanders galleys each loaded 180 bushels of biscuit, a bushel being at least 95 lbs in weight. Each oarsman was allotted 18 ounces of biscuit per day (such ship's biscuit, often called 'Biscay bread', being the origin of hardtack). Since the galleys would make regular stops in port along the way, fresh produce could be had there, at least until they needed to cross Biscay and leave the relative safety of shoreline anchorages. It was certainly not all hardtack and beer. The Flanders galleys around 1440 allotted daily either 1 lbs 6 ounces of biscuit to each rower or 2 lbs of fresh bread, to which was added 5 lbs of cheese per month, and an allowance of 5 shillings per month for wine and 4 shillings of beans per month.[17]

When in 1465 the *Edward Howard* was being readied in Dunwich (almost all of which has since been lost to the sea), the expenses for a complement of twenty-six men and one child on the payroll comprised four dozen loaves of bread, four barrels of beer, rye, herring, saltfish, fresh fish, a cheese, and the flesh of a whole beast (unspecified). More bread, beer, beef and salt plus fresh fish were bought at Orwell, and ale (lacking beer) was purchased at Walberswick. The bill came to 36 shillings. Given that the run to Bordeaux took an average of ten days, it is reasonable to suppose that this floating larder was for just such a voyage, perhaps to bring back wine.

For a voyage from Bayonne in France to England, two galleys and a galliot were newly refitted for the English Crown. Their victualling comprised twelve pigs and a piglet ('a small one'), huge quantities of bread (one baker alone provided 500 loaves, which were stored beneath a sail at sea), napkins, dishes, platters and saucers, 260 mackerel, 20 tuns of cider, firewood and candles.[18] In this case, however, the list is surely a cargo of foodstuffs as Bayonne has become known for its celebrated ham. The crew may have only had the piglet and lots of mackerel to eat; the rest of the pigs may have been for sale upon disembarkation.

We know nothing of what sort of ship the *Edward Howard* was, but if crewing is anything to go by the record of *The Catherine* of Winchelsea in 1438 may give a clue. *The Catherine* was noted as a balinger, and carried a crew of twenty, similar to the *Edward Howard*'s twenty-six, suggesting the latter ship might have been a balinger too. *The Catherine* was only noted in detail because it was burnt under the walls of the coastal Crotey Castle in France during Henry VI's siege there, leading the king to pay recompense to its master.[19]

Alternatively, the *Edward Howard*'s crew of twenty-six may have put it in the class of a larger carrack such as *The Trinity* of Bristol. Two sets of instructions in 1483 suggest that twenty-six was not an uncommon complement for this ship. The *Caravel of Ewe* and the *Elizabeth* (home ports unknown) were made available for seakeeping operations under the boy-king Edward V, and each is noted as having a crew of twenty-six soldiers and mariners.[20]

When the 300-ton *Trinity* was working out of Bristol in 1480–81 it carried a crew of twenty-eight including some soldiers for defence. Its purser's accounts relate numerous quantities of biscuit taken on for crew's meals, but also various fresh elements and beer – a usual mix. This could be further supplemented if the ship was working on high days or holy days, when different fare was either allowed or encouraged.[21] It would not have been encouraged to partake in anything which was specifically related to cargo, however, most if not all of which would have been stowed, crated or slung, often sealed in such a way as to be out of the elements and parcelled according to its individual shipper or end purchaser where known.

At the other end of the scale, the port books for Elizabethan Rye list twenty-seven fishing boats going to fish off Yarmouth between 1565 and 1596. They carried a crew averaging ten men and two boys, with few variations.[22] Rye's Elizabethan trading ships, almost all under 40 tons, were crewed by six to ten men, depending upon their tonnage. Even when in port and 'stood down' a ship needed to be looked after. In 1518, Henry VIII's navy amounted to twenty ships and each was in port, moored on the Thames. Each one had between one and four men as skeleton crew aboard, except for the flagship, the *Henry Grace à Dieu*, which had twelve, and the *Great Galley*, which had to be moved by oarsmen and so required a skeleton crew of twenty.[23]

When the Crown was paying for a special seakeeping fleet during the politically hazy days of 1483 as Edward IV's drained coffers passed seamlessly via the young, uncrowned Edward V to his supposedly wicked uncle Richard III, a large state carrack was victualled for Sir Roger Coben, one of a number in a fleet for 2,000 marines to keep the sea as England teetered on the brink of civil war once more. We must conclude that Sir Roger commanded a well-watered crew, as can be seen:[24]

> Paid for by Sir Roger to Richard Alder at The King's Head, (London) Bridge Street, Vintner:
>
> Flour, beef and eighty fish, a pipe of good wine, sixty pipes of wine @ 8s per pipe, a pipe of dull beer, a barrel of good ale, twenty pipes of beer 'and other stuff!', expenses to the steward of the ships for purchases, expenses to the purser for fuel, bordes and fresh accates (?), to the tallow chandler for candles, to the smith in The Tower for a great kettle and a great trivet, for a great pan and other stuff for the kitchen (galley), bought in London, for crayers and bottes to bring the stuff to the ship, to the under-purser for fresh accates (?) and fuel, to Wm Clark at Sandwich (?pilot?), to Sir Roger in wages for 133 men that were with him in the shippe, as by their names 10s the pece, Wm Fissher for the wages of twenty-six men, 10s per man, Edmund Hynsle wages for forty men, John Ashley wages for four men, To the purser for two men, which is in all seventy-two men.

The payments and expenses totalled almost £230, a considerable sum to claim from the Crown as expenses for victualling a single ship. There were further extraneous payments to 'lodesmen', who were paid to conduct it with some 2,000 men downriver to join the fleet for offensive operations. These were lightermen whose vessels specifically provided inshore taxi services and the carriage of freight from the anchorages to the wharf and vice versa. Merchant ships in royal service were numerous. Some, called 'showtis', waited in 1444 for royal freight to come from the Tower and two other addresses in London. They waited at Tilbury in Essex and at The Pool, east of London Bridge, where they would transfer their loads to bigger vessels.[25]

In 1536, right at the end of the period covered by this book, we have a list of victuals bought for the (naval) ships of Henry VIII. They indicate that some effort was made to ensure crews were sufficiently cared for and the ships themselves were well fitted out, boasting a chemist's shop, surgical tools (not found on most merchant vessels!), a carpenter's shop and even the materials for building the oven deep below decks. The purchases were as follows:

> Bisquitt, meale, biere, byef, poerke and bacon, seasoning, butter, cheese, oatemeale, salte, mustarde seede, vinegar, sweete oyle, fish of Lynn, the best Rumeney, firewood, candells, soape, paper, surgeons kit, balance pans and weights, apothecary's remedies, a hand mill, canvas, netting hand tools, mattresses, salting pan, barrelles, handbarrowes, grindstones and whetstones, carpenter's tools, 100s of nails, wedges, a smith's andvile (anvil), and brick, tile and stone for an oven.[26]

Food and water were carefully calculated to last the duration of the voyage, including the planned legs between ports. Foul weather, supplies being spoiled by sea water and journeys simply taking too long could be disastrous, as Brother Felix Fabri found out off Paphos in 1480: 'After two days' wait, we put out, but adverse winds drove us off course, and we tossed about hove-to until we began to run short of provisions.'

On another occasion he notes that the captain and all the ship's officers were so worried about the freshwater situation that they denied any to the animals they had on board for butchering, reserving it only for human consumption. Fabri, who was clearly not short on compassion, noted the animals' piteous plight as one by one they perished, forced to lick the salty night-time dew that formed on the planking.

English armies, for both personnel and freight, needed huge numbers of ships of all nationalities, as the royal whim dictated. The French campaign of Henry V in 1417 took hundreds of English vessels as well as dozens from the ports of Holland. In 1427, Henry VI served notice to the ports of London, Sandwich, Dover, Winchelsea and other Cinque Port towns to assemble (the words used are 'detain and seize') every vessel between 20 and 140 tons to take the army to France.[27] As a result, trade might be suspended at short notice since the king had requisitioned just about everything that would float. In the 1520s, under Henry VIII, that policy would spell disaster and figure strongly in the end of the annual Flanders galleys from Venice.

Life at Sea

For Brother Felix Fabri, on his second pilgrimage to the Holy Land in 1483, his observations of weeks spent at sea in a crowded galley are illuminating. He lists pastimes to stave off long hours of boredom. He also notes that others turn to drinking, especially Saxons and Flemings 'and other men of a low class'. One might imagine he is slightly biased against those from northern Europe.

Fabri noted that there were numerous games played – and much betting, 'some of them with a board and dice, others with the dice alone, some with cards, others with chess boards, and one may say that the greater number is engaged at this pastime'. Judging from the numbers of bone dice, bone and jet counters and chessmen found on archaeological excavations right across Europe, especially urban ones, the ubiquity of gaming is unsurprising. Hundreds of pieces and dice must have been dropped on board. Gaming tables were imported up and down England's east coast in Hanseatic ships.

Fabri also listened to a lot of music on board, as some 'sing songs, or pass their time with lutes, flutes, bagpipes, clavichords, zithers and other musical instruments'. Again, music-making was far from the preserve of professional musicians, and tuning pegs of every kind are a common find on English and Welsh excavations, both urban and rural. Many instruments figure in the import lists of the Hanse at both Lynn and Hull.

Some sailors discuss worldly matters, he says, while others read books, pray with beads, sit still and meditate or shout aloud for lightness of heart. Some laugh; others whistle. Some work with their hands, while others sleep out of laziness – and some to excess. Others still spend their time in physical training. And some are more contemplative and observant, watching their surroundings and those in them. Some, he says, even write travel books in their spare time – patting himself on the back for his own choice of pastime. Brother Felix paints a picture as varied as one might see in any late medieval town; 200 or more people thrown together in a small space for weeks on end, with nothing to do except work and try to get along with their neighbours.

Finally, he turns to unpleasant aspects of a voyage. Those same 200 or more confined are filthy and smelly, and he relates the lengthy daily ritual of hunting and catching lice and vermin – and the broken sleep if they ignore them.

With sailors and rowers on deck and pilgrims and their luggage between decks, overcrowding was certain. Fabri laments that every morning and night bulky bedrolls must be rolled up and stowed and unpacked again before sleep. Hung on nails above their heads, they were thus kept out of the way during the day. He was fed up with this constant toil. Fabri also remarks on the untrustworthiness and thieving tendencies of the rowers (whom he again calls galley slaves). He complained that if something wasn't nailed down it would walk, for which reason the rowers were forbidden to go below and the passengers discouraged from mixing with them at all.

It wasn't all evil smells and poor relations, however. Early in his 1483 voyage, on 2 June, their departure called for the ship to be dressed. The fo'c'sle was hung with a tapestry all around and the galley was dressed with seven large silk banners, depicting the Holy Sepulchre of Jerusalem (the largest banner, white with a red cross); Venice and St Mark (the winged lion, forepaws on the sea, hind paws on the land); the arms of Pope Sixtus IV (a green oak tree with golden acorns and the keys of St Peter against a sky blue background); the captain's banner, described as colourful; the arms of Venice and those of the captain together; and two banners, both alike, depicting a black lion on a white background.

Later there was an onboard party marking the eve of the feast of St John the Baptist, after a tough day battling a heavy Aegean swell. The crew took out forty wood-and-horn lanterns ('lanthorn', the origin of lantern) and hung them from bow to stern using the masthead above the rowing benches. The whole ship was lit up and everyone gathered on deck. Fabri rejoices: 'Thereupon the trumpeters began to blow their trumpets, and the galley-slaves and other sailors sang, rejoiced, chanted, danced, and clapped their hands; whereat all who stood roundabout were wrought upon by the shouts of gladness and the clapping of hands to rejoice at the respect paid to the most blessed forerunner of our Lord.'

Curiously, Fabri notes that he had never before encountered the practice of clapping hands in joy (although he quotes its use in Psalm 46), nor could he believe the sheer exhilaration of the moment as everyone joined in. He was apparently no partygoer.

The Choice of Port Destination

For a foreign trader looking to land a valuable cargo, perhaps owned by a dozen different shippers and investors, the choice of the right English port was critical. For old hands the choice had already been made by their forebears in countless voyages over decades or more, but any new venture meant the available ports were scrutinised in a league for safety, practicality and unloading fees and tolls. Such, for instance, was the choice set before the Florentines when they decided to send their first state fleet to England in the late 1420s.

The first and foremost consideration was a safe anchorage. In a century in which piracy and casual violence was rife, safety might be indicated by how well protected they might be from sudden attack. However, primarily this concept refers to the anchorage of the ship while waiting to unload, overwintering if necessary and waiting to load up before departure. A landlubber tends to think that in a storm a ship heads for port, but at such a time ports can be hugely dangerous. No one wants to be in an unfamiliar port when a storm hits, since the movement of vessels becomes unpredictable, and disaster comes from anything with which they might make unplanned contact. When a swell rises the clearance beneath the keel changes unpredictably, so depth is key. The fastness of the anchor and the quality of the mooring cable come to be relied upon, the normally welcoming wharf-side or quayside becoming an anvil against which the ship is beaten, and every other ship nearby becomes a potential battering ram or seaborne missile if its cables break or the anchor drags. The incoming or outgoing tide then carries with it assorted bobbing crates, barrels and other weighty receptacles amid a heaving, grating meniscus on the surface, while rolling like a mincing machine just beneath are splintered wood, shredded rope, canvas and, sadly, drowned and broken bodies. It is as bad as being on the rocks.

When a storm threatened, a surprised vessel in an unfamiliar anchorage would seek to escape to a known 'haven' or 'road' – a deepwater offshore anchorage – and ride it out, hove-to (stopped) and anchored to ensure a heading, so that the ship remained bow-on to the current and not beam-on and rolling with every wave. If an unwary captain did not get his vessel away from a quay and other boats in a storm, he was likely to find it floating as matchwood in the harbour or see its masts alone sticking out of the water.

Brother Felix Fabri, aboard a Venetian galley to the Holy Land in 1480, described the uncertainty of hurriedly trying to find a safe anchorage when bad weather was closing in:

> We came to a wide channel in which we caught the wind very heavily, nevertheless we tried to anchor in the middle of it; so, we swung the sounding-lead, and found too great a depth. We therefore sailed further; but when darkness fell, we could go no further without great danger. We took another sounding and found the bottom, but still very deep; nevertheless, we let go our biggest anchor to hold the galley. But when it reached the bottom, it found neither rocks, stones nor sand on which it could grip but dragged over the bottom after the galley, to our great concern. With enormous effort the anchor was weighed, and dropped in another place, where it again followed the galley like a plough following a horse. It was then hauled in again and we dropped it in a third place, where it caught upon a rock. The galley stopped, pulled the cable taut and veered from side to side. Then it slipped once more and began to drag again, but suddenly caught on another rock where it stuck fast. There we hung throughout the night.

No doubt a long night of worry.

The second consideration when choosing a destination was the port's access to the markets of the investing shippers. By the 1420s anyone with a great ship, be it galley or carrack, had perhaps half a dozen major southern ports from which to choose: London, Sandwich, Southampton, Poole, Dartmouth and Falmouth. In the north it was Hull, Boston or Lynn. London was a shared destination for most, at one time or another. In the West Country one can add Plymouth and Bristol to the premier league of ports. These had the best access to the road network and a speedy exit for imported goods to inland markets as far as the Midlands. If a sailor's merchant clients already had guild connections with their English counterparts, they might already have established routes in and out and the choice was already made. In late medieval England, roads comprised little more than the old Roman network, at best unkempt, at worst badly degraded, but each year carrying far more traffic than was ever intended.

Thirdly, but no less importantly, came the accessibility of the port from the sea. With so many small harbours around England's coasts, sailors had to choose carefully. There needed to be sufficient depth of water in a port, not just outside the harbour but all the way into its chosen berth beside a wharf. While ships' boats or lighters might be able to journey out to unload smaller crates and packages from ships by hand and transfer passengers, a harbour that dried out at low tide was useless if one had to approach in a galley or carrack of 500 tons' burden or more. Just half an hour resting on rocks might be enough to break the back of a fully laden boat or prise up its meticulously contoured hull planking. Status as a dry harbour was enough to ensure that fishing village after fishing village, from Mousehole to Robin Hood's Bay, never became anything more than that. To coin the title of Tim Marshall's 2015 bestseller, we are prisoners of geography. That is as much true at the small scale as it is in international geopolitics.

The fourth concern was the need to keep the ship in good shape. It is rare that a vessel does not show signs of use: worn blocks, a loose rudder, split masts and torn sails, frayed halyards and leaking joints. Boatyard facilities were, and are, a prerequisite of a suitable port.

Lastly, the crew needed safe and welcoming quarters while in port, an assurance that sometimes fell painfully short in the regular heavy swell of anti-foreign feeling which characterised trading into

England and Wales in the fifteenth and sixteenth centuries. Stays during unloading and loading could be lengthy. Places such as the Cistercian Netley Abbey, Southampton, known for its welcoming reception of foreign mariners in port, were indispensable.

These same considerations prevail to this day and are no different for any boat owner wishing to berth their vessel anywhere outside a home port or familiar anchorage. In the middle decades of the twentieth century a series of books was published for boat owners which highlighted the merits and disadvantages of every port around the English coast, showing how these same issues were tackled by each new generation.[28] Below I quote briefly from K. Adlard Coles' marvellous passage notes as an illustration of these recurring but vitally important questions, each one borne in mind before every voyage or before the signing of contracts to land imported goods. The reader should bear in mind that the answers quickly went out of date – they describe 'modern' ports and facilities from 1939 to 1973 (in five editions), for pleasure craft undoubtedly much smaller than almost all the great ships of 1400–1540 but concerned with the same issues. The changes at those ports in the intervening centuries cannot be overstressed, but the considerations have remained constant.

We begin with notes for Southampton, one of the three favoured ports of the north Italians, and the destination Aubrey de Selincourt called 'the finest natural harbour in the world'.[29]

Southampton

Tide rises: 13ft Spring, 10.5 ft Neaps; Depths: Deep harbour for ships of any size.

Southampton Water is a natural harbour which has been used by ships of all kinds from time immemorial (true even in the fifteenth century). It is an almost straight stretch of water, measuring some 6 miles from Calshot Castle to the Royal Pier. Navigation is easy in any weather bar fog. So far as facilities are concerned the town provides everything that can possibly be required. It is an easy journey [to and] from London.

When entering Southampton Water strangers will (between buoys) run north-west close to Calshot Castle. Those approaching from the west may take a short cut over the end of Calshot spit in 1¼ fathoms (90"/2.25m) low water (steering between buoys). Approaching from the eastward keep well offshore between Hillhead and Hamble as the shoal water extends a surprisingly long way from the shore. Whether coming from the east or west remember Bramble Bank, situated in mid-Solent. In spite of being such a well-known danger many still go ashore on it.[30]

These are the primary reasons why Southampton in the fifteenth century had long since picked itself as a preferred port and continued to do so. It may be compared very favourably with the less-than-glowing report that the same volume relates for modern Sandwich, increasingly disadvantaged since the later fifteenth century by a long series of maritime woes.

Sandwich

Tides: The ebb runs for 9 hours and the flood for 3 hours at Sandwich Town, but the current continues upstream for a short time after High Water and downstream for a short time after Low Water.

Depths: Entrance channel and river shallow. At High Water springs navigable with a maximum draft of 10ft (3.04m) or 6½feet (1.98m) at neaps as far as Sandwich.

Pegwell Bay dries out except for a narrow gulley carrying the river water. The channel is well marked (by buoys) upon which to steer. Buoys moved from time to time to account for shifting sands. Approach only in good weather.

Dubious 10ft mean high water spring and 6½ft mean high water neaps as far as Sandwich, with sludge bottom. Do not attempt to enter at night or in fog without local knowledge. At Sandwich the bottom is mud over chalk. For deep draft boats it is wise to prepare for drying out by the wall as the layer of mud is not very deep.[31]

For Sandwich, these sparser notes may be favourably compared with Michael of Rhodes' description of entering Sandwich around 1440 (see above). 'Proceed with care' should always be borne in mind.

Others along the south coast elicit mixed reviews, and even allowing for the centuries that elapsed between 1540 and 1973, the less-than-ringing endorsements are seen to be little more than updates on what John Leland said of many of them – or, more pointedly, what he did not say about them – back in the mid-sixteenth century. Some had garnered what were undisguised bad reputations as unsafe anchorages and harbours, such as Appledore and Mousehole, a drying harbour where in 1973 the available draught just outside the harbour was a mere quarter-fathom (18 inches).

This is more than sufficient to show why Albizzi, captain of the Florentine state galleys, might in 1429 use Mousehole Bay as the first of his seamarks on sighting England but could never begin to contemplate Mousehole as a shelter for his galleys in the event they arrived in bad weather. He would probably have to anchor off Falmouth, Plymouth or Dartmouth.

In a carrack, the weight of a prominent fo'c'sle and sterncastle would have made the pressure on the keel and tight planking intolerable if it came to rest on the bottom, and its back would break, so no thought of a drying harbour could be entertained. Although it is not an intention of this book to look at ship design in all its various forms (others have done this admirably), it is worth noting that in respect of the greatest Mediterranean visitors to these shores, the north Italians sailed galleys with straight, jointed keels. A typical great galley of 1445 (only a little larger than a Flanders galley of the previous generation) had a beam of almost 6 metres and a length approaching 50 metres, weighing 600 tons. There were few oaks to be found with heartwood longer than 8 metres (and everywhere their use in ships would compete with the needs of building projects on land) so such a boat keel would need to be jointed in at least five places. Unfortunately, we do not know their maximum draught, but fully loaded and with straight keels, for their oars to sweep effectively (and without clashing) they would have ridden relatively low in the water, with minimal freeboard.[32]

I conclude with K. Adlard Coles' description of another excellent harbour; it was a good choice in the fifteenth and sixteenth centuries but was disadvantaged by its great distance from everywhere except the West Country.

Falmouth

Tides: 17.2ft spring, 13.8ft neaps; Depths: The eastern entrance channel has 7 fathoms mean low water spring and the western one 3 fathoms (42 ft & 18 ft). Black Rock lies between the two and uncovers at half-tide. The main channel River Fal is deep as far as Ruan Creek.

Falmouth is the most westerly of the deepwater natural harbours of the south coast. The harbour and neighbouring rivers and creeks provide one of the best centres for sailing in the south of England ... beyond the docks there is a good anchorage and first-class facilities. On the opposite side (on the eastern arm) is St Mawes, which offers clean anchorage in beautiful surroundings. The central arm (of three) is the northern arm of the River Fal, largest and deepest arm which forks 5 miles up, the northern creek leading to Truro.

The entrance is deep, easily navigated, although very rough during onshore gales blowing against an ebb tide but is considered one of the safest on the south coast.

Anchorage and moorings. 1. Outside a good holding ground, protected from the west, suitable for large ships. 2. Carrick Road (centre of harbour; its name is no accident – Carrack Roads) and above. This is used by large vessels, but there is a big swell in southerly gales. 3. St Mawes Creek: in offshore winds or settled weather there is a delightful anchorage south-east of St Mawes harbour in about 8ft. Seven other anchorages in lesser water.[33]

While all these descriptions are merely extracts from a much wider series of very detailed observations of almost every harbour from Ramsgate to Penzance (with equivalents along other coasts also published), they respond to questions and concerns expressed by every generation of seafarers. They may be compared in detail to the observations which can be found in the writings of William Worcestre around 1480 for the port of Bristol and summarised in the next chapter as part of a gazetteer of ports in the fifteenth and sixteenth centuries; he listed the same things and painted a picture of a natural haven opposite a port town that had the safety and welfare of crews, the ships, valuable cargos and influential shippers in mind as the medieval port there reached its height, its prosperity very much the result of its geography combined with the foresight of its leading citizens.

Like William Worcestre, it could also be a landlubber who recognised a bad port when they saw one, such as Brother Felix Fabri, who arrived at Jaffa near the end of his second pilgrimage to the Holy Land in 1483:

It is very difficult and dangerous to make one's way into this port from the sea, and I believe there is hardly such another abominable harbour to be found in the whole circuit of the sea; for no great ship, from whatever quarter it comes, can enter the harbour, but must stay outside and find an anchorage by sounding: for out in the deep sea as far as the flight of an arrow there are reefs and steep rocks and shoals and stones rising up from the water ... nor can even small boats pass through except in one place ... and unless the pilot or boatman be careful the water takes hold, hurls the boat against the rocks, smashing it into a thousand pieces.

Despite everyone's best efforts, inevitably the weather and the seas took their toll on all vessels. While a great ship might be expected to give twenty to thirty years of good service, it did not come without considerable expense in maintenance and repairs. Any ship which arrived safely after a rough Biscay or North Sea crossing, having negotiated either the Mediterranean or the Baltic before that, might need considerable attention: tarpaulins and hatches ripped away, torn sails, rigging and other ropes snapped or fraying and some timbers beginning to shake, plus joints alarmingly prised open. These were matters for the boatyards. Archaeological excavations have found elements of an early fifteenth-century boatyard just off the old town quay at Poole, including stocks of timber knees and other structural elements, both new and recycled, stockpiled ready for use or reuse (in the event bundled into the remaking of a new wharf). William Worcestre in his writing on Bristol mentions stores of spare anchors and stacked fir trunks ready at the quayside for masts, spars and jibs as needed. At Newport in Gwent, perhaps the best theory on the fate of the excavated mid-fifteenth-century Newport Boat is that it collapsed in its dry dock while being worked upon, blocking the dry dock, which had to be filled in, entombing the vessel. A recent collapse of this sort happened on 22 March 2023 at the port of Leith in Edinburgh when the 250-foot RV *Petrel*, a US Navy vessel of 3,371 tonnes, was blown over in high winds, injuring thirty-five people. Even with modern engineering methods, it was not righted until May.[34]

At some point, all oceangoing vessels needed to careen and clean their hulls. This involved scraping the barnacles and accretions from their undersides and then recaulking the seams with freshly oiled hemp. The algal growth of just a few weeks could slow a vessel right down to the point where a ship might struggle to make headway in difficult seas. The tidal race in and out of the straits of Gibraltar (where the cold Atlantic Ocean swell meets the warmer enclosed basin of the Mediterranean Sea) would strain every joint on anything but a well-maintained boat in competent hands. The *Trinity* of Bristol in 1480 followed English tradition by calling at Puerto de Santa Maria in southern Spain, where it could be drawn up on a soft, sandy spar, heeled over onto a specially designed carriage and the hull careened without the ship breaking its back.[35] It could then be freed from its carriage and, with the help of judiciously placed ballast, be encouraged to right itself on the rising tide, ready once more.[36]

4

DESTINATION ENGLAND AND WALES

The map of places passes.
The reality of paper tears.
Land and water where they are
Are only where they were
When words read here and here
Before ships happened there.
                    Laura Riding, 'The map of places'

The Many Ways to Market
A huge number of ports made up the fifteenth-century rollcall of harbours at which inbound goods might be unloaded. The larger examples stand out, of course, and are listed by Williamson (1913):

[East coast] – London, Lynn, Dunwich, Boston, Scarborough, Whitby, Hull, Newcastle, Yarmouth and Ipswich; [South coast] – Southampton, Sandwich, Rye, Winchelsea, Dover, Folkestone, Plymouth, Dartmouth, Portsmouth, Weymouth, Exmouth; [West coast] – Bristol, Chester, Teignmouth.

The influential Eileen Power once set down a list of the smaller ports which also played a part, however small, on the south and south-east coasts: Brightlingsea, Rotherhithe, Walberswick, Rainham, Bradwell, Maidstone, Milton, New Hythe, Milhall.[1] Close attention to any stretch of the English coast can, in addition, add groups of other harbours or launching places and landing beaches, such as Poole, Lydd, Dungeness, Hastings, Hythe, Sittingbourne (Ashford) and Romney, all on the south coast and some at least briefly working ports, with or without a nearby safe anchorage, while shifting sands, shingle banks and salt marsh islands permitted coastal access for limited periods. Some had been snuffed out even before the fifteenth century.

A host of smaller coastal towns and villages were occasional ports of call, although some necessarily only for the smallest vessels: Minehead in Somerset, just out of the Severn Estuary, Brixham in Devon, today known for its fishing boats, and Mousehole in Cornwall, remarked upon by Albizzi. In some, such as Hastings and Deal, there was no harbour at all, just a beach onto which boats were winched using capstans or ground-anchored winches called horses. Preferred for the big ships was a discrete offshore anchorage served by lighters with which to land off-loaded goods. Some river estuaries or creeks also made for comparatively safe anchorages against bad weather, and many such creeks along otherwise dangerous, rocky shores sufficed to send a few goods ashore if tides permitted. Some erstwhile ports have since been lost to erosion by the sea. Dunwich in Suffolk in this way was lost having once been a thriving port town. On the other side of the country, Abergwaitha in Gwent was similarly lost. The same erosive power of the sea also moved sand and shingle around in such fantastic volumes that harbour mouths became choked, denied their sea access. The process never ends, and many were entirely lost to merchants in this way.

Destination England and Wales

The selection of ports which appears in the following chapters is not too dissimilar. History has left us with a near-contemporary description of the anchorages and port facilities through the work of the sixteenth-century antiquarian and librarian John Leland, whose state-sponsored journeys around England and Wales from *circa* 1540 have given us some memorable accounts, however brief, of the towns, villages and harbours he visited. It is not an exhaustive list, and many small harbours and landing places do not appear here as a result. It differs only a little from Williamson's 1913 list. Eileen Power's extensive list of 1937 is not reproduced here, not least because Leland did not detail East Anglia, although there are a few introductions of my own.[2]

In a manuscript volume preserved in the British Library[3] is a list of the places a contemporary Tudor considered to be the ports and harbours of England and Wales. It is an interesting list, grouping supposedly secondary ports along with their potentially dominant neighbour, but it is far from geographically consistent:

Kingston Sup[er] Hull, Grymmesbye et Scarborowe; Boston; Lynne; Yarmouthe, Blakeney, Cromer, Walberswick, Southwold, Aldeburgh, Woodbridge; Gippeswic [Ipswich], Colchester, Maldon; Sandwyche, Dover quondam, Milton and Porchester; London; Berwick upon Tweed; Caerlisle; […]; Ar … (?)., Nova … [New Romney?], […], Pevensey, Hastyngs, Winchelsea, Rye, Romney, Lympne, Folkeston; Southt [Southampton]; Poole, Lyme and Weymouthe; Bristoll, Bridgewatter, Mynehedde; Plymouth, Looe, Trem [unclear], Fowey, Penryn, Falmouth, St Ives, Padstow, Mounts Bay; Chester, Milford, Carmarthen, Conwy, Exeter, Dartmouth, Barnstaple, Ilfracombe…

Although not closely dated, the document is bound in with others of 1522–25 so is likely to be of that date. It contains some perhaps unexpected inclusions, such as Colchester and Bridgwater, both being essentially inland up long river channels. And since they are included, why are Norwich and York excluded? We do not know. The order is sometimes awry if any real progression was intended, and it may have been a preliminary list for discussion. It does however, to some extent equate with the list I have chosen to highlight in the following chapters.

I have chosen also to address a 1524 list of 'havyns, crickes and roodys' on Anglesey and North Wales found in the British Library. This has outstanding local topographical detail and is arguably without parallel.[4] It lists twenty anchorages and mooring places on Anglesey alone 'where any shippe or balinger or any other vessell may enter or land', to which it adds a further twenty-four in Caernarfonshire and four in Merionethshire. They include Holyhead and Amlwch – names followed up by Leland, Conwy and Barmouth.[5] All are in their sixteenth-century antecedents, written as heard – probably by an Englishman – and there is the challenge of some not having made it into modern Welsh with certainty, even as actual places. The intervention of the likes of a modern container port (Holyhead), an airbase (Cymyran Bay – RAF Valley) and a nuclear power station (Cemlyn Bay) don't help. However, with 'Llanviangell yn Traythe' coming down to us as Llanfihangel y Traethau and translating into English as 'St Michael's in the Beaches', inclusion in a portolan or passage notes was entirely appropriate, then and now.

London, Southampton and Sandwich stand at the head of our principal ports, and they appear regularly throughout this volume. The Italians with their great galleys generally made for Southampton and London, with Sandwich as their secondary destination.[6] The best-documented period for our purposes is 1435–56, during which only the Venetians regularly visited London. The principal port for other Italian vessels, mainly Florentine and Genoese, was an annual choice between Southampton and Sandwich. Otherwise, they had Falmouth, Plymouth, Dartmouth or Poole to call at if

The windswept Mynydd Bodafon looking out to Dulas Bay anchorage, Anglesey. Photo by Sara Elin Roberts.

they wished, or Bristol beyond, on the way to Ireland, which was then a very much smaller market.

From Michaelmas 1443 to Michaelmas 1444, which was a typical year, twenty-one Spanish and Italian ships called at Southampton. Among them, eight large carracks and one navis were Genoese or from Liguria, Genoa's coastal region. Between 1439 and 1445 an average of eleven Genoese ships arrived annually at Southampton, most of them carrying woad and alum. When the carrack of Genoese merchant Percivale Grillo unloaded mainly alum at Southampton and then stayed for two months during the depths of winter 1443–44, it did so alongside two Florentine state galleys returning from Flanders, two private Venetian ships, one Spanish, one Greek/Aegean and one other. Conversely the Florentines sent their annual state galley fleets year after year to Sandwich and Southampton, and any returning from Flanders not filled to the gunwales were encouraged to top up their outgoing cargoes there too, providing they had their safe conduct guaranteed. In portside inns, brothels and chapels most of the languages of Europe would have been heard. The Florentines alone allowed themselves forty-five days for loading at Southampton. By 1520 the Venetians allowed sixty days at Southampton after twenty-five at Sluys, so there was plenty of opportunity for relaxation, exploration or mischief.

In this same period the Venetian brothers Andrea and Federico Corner, shipping goods on the Venetian state galleys, sold almost £12,000 worth of goods out of Southampton, while in 1441 their inbound wine receipts at Southampton totalled £1,700, while another carrack took their pepper to Bristol, which was a gateway to Wales and a second gateway into the English Midlands.

The inward goods from Southampton were not necessarily unloaded beneath the walls of the city, although they did front the harbour and give direct access. The principal mooring lay off the western shore of Southampton Water at Calshot Spit, on which Calshot Castle was later built. There even the massive Venetian state galleys could ride at anchor, and there the Signory of Venice instructed them to berth safely for their extended stays.

Southampton enjoyed two principal busy routes inland, along which its imported woad, alum and much else travelled, as indicated by its Brokage Books. The first ran from Andover through Newbury, Abingdon and Oxford to Banbury (which, remarkably, is mirrored today by road traffic taking the M40 and A34 almost to the coast). The second route was specifically for the Coventry and Warwickshire wool-exporting centre and ran from Romsey through Whiteparish, Salisbury, Marlborough, Burford, Stow, Chipping Campden, Stratford-upon-Avon and Warwick before arriving at Coventry.[7] Coventry and to a lesser extent Warwick and Stratford upon Avon eagerly consumed whatever came back from the port on the return legs. This second route was a three-to-four-day journey by oxcart and one which was plied regularly by whole ox-convoys to and from Southampton, the north Italian sponsors seeking superior woollen cloth from both the Cotswolds and the wealthy merchant producers of Coventry and Warwickshire, across to the Vale of Evesham. Southampton Brokage Books record without comment the monotony of the constant woad convoys along the route to Coventry, a city which also had negotiated keen trading privileges at Bristol and sought numerous foreign merchants on its statute merchant rolls. By comparison with Southampton, goods coming in via Sandwich generally went via London, as did most of the cargos from other, smaller south-eastern ports.

At London, even the most cosmopolitan onlookers were excited when news travelled upriver announcing the approaching Venetian state galleys. Crowds would gather at Rotherhithe to greet them and anticipate their unloading, a task which may have taken some time and been delayed by customs bureaucracy. Out-of-London goods generally made their way along former Roman roads, the Ermine Street northwards and Watling Street north-westwards, although by then they were in poor condition and probably congested with pilgrims, monks, traders, embassies and all manner of travellers. The magnet that was London generally ensured that much of what entered the city, whether from its own Thames wharves or arriving overland from south-eastern ports, stayed to be consumed there, either formally or spirited away as bribes, as under-the-counter purchases or bought in a hundred small purchases at the galley-side market set up by the rowers themselves. By the mid-fifteenth century most well-to-do gentry, previously ensconced only in far-flung manor houses and castles, also had residences in or near London so that they could benefit from a closer proximity to the capital with its political intrigues, and also in order to make an outward show of opulence which might project their status among their peers. Italian finery and eastern delights, however they might be secured, only added to their prestige.

One thing seems very clear from the distance of time: the most successful ports were on the south and east coasts. Herein lies one of this country's inherent geographical reasons for the enduring – and much discussed – economic north–south divide. It is an insurmountable truth that to lie on the south or east coast is to experience an ease of import from the continent of not just goods but people and new ideas in manner and quantity that the west or the north could not attract, because of relative distance and the comparative difficulty of the longer sea crossing, followed by the tortuous roads. Lying along the coasts and between the ports, the unnavigable and treacherous places remain just that. The southern and eastern ports, directly facing the continent, soaked up European imports and wealth first, most and longest; their facilities continued to grow, and their road networks grew with them. More than anything, however much enduring social divisions are reviled, the basics of our economy have been dictated by geography in so many ways. The tone was set from the beginning by the contrast between the south and east's quick landfall, deepwater anchorages and short road journeys and the north and west's poorly connected, far-flung harbours with high cliffs and shifting sands.

Many smaller ports and harbours, if they ever saw much beyond catches of fish, were used for 'coasting', the process by which goods were moved from bigger ports to smaller ones around the coast. This form of secondary distribution often takes account of the fact that only a few places were well linked to the principal medieval road network, but anywhere on the coast could, weather providing, land smaller vessels for the local distribution of lesser cargoes – a crate here, a barrel there. They were also staging posts for goods out, such as the *Trinity* of Barton and the *Tusewyn* of Newcastle-upon-Tyne, which together in 1436 took a very practical 7,000 lead mallets, 500 mattocks and 2,720 shovels, spades and scoops from London to Sandwich and thence to Calais for the army in France.[8]

For every large vessel that came into a large deepwater port, there were probably any number of smaller vessels which were designed to coast along to the next stop, negotiating tidal estuaries and narrow creeks, some going a long way inland, but they would never be robust enough to take to the high seas; smaller than a 40-ton balinger, many probably never went out of sight of land. Numerous such vessels have been excavated since the mid-twentieth century across areas of polders (land reclaimed behind dykes) in the Netherlands, where they once plied the Zuiderzee and other inland channels in that country's ongoing negotiation with the North Sea. Regionally, each type continued to evolve, always powered by the wind, sometimes with added oars for manoeuvring. Some survive today in their most refined forms, such as Norfolk wherries. Today we might generally call them all skiffs or lighters, but they knew a variety of local names in the medieval period. Lacking a freight-carrying equivalent in the current day, their berths in many a small seaside harbour have been taken by yachts and pleasure craft.

Some small port towns, usually those that lay up creeks and rivers, could become their own bar to development. Without great foresight, their expansion for the purposes of landing everyday staple goods – thereby stocking local larders – got in the way of a wider variety of imports. Usually this was because one or more bridges would be built linking the two sides of the creek or river, which was better for local communication but a physical barrier to all but the smallest boats wishing to sail up the creek, necessitating unloading downriver of the bridge. Likewise, not all fishermen had robust enough boats to go out to sea for their catch and on numerous occasions the sinking of fish traps and fish weirs, or banks of wicker fish traps in a wide frame, impeded navigable channels, to the chagrin of local authorities and the detriment of the wider mercantile community. Colchester struggled along these lines. Few boat owners would run the risk of damaging their vessel or of stranding a cargo being caught on a fish weir, not to mention the lawsuit which might ensue from disgruntled fishermen banding together to seek restitution for a smashed-up weir.

Contemporary Views

Numerous ports and harbours were noted by John Leland, who was on the royal staff of Henry VIII. His surviving descriptions from the 1540s are unique in their generation, although the list of ports he visited is limited by the journeys he made, many of which lay only inland. Some touch upon the coast almost by accident simply because he took the coast road for part of his journey. Frustrating for the modern reader is the fact that the questions he asked and the observations he made are neither consistent nor similarly set out. I am much indebted to the scholarship of Lucy Toulmin Smith, whose 1964 work editing and interpreting Leland's itinerary remains unsurpassed.[9]

Leland's work is nonetheless unique and deserves presentation in the following chapters where ports are of note, with his tricky spelling preserved. The harbour facilities he records vary considerably, but generally may be related to the group of structures which today we might call the harbour wall, dock, quay, pier, wharf, jetty, mole or breakwater. To landlubbers the differences might be academic, but most people will have a somewhat informed idea of how each might look. Like today, his use of 'rode' (road) is indicative of a deepwater anchorage – a haven, usually offshore and not within a harbour. The word 'harbour', meanwhile, he conflates with 'haven', which is properly a safe (usually deepwater) anchorage. His use of 'bosom' at both Scarborough and Robin Hood's Bay (a dry harbour) is less clear but surely implies a welcoming berth for a beleaguered boat.

Destination England and Wales

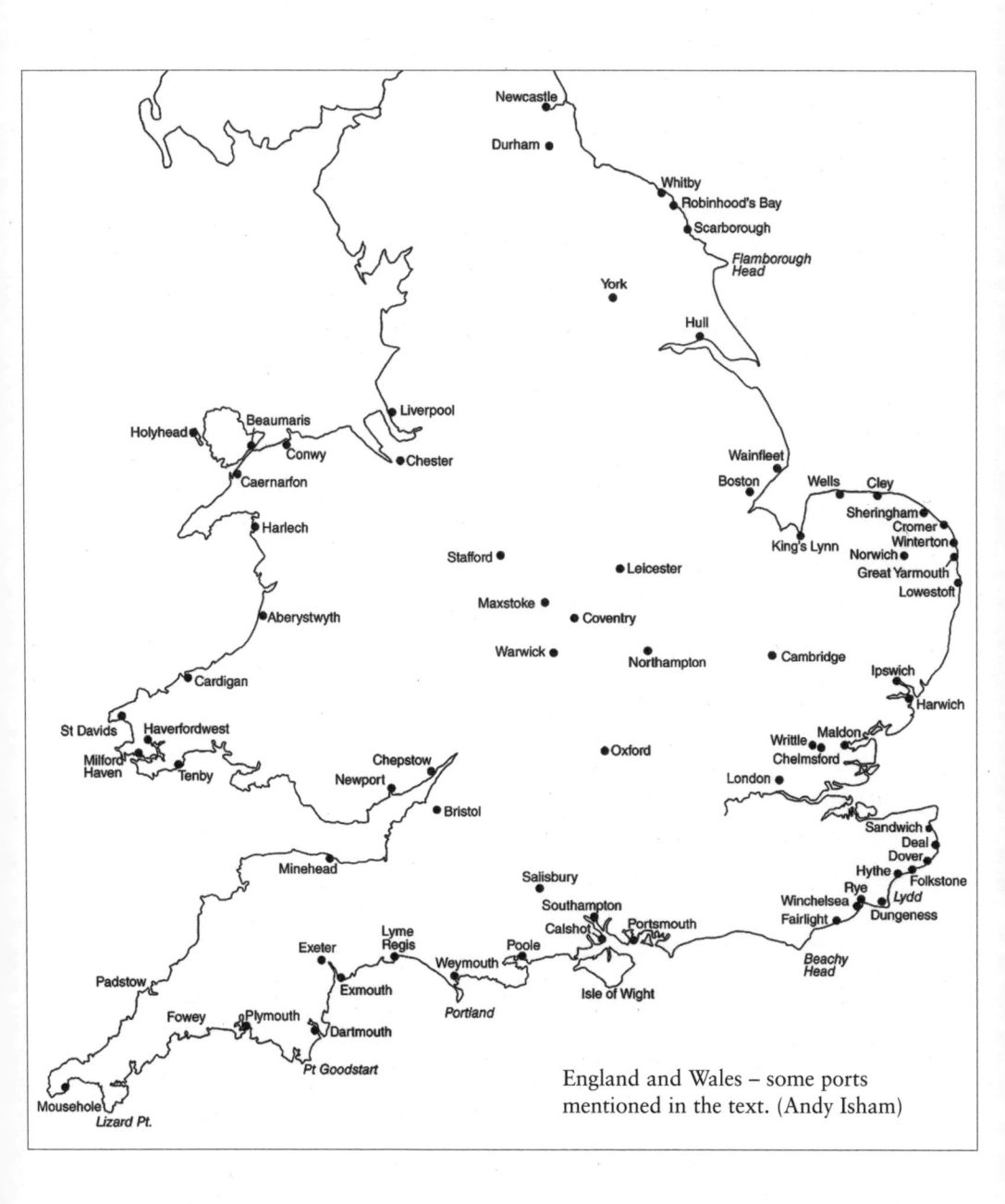

England and Wales – some ports mentioned in the text. (Andy Isham)

In addition to John Leland, the following work draws on the writings of William Worcestre, whose keen observations of Bristol in 1480 mean that we have the kind of detailed description of the harbour works and facilities which we lack for almost every other port.[10] I have also chosen to add the later journalled observations of a travelling Dutch artist, Willem Schellinks, whose writings of his sojourn in England in 1661–63 are so keen that he may well have been acting as a spy at a time when England's relations with Holland were rather rocky.[11] Although more recent than the focus of this book, a comment by Schellinks on the topography adds a further layer of detail at a time when most places had still to be developed. Many of his drawings have survived as well, including forty-one of England, in the collections of Vienna's National Library of Austria. To these may be added the portolans of Michael of Rhodes and Karl Koppmann, the diary of Luca di Maso degli Albizzi and the map of Lucas Wagenhaer. Taking all of these into account, a firmer grasp of our coasts in the fifteenth and sixteenth centuries can be had.

In the following chapters are set out the ports, some of the facilities and a flavour of the welcome that visitors might receive as they neared our coasts. Having chosen where to land, the rest was in the hands of their English and Welsh trading partners, the port authorities and the vagaries of local people. And as we shall see, the welcome, like the facilities, varied.

5

WEST COAST PORTS

Away in the lovable West,
On a pastoral forehead of Wales,
I was under a roof here, I was at rest,
And they the prey of gales;

Gerard Manley Hopkins,
'The wreck of the *Deutchland*', s. 24

Lancashire and Cheshire

Liverpool is by and large a post-medieval and modern port, but it has medieval beginnings. It does not figure in this book anywhere except here, since it is mentioned in the 1540s by John Leland: 'Lyrpole, alias Lyverpoole, a pavid towne, ... Irisch marchauntes cum much hither, as to a good haven. At Lyrpole is small custume payid that causith marchauntes to resorte. Good Marchandis at Lyrpole, and moch Yrisch yarn that Manchester men do by ther.'[1]

Location alone meant that the Irish market would come to dominate in Liverpool, but for the moment it would not compete on even terms with the port at Chester, the main concern of which was staying open despite silting of the Dee Estuary.

The fifteenth century opened with the Dee Estuary already under considerable pressure from the Irish Sea, which has a fearsome reputation. In 1396 the monks of St Werburgh's Abbey, Chester received special dispensation from Pope Boniface IX to reappropriate one of their churches well inland since most of their farmlands along the seashore had been 'irrecoverably destroyed' by the tides.[2] Even the relatively sheltered Dee can be a truly wild place as spring tides funnel between hilly north-east Wales and the much flatter Wirral. There the land narrows down the weather bottleneck that opens into the Cheshire Gap, providing the nor'westerlies direct access to the English interior. It is regrettable that Chester's maritime import–export records and its documentation concerning Ireland does not survive as it would surely facilitate a direct comparison with the trade between Bristol and Ireland.

As early as the late twelfth century, the old Roman city of Chester was celebrated by a Bendedictine chronicler, Lucian, as a cosmopolitan port, with ships arriving from Aquitaine, Spain, Scotland and Germany.[3] At the start of our period the port, though ailing, was still very much functioning. In 1402 a royal ship paid freightage there when it set out for Dublin and returned with Prince Henry (later Henry V) together with the furniture and ornaments of a chapel which had belonged to the late Richard II.[4] Although previously a relatively easily accessed port, with regular storms such as noted above, Chester had ceased to be in the forefront by the later fifteenth century, since the Dee Estuary was becoming silted. The city does get a mention by Leland: 'Wyrale begynneth lesse than a quarter of a mile of the very cite self of Chester, and withyn a two bow shottes of the suburbe without the northe gate at a little brooklet caullid Flokkars Broke that ther cummith into Dee River, and ther is a dok wherat at spring tide a ship may ly, and this place is caullid Porte Poole.'[5]

Leland's description indicates that what remained of the old Roman harbour basin was still accessible but only at the high spring tide. This made it a relatively unreliable destination for extensive trade and a dicey place to tie up in case a ship entered but then could not leave. It would have to leave with lighter return cargo than it imported if it was to be sure of riding high above old channels that were still accumulating silt. Leland mentions an 8-to-10-mile sand bar accumulated at the mouth of the Dee.[6] Despite these drawbacks Chester continued to maintain regular contact with Ireland, and coasting trades across the north Wales coast and up around the Wirral into Lancashire and Cumbria meant that it remained a destination worthy of regular imports, especially from Ireland, if only in smaller amounts than might have been desired. Even as the city's port silted up, the civic authorities tried to retain trade by building a new haven in the Dee Estuary, but this was a failure. Its dwindling overseas trade in the sixteenth century passed inexorably to Liverpool – the Mersey unaffected by silting.

If a great ship might not risk approaching, many a flat-bottomed barge and lighter could still land. Certainly, excavation shows that for its location the city did not lack any of the general imports enjoyed by many other north Midland towns, although its location on the old Roman road network did ensure that it was still linked to the Midlands and their extended overland trade routes. It is inescapable that many of modern Chester's fine medieval buildings have survived so well simply because the late medieval drop in trade reduced the impetus for widespread redevelopment in the early post-medieval period. Even if it was of dwindling relevance in the scope of this book, its old walled town remains an utterly lovely gem in modern Britain's crown.

North Wales

There are few places on the north Wales coast that are sufficiently safe from the winds of the Irish Sea to provide safe anchorage. Sheltered creeks are mostly relatively narrow and not all that sheltered, such as Degannwy, close to Conwy, where there was a ferry across the narrows. Sea walls barely cling on towards the hunkered-down leviathan of the Great Orme (Gogarth), and windswept bays shake in the teeth of a northerly gale. Edward I had built his castles where he could find the first shelter to the west of these sites of Mother Nature's elemental power. Further west, Conwy, and the river on which it stands, are mentioned several times by Leland, but the existence of its harbour only once despite its long quayside next to the town's thirteenth-century defences.[7] It began the fifteenth century in the hands of the rebellious Owain Glyndwr, and the defences were always suspect, requiring regular attention. By Leland's day both castle and town were very much in decline.

In a remarkably detailed – but anonymous – 1524 gazetteer for Anglesey, Caernarfonshire and Merionethshire, the principal deep anchorage on the north coast of the mainland was said to be at 'Aber Kerrek Twynyon' (Abergele Roads), while Conwy was also noted. There were a host of small creeks and bays around the Llyn Peninsula, which are listed, but their isolation meant that they had little purpose other than for shelter in the teeth of the Irish Sea's worst weather or for coasting to their equally isolated communities. They were key to a thriving trade with Ireland and made for many a brief rest against adverse winds, but proper landing places were few. Most of the little bays and coves named in 1524 still carry the same names on a modern map. Of particular note is the haven in the middle of St Tudwal Bay at Pulleth (Pwllheli), mentioned in the 1524 list.[8]

On the first sea atlas printed anywhere in the world, that of Lucas Wagenhaer in 1585, are found Anglesey itself (with no further data), Bardsey Island (probably as a seamark), Abergali (the anchorage at Abergele Roads), Carmania (possibly Caernarfon) and Mons Inis (probably Cader Idris as one huge seamark!).

The Menai Straits approach to Caernarfon is not mentioned at all, despite the town defences having a very serviceable quayside

Conwy Castle, Clwyd, near the former Watergate and castle quay (now lost). Photo by Walton Hudson (1932).

under the walls, not unlike nearby Conwy. Like Conwy, however, Caernarfon saw the fifteenth century open with Owain Glyndwr banging at its gates, although as his rebellion faltered his French backers were soundly defeated by the English at sea in 1406. In the ensuing years both castles became prisons for the captives and hostages of victories over France, such as Agincourt (1415) and Harfleur (1417). Another group of noble French prisoners was moved, twelve to Conwy and twenty to Caernarfon, for whom expenses continued to be paid up to 1424.[9] Both towns were almost certainly supplied directly through their own quays by coasting from Chester or via the small bays or creeks along the Llyn peninsula. There the hostages were far out of normal French reach but would expect to be kept in the manner to which they were accustomed. In 1538, Caernarfon was described as 'moche ruynous', neglected once English policy towards a peaceful north Wales rendered superfluous the huge defences of the old Edwardian castles and their surrounding towns.

Seas of Plenty

On Anglesey itself, Leland mentions a harbour at Amlwch (Amlogh on the 1524 list) on the north-east coast[10] and a crossing over the Menai Strait to the mainland at Beaumaris.[11] He may not have been aware of the 1524 list but it perhaps shows that Leland was a landlubber as opposed to the compiler of the 1524 list, who noted the aforementioned twenty Anglesey creeks, bays and havens suitable for laying up a vessel in adverse winds. He may have been English-born or educated as his spelling of Welsh falters, although his familiarity with local topographic names in detail, such as 'the roade of the table rownde' (off Dinas Sylwy, in sight of Bwrdd Arthur) and the beautifully named Llanfihangel y Traethau (St Michael's in the Beaches – once on a tidal island),[12] suggests he might have lived locally.

At Beaumaris (not on the 1524 list) the unfinished castle had a tidal dock, the only glimmer of aid in a portion of the shore dominated by vast acres of sandbanks called Lavan Sands. Leland also notes of Anglesey the very high tidal race in the Straits, the rocky shoreline, and the raging waters, all of which militate against good landing places. The 1524 list prefers to ignore the straits altogether. This wariness of the tide of course comes centuries before the bridges were built. Bangor is noted as a market town, with two fairs a year, but no mention is made by Leland of its Irish links. In the 1320s the Franciscan friar Simon fitz Simon, travelling from Ireland to the Holy Land, crossed to Bangor via Holyhead, across Anglesey and on to Chester.[13]

Pwllheli and Criccieth are given short shrift by Leland, who notes they are rundown and have been so as long as anyone can recall; a reference to 'the prince' relates to its ruin coming after the fall of the last independent Prince of Wales. Leland notes 'a good haven roode' at Penrhyn Du.[14]

Further south, Harlech Castle, like Conwy and Caernarfon, had its own landing stage, if not a quay. It may have assumed greater importance in 1403–04 when it was captured by the forces of

Owain Glyndwr, allowing him to be provisioned or reinforced from the sea; however, a previous attempt to resupply its royalist garrison had seen the rebels capture both ship and provisions.[15] Although the castle was retaken by English forces as the rebellion was put down, it was a stern lesson about how supply and defence (and tolls upon that supply) could become a matter of pointed offensive action in war. None of the north Welsh castles were easy to supply, not least because of their distance from England, and their vulnerability to siege was known to contemporaries. Harlech was in open revolt once more during the 1460s, a lingering Lancastrian outpost in a Yorkist-ruled country. It finally fell to Lord Herbert for Edward IV in 1468.

Barmouth is noted in the Welsh as Aber Mawthach, but the approach is clearly written off as tidal.[16] It lies in Merionethshire, in the fifteenth century even more isolated than today, although in 1524 the county warranted a mention for anchorages at Aber Artro south of Harlech, Aber Dysynni and Aberdyfi.[17] Further south, Aberystwyth is mentioned only briefly by Leland, not for its marine links but only to say that its market was better than that of

Aberystwyth, Ceredigion: A good market according to Leland – its dock facilities less clear in the sixteenth century but with good anchorages nearby. The photo shows the unfinished hotel of 1864 by J. P. Seddon, turned into the University College of Wales, and nearby pier. Photo by Walton Hudson (1935).

Cardigan! It was described as 'once walled'. Of the two, however, it is Cardigan, or more properly its neighbour 'Stahlmuyl' – nearby St Dogmael's – that appears on Lucas Wagenhaer's map of 1585. At Fishguard, Leland notes only that 'here is a little haven, havynge a resort for shippis'.[18] That was enough for many local boats.

South Wales

> *The summer day on which in heart's delight*
> *I saw the Swansea Mumbles bursting white.*
> John Masefield, 'Biography'

For South Wales an effusive observer is the fastidious William Worcestre, who, writing in 1480, listed the southern Welsh ports sending their produce to Bristol, where they were assigned their own anchorage near a quay called 'the Back'.[19] There, he notes, were ships from Tenby, Milford Haven, Haverfordwest, Laugharne, Llansteffan, Kidwelly, Swansea, Neath, Cardiff, Usk, Caerleon, Tintern Abbey on the River Wye, Chepstow and Betysley Water (possibly Beachey) on the River Wye. Although he makes no mention of the maritime facilities in these tiny havens, some of them warranted later mentions by John Leland.

Curiously Milford Haven, for Leland, gets no mention, other than to note the irregular creek on which it lies. It was certainly on the radar of the mid-fifteenth-century Baltic mariner Karl Koppmann, whose *seebuch* notes it as 'Mylvorde', and it is labelled on Wagenhaer's 1585 map as 'Muijlfoordt'. Nearby the strong, walled medieval town of Tenby ('Timbij' to Wagenhaer), does attract comment from Leland as to its situation: 'The Severn Se so gulfeth in about hit, that at the ful se almost the thirde part of the toune is inclosid with water.'[20] It was from Tenby that Jasper Tudor and the young Prince Henry (later Henry VII) escaped to Brittany by boat. Leland notes, 'Tinby ys a walled towne hard on

Right: Plate 1. Church of St Nicolas, North Stoneham, Southampton: 1491 tomb ledger slab of Slav rowers or merchants. The inscription reads, 'Sepultura de la Scola de Sclavoni ano dni MCCCCLXXXXI (1491)' (2023).

Below: Plate 2. Drawing by Willem Schellinks of 'Turkish slave' rowers powering an Italian galley. (Courtesy of The Austrian National Library, Vienna)

Plate 3. Gent, Belgium: fifteenth-century carving of a fully rigged great ship. (Courtesy of STAM – Stadsmuseum Gent, on loan from Historische Huize, Gent)

Plate 4. Bruges, Belgium: the former 'English House', now 15 Spiegelrei (2023).

Plate 5. Bruges, Belgium: Hanseatic League HQ from 1478, now part of a hotel at 1 Oosterlingenplein (2023).

Plate 6. Damme, Belgium: the former herring market with huge Hanseatic salt requirements (2010).

Plate 7. '*Die Statt Aldair*', detail from 1579 edition of *Cosmographia* (1542) by Sebastian Munster (1488–1552). Extract from map of Aldair (Cairo), the principal Venetian spice market. (Private collection)

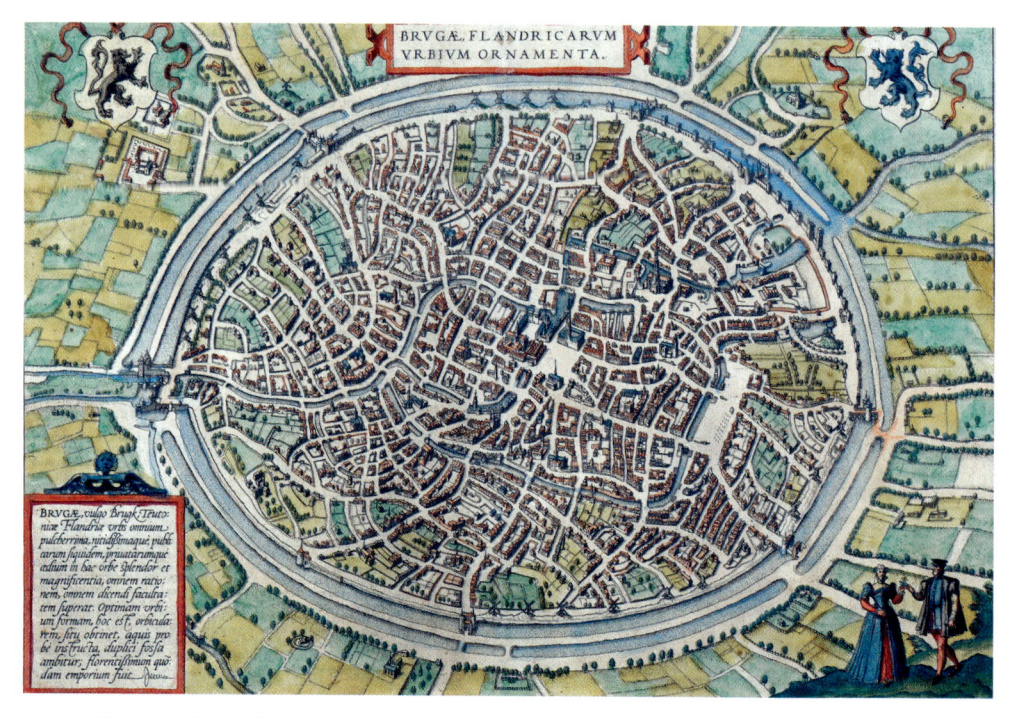

Plate 8. Sixteenth-century Bruges. (Courtesy of the Rijksmuseum)

Plate 9. King's Lynn, Norfolk: the colour-washed corner building (Hampton Court) fronts a courtyard with former loading bays onto the river and served the Hanseatic League (2020).

Plate 10. King's Lynn, Norfolk: Hanseatic warehouse of the 1470s, stretching down to the River Great Ouse (2020).

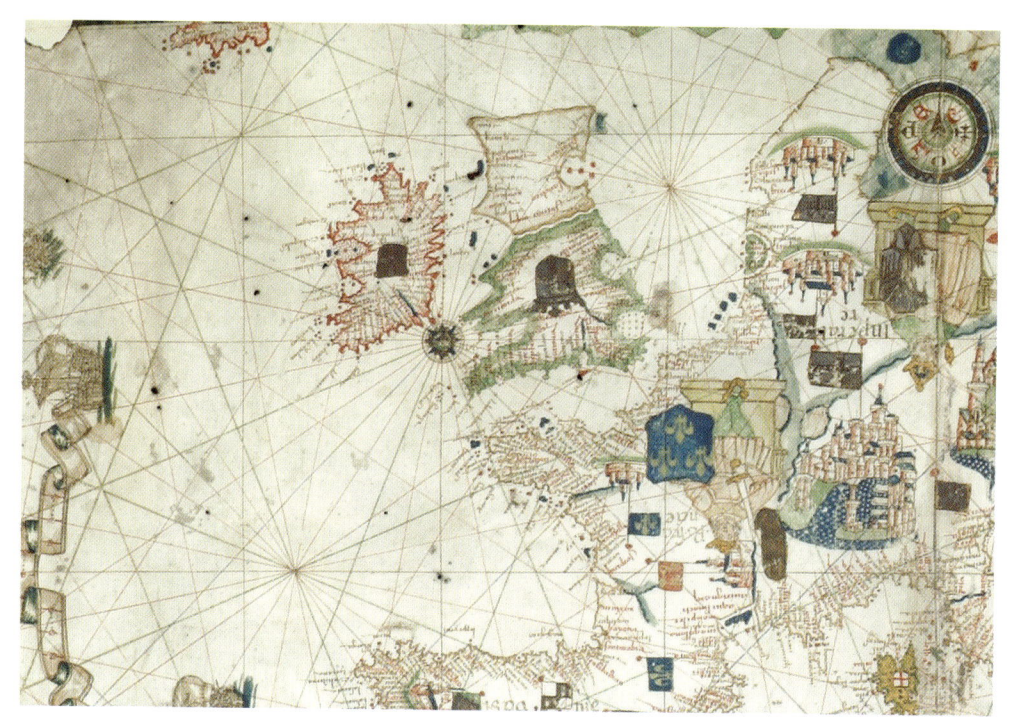

Plate 11. The British Isles on a navigational map of Europe, North Africa and the Middle East, on hide, by Jacobo Russo (1528), drawn to be viewed from the north. (Courtesy Birmingham Museums Trust, licenced under CC0)

Above left: Plate 12. Gent, Belgium: model exhibit of a medieval crane. (Courtesy STAM - Stadsmuseum Gent)

Above right: Plate 13. St Nicholas, patron saint of sailors, with a ship in stained glass, from the parish church of St Nicholas, Bulwick, Northamptonshire (2013).

Plate 14. Winchelsea, Sussex: town gateway approach up from the former harbour, now silted up and landlocked (2019).

Plate 15. At Quarr Abbey on the Isle of Wight the Cistercians maintained their own ships and kept a welcome for other mariners. Here abbey remains have been converted into a lodge (2023).

Plate 16. Sandwich, Kent: favourite port of the Florentines. Pictured is the Barbican gateway (2014).

Above left: Plate 17. Sandwich, Kent: the Fishergate. Medieval with post-medieval top storeys (2014).

Above right: Plate 18. For a Venetian rower the seaman's portion had to pack into a chest measuring 110 by 45 by 45 centimetres and be neatly stowed. It contained pepper, ginger, fruit, silk, wine – whatever he chose to sell.

Plate 19. Bruges, Belgium: canal approach to the medieval Poorteresloge on Jan van Eyckplein (2023).

Plate 20. St Mawes Castle, Cornwall: one in the chain of 1540s 'fortlets'. this one, with a twin at Pendennis, was built to deter an attack on Falmouth harbour (2008).

Plate 21. Hurst Castle, Hampshire. Perched on an exposed spit, another in the chain of 1540s 'fortlets' covered the Solent, with another opposite at Yarmouth, Isle of Wight. In the far distance are The Needles, a seamark on Michael of Rhodes', Albizzi's and Koppmann's passage notes (2012).

Plate 22. Three coins, all depicting on their reverse the ship of state. *Above left*: Gold ryal of Edward IV's coinage reforms, minted in Coventry [Acc no 1960/178]. This was the standard toll at Elsinore. *Above right*: Gold angel, also of Edward IV's coinage reforms, 1480–83, excavated at Coventry Charterhouse 1981 [Acc no 1981/68/1]. *Left*: Copper alloy Nuremburg jetton, fifteenth/sixteenth century, excavated at Coventry Charterhouse 1987 [Acc no 1987/2/21]. (Herbert Art Gallery and Museum, Coventry)

Above left: Plate 23. St Botolph's Church, Boston, Lincs: seamark when navigating the Wash. Now known as the Boston Stump (2008). (Courtesy of Mike McBey under Creative Commons 2.0)

Above right: Plate 24. A fifteenth-century ship in the Rose Window, St Lawrence's Church, Ludlow (2012).

Below: Plate 25. 1454 tomb effigy of William Beauchamp, Earl of Warwick. A continental tour-de-force: gilding by Bartholomew Lambespring, 'Docheman'; there was also a reredos by Christian Colborne of 'Germany' (2012).

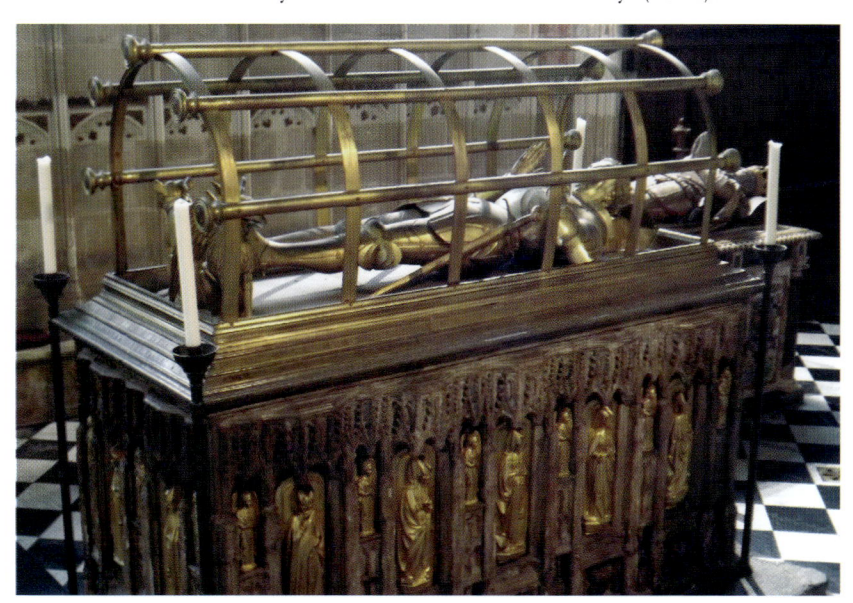

Plate 26. Clos de Vougeot, Côte-d'Or (21), France: Froissart wrote of the French wine trade that it was a 'great pleasure to all estates and degrees'. The beams of this medieval Cistercian wine press were saplings under Charlemagne; it last pressed in 1963 (1988).

Above left: Plate 27. Jerusalem Church, Bruges, Belgium: black marble effigies of Anselm Adornes and his wife, Margaretha, from a resident family of Genoese merchants, 1483 (2023).

Above right: Plate 28. Italian Maiolica plate dated 1535 showing the death of Palinurus, Aeneas' steersman on his galley. Palinurus dozed off and fell overboard to his death – from Virgil's *Aeneid*, book V. (© Victoria and Albert Museum, London)

Plate 29. 1662 drawing by Willem Schellinks of Fowey, Cornwall; Polruan to the right. Blockhouses on each shore and cannon high on the cliffs to the left. (Courtesy of the Austrian National Library, Vienna)

Plate 30. Netley Abbey, Southampton: abbott's lodgings. Foreign mariners were welcomed here by the Cistercian monks, a fact still noted at its dissolution in 1536, but which failed to save the house (2023).

Plate 31. Calshore Spit, Southampton Water, Hants: a glimpse north across the former anchorage of the Italian state galleys, guarded from the 1540s by Calshot Castle (2023).

Plate 32. Calshot Castle, Southampton Water, Hants: the castle and environs by Samuel and Nathaniel Buck (1733). (Private collection)

Plate 33. Remains of the Watergate, Southampton, Hants: the goods of the Italian galleys landed here (2023).

Plate 34. Contemporary depiction of a late fifteenth-century galley by Conrad Grunenburg (*c.* 1415–94). (Courtesy of the Baden State Library by Creative Commons 4.0)

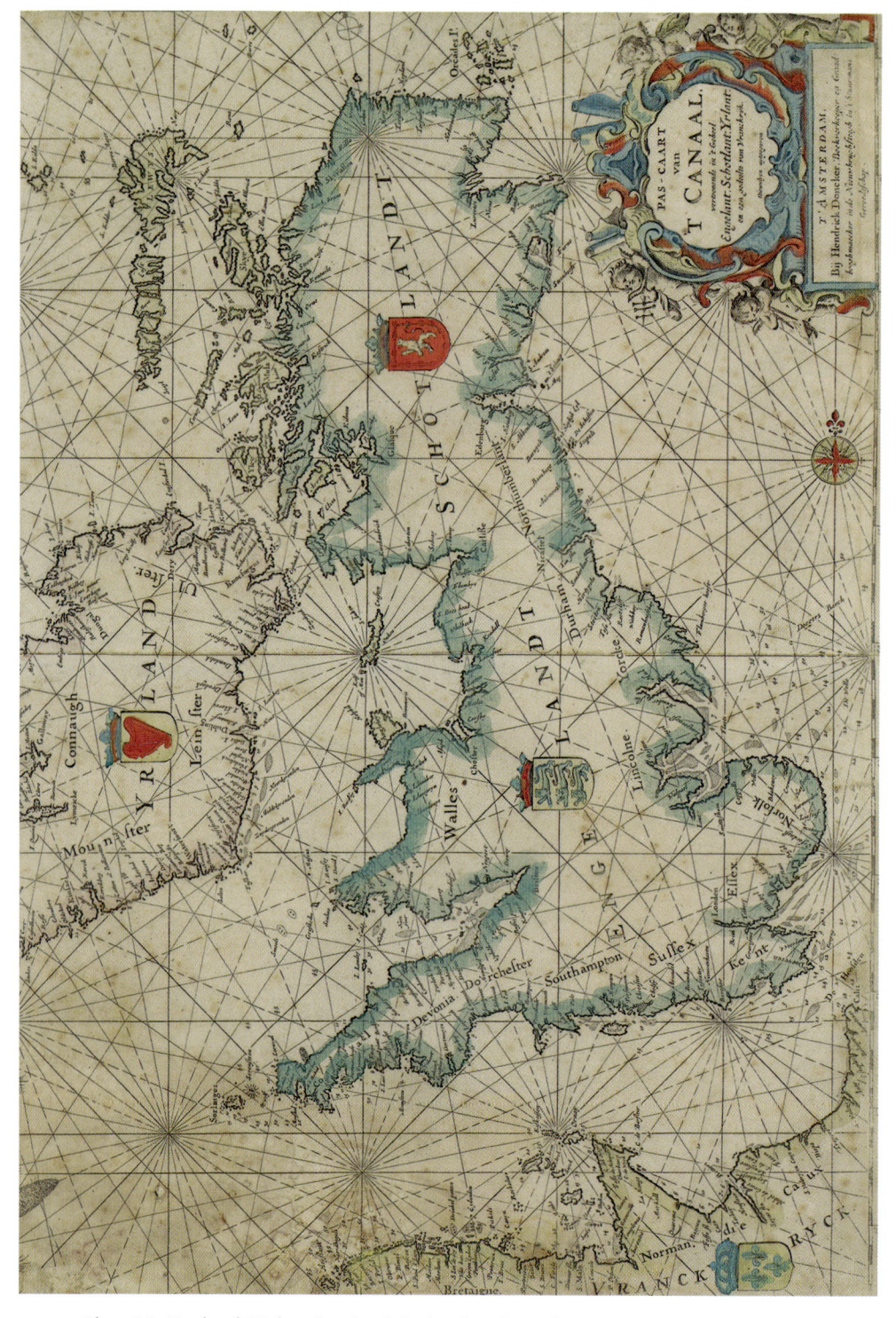

Plate 35. England Wales, Scotland, Ireland and northern France: navigation map by Hendrick Donckers (1668), including depth soundings, rocks and shoals. Designed to be read from the Netherlands. (Private collection)

the Severn Se yn Penbrookeshire. There ys a sinus and a peere made for shyppes. The towne is very welthe by marchaundyce.'[21] 'Sinus' in his description may refer to a close-fitting dock, hollowed out of the land, which extended the loading and unloading facilities with ease and could be used to 'clamp' a vessel between its sides for repairs. However, it does not imply a safe anchorage. Tenby is in fact today the location of a preserved merchant's house of *circa* 1500, laid out as it might have looked in its heyday.

At Aberavon there is mention, but no detail, of 'an haven for shippes at the mouth of this Avon'.[22] There is a reference to a stop a little further on at Neath: 'There cummith up shippelettes almost onto the towne of Nethe from the Severn.'[23] The Aberavon haven was key to its longer-lasting success.

All in all, Leland gives a relatively even coverage of the Welsh coast, but without the local detail afforded by the extensive 1524 North Wales list. Lucas Wagenhaer's 1585 list of labels on his printed atlas establishes the leading ports with wider appeal. After

Tenby, Dyfed, where lay 'a sinus and a peere made for shyppes'. Photo courtesy of Jonathan Pinsent, 2023.

Chester, his list, not always necessarily in correct order (suggesting he was perhaps not familiar with the coast), appropriately contains both ports and coastal landscape features, preserved here in his spelling: Anglesey, Abergali (Abergele Roads), Bardsey Island, Carmania (Great Orme, Conwy or Caernarfon), Mont Lois (Cader Idris), Stalmuyl (St Dogmaels); Lijpoort (New Port), St Davidt (St David's Head), Muijlfordt (Milford Haven), Timbij (Tenby), Armuizin (Carmarthen).[24] The Wagenhaer map labels then jump via Lundij (Lundy Island) to the Lizard and southern Cornwall, missing out north Cornwall, north Devon and Somerset altogether. The fifteenth-century mariner Karl Koppmann had a shorter list in his *seebuch* as his itinerary jumped across from South Wales to Ireland. Instead of Tenby he noted Caldey Island, presumably because he was unaccustomed to calling at Tenby and therefore steered clear of it. He did note Lundy and Milford Haven, however.

At Aberthaw, Leland notes a 16-mile ferry crossing to Minehead in Somerset.[25]

Of Usk, Leland is quite damning: 'From the haven mouth of Wisch (Usk) to the mouth of Remny, where no haven is or cumming yn meete for shippes, a vi miles. On this shore is no very notable thing.' Similarly Newport, home to the inimitable Newport Boat excavation of 2002, merits no maritime mention by Leland; with some finality he notes that 'the towne is in ruine'.[26] At Newport, maintaining status and staving off ruin was a regular theme, as can be seen by its apparent mid-century fame, which reached the ears of Rome. In 1445, Pope Eugenius IV granted indulgences to all who would visit Newport church and contribute to repairing its bridge on the road to St David's.[27] It was described as 'in the remoter part of Wales and the bounds of the earth and has a very famous seaport'. This suggests that Newport, in papal eyes, was a principal port for foreign pilgrims to St David's, such that maintaining the way there could attract papal indulgences. The excavated Newport Boat, seemingly a capsized Basque-built merchantman of about 1449, has sadly left no trace of its last cargo, probably long since unloaded and dispersed (whether foodstuffs in crates or pilgrims on foot) before the boat was left high and dry for its final, fateful repairs which were never finished. Its discovery is testament to the contribution that archaeology can and does make to our historical understanding, not least when the low level of contemporary historical data leaves the likes of both William Worcestre and John Leland unmoved. Clearly there were, or had been, considerable dry dock repair facilities at Newport, but they either failed to impress Leland and Worcestre or did not catch their eye; perhaps the facility had already been filled in by the time of their visits.

By comparison with England, Leland's notes on the Welsh coast are sparse and almost cursory, but that may be because the west did not face England's enemies in his day and was therefore not so relevant. One must imagine that many small coastal villages and towns required marine access but that tides, rocky creeks, bridges and poor inland road connections all militated against regular or noteworthy overseas links – and most of all they were disadvantaged by the absence of a safe deepwater anchorage. Worcestre's list and the notes of Michael of Rhodes show that there were indeed tiny havens dotted along the south Wales coast but that their boats, even combined and regularly sailing into Bristol, only warranted a quay ('the Back'), which they shared with ships from Somerset, Devon and Cornwall.

Gloucestershire/Avon

One of the principal ports of late medieval England, Bristol's anchorage caught the attention of both Worcestre in 1480 and Leland around 1545. It is also mentioned by Koppmann in his mid-fifteenth-century *seebuch* as 'Brustouwe', only referring to St Katherine's (Hospital) there. Likewise, most of Worcestre and Leland's writing is about the town itself, and Leland stumbles upon the harbour works almost at the end, paying no attention whatsoever to the place Bristol held in the wine trade or the far north Atlantic, even though these links were barely diminished in his time, and indeed were probably growing:

> The shipps of olde tyme cam only up by Avon to a place caullyd the Bak, where was and is depthe enowghe of water; but the botom is very stony and rughe sens by polecye they threnchid sowhat a-lofe by northe west of the old key on Avon anno 1247 and in continuance brynginge the cowrse of From river that way hathe made softe and whosy harborow for grete shipps.
>
> Hunge Rode (Hungroad) aboute a three miles lower in haven then Brightstow ... about a myle lowere is Kyng's Rode, ... Ther is a place amongst agayne Hung Rode caulyd Portchestar ...
>
> Sum thinke that a grete pece of the depenes of the haven from St Vincents to Hung Rode hathe be made by hand. Sum say that shipps of very aunciant tyme cam up to St Stephanes church in Brightstow.[28]

The tidal range of the Avon at Bristol can be a problem. The Dutchman Willem Schellinks in 1661 visited Bristol and noted that the water rose and fell between 24 and 28 feet, in for four hours and out for six. Downstream he was aghast to note it was as much as 48 feet. Such is the Bristol Channel.[29]

Although his mentions of port facilities are very much scattered around in his incomplete notes, Worcestre was far more effusive. Moreover, he was a compulsive recorder of plans, measurements and layouts and while this can make for difficult reading it has a wide appeal for a variety of readers. His description makes clear Bristol's advantage in having various safe deepwater anchorages where even the largest ships could anchor safely. This led to the development of considerable maritime facilities, detailed in Worcestre's account: 'There is a ship-building place near the Marsh Gate ... where poles and masts of fir and anchors lie ... the Key (quay), where great ships lie on the mud at the western end of the (paved) quay.'[30] This quay was long enough (346 steps/paces) to have six parallel roads leading off from it, and was heavily defended with walls and towers. It sported a triangular open plaza on which stood both a conduit head and the customs house. Bristol gained great kudos from its shipbuilding, such that the town sought to regulate it (and levy fees for crane usage among other things). In 1475 a civic ordinance required that anyone wishing to break new ground to dig out a new dock for ship construction had to get mayoral permission.

Next is Worcestre's previously explored mention of 'the Back, ... a slip(way) going to the River called Avon Water, for working clothes and loading the vessels and ships that come to the said Back'. Elsewhere he lists the Welsh ports whose vessels were assigned a berth at the Back, together with coasting vessels from Somerset, Devon and Cornwall. They moored their vessels on the rising tide, unloading just as the higher sea levels, relative to the dock, made their task easier.

Worcestre notes that many merchants and mariners congregated and lived on Marsh Street, benefiting from their own chapel on 'the Back', and that next to the nearby Marsh Gate was the publicly owned town crane, which had considerable foundations and was very firmly fixed to the ground, probably using a set of timber crosstrees such as were employed in contemporary post-mills.[31] Powered by one or two massive treadwheels, it could be used to load or unload, step heavy masts, rig ships and even hold small ships clear of the water while repairs took place. Exeter had a crane of its own constructed in 1564–67 for its brand-new quay. In towns where most buildings were of one, two or at most three storeys (except churches and castles), a working dockside crane, with its creaking moving parts and wide clearance, must have been quite a sight, perhaps attracting mesmerised small children the way mechanical excavators still do today. Some evidently had names in the way siege engines did: on a London wharf stood one called the Heydox crane (the meaning is unclear – possibly it merely means 'high docks'). This needed repairs when the lifting of Edward IV's new tomb broke it – possibly the jib snapped.[32]

Also at 'the Back' was, says Worcestre, a house and lodging for public benefit called a 'cloth hall'. It was set up by Robert Sturmy (drowned at sea on 23 December 1446) for the lodging and hospitality of foreign merchants and other gentry. Being crowded together in a place like this was meant as a gesture of welcome but it also provided security. Unfortunately, it also meant that in times of overt racism ringleaders would know exactly where to head!

Worcestre lists the countries known to him whose produce flowed into Bristol in 1480. He states that their (great) ships would moor at Blackstones on the River Severn and at Hollowbacks, 4 miles from Bristol, beyond Hungroad. There they would wait for the incoming tide, and because of the great tidal range there was something of a mad rush when it turned, with all eager to weigh anchor and set sail towards Bristol as the rising tide deepened the final approach. There were ships from Spain, Portugal, Bordeaux, Bayonne, Gascony, Aquitaine (by 1480 part of the Kingdom of France), Brittany, Iceland, Ireland, Wales 'and other countries'. As a principal wine port it is no surprise to discover that William Worcestre makes mention of Bristol's countless cellars and vaults, street by street, and in particular a row of huge, deep cellars just behind the quay.

In 2021, archaeologists reported in the British press that microbial evidence from samples in cesspits linked Bristol with towns on the German Baltic coast. Indeed, as early as 1891 historians noted that the Hanse had a permanent presence in Bristol.[33] It would be strange had these exceptional merchants *not* had a base there, even though it lay on the opposite side of England from their usual focus. The mentions by Worcestre and Leland make it clear that

West Coast Ports

Bristol was a major destination for the most serious merchantmen, with its (admittedly tricky) deepwater access right up to the town, together with several expansive anchorages away from the quays.

Bristol was at the forefront of navigation up the Atlantic coast of Ireland and up to Iceland, increasingly visited from the 1420s to the 1460s. Diplomatic problems ensued from 1467, when men of Lynn and Bristol conspired and murdered the Danish governor of Iceland; the trade never ceased but some was forced to divert via the Hanseatic staple at Bergen in Norway. Meanwhile Bristol's slice of the Icelandic cake dwindled.[34] Nevertheless, the city would spearhead England's (and Europe's) quest for new lands at the end of the fifteenth century.

Bristol was the principal point of entry for goods from Ireland. In 1516 as many as forty-two Irish vessels, mainly out of Waterford, regularly plied the route to Bristol. They brought mainly fish, but this was dwindling as cloth gained greater favour. Between the late 1400s and around 1540 Anglo-Irish trade increased steadily by a startling 65 per cent. Irish ships accounted for two-thirds of the trade in 1516, but even that was increasing, bolstered by the growth of Liverpool.[35] It gives real context to John Leland's comment about the high numbers of Irishmen he encountered in Minehead.

Somerset

Minehead itself is noted by Leland only as a 16-mile ferry-crossing point to Aberthaw in Wales.[36] The process by which the sea has retreated from Minehead leaves the village now half a mile from the shore, with the nearest anchorage at Porlock Bay, 'a meatly good rode for shippes' – again, a good offshore anchorage but with no indication of landing facilities. Leland also noted that the town of Minehead 'is exceding ful of Irisch menne'. This may have been a reference to the fast-growing trade with Ireland, a relatively short crossing from here, but equally they may have been because their skills were in demand locally.

Seas of Plenty

Minehead, Somerset, a mid-twentieth-century tourist beach, apparently full of Irishmen *circa* 1540. In 1480 it was first stop for the *Trinity* of Bristol to pick up senior crew. The anchorage, 'a meetly good rode', lay beyond the headland in Porlock Bay. Photo by Walton Hudson (*c.* 1960).

Appledore, North Devon – a difficult approach: a shifting sand bar to port and a rocky shelf to starboard (2013).

North Devon

Appledore is noted by Leland,[37] but only because it was not a recommended harbour: 'Appledre village ... the haven entery is barrid with sande, and the enterie into it is very daungerous.' This was no ringing endorsement. The shifting sands deposited by the tide had left a difficult approach for anyone wishing to anchor there.

North Cornwall

'Padelstaw' to Koppmann in the mid-fifteenth century, Padstow is today a pleasant tourist destination and still enjoys a notable fishing fleet. Leland said of it that ships were only able to enter on the rising tide and that it was one of few places, along with Lelant and St Ives, where 'the balinggars and shyppes ar saved and kept fro al weders with keyes or peres'.[38] It occasionally attracted Spanish shipping, and not necessarily with good intent – a document of 1483 records the young Edward V giving instructions for a ship despoiled at Padstow to be returned to its owner, Roderic de Balneseda.[39]

Sailing around Land's End towards Newlyn and the south coast, Leland notes an absence of harbours and wharfs at St Just and states that local boats were drawn up onto the beach by means of capstans. He mentions that local fishing was fair-weather only, as any swell would likely see the boats run aground.[40]

6

SOUTH COAST PORTS

Holes in maps look through to nowhere.
Laura Riding, 'The map of places'

South Cornwall

It would be strange not to mention the much-loved tiny Cornish village of Mousehole, Albizzi's first seamark and his eastwards turning point as he approached England on his first voyage in 1429–30. He called it the Golfo di Musuofulo – Mousehole Bay. Had he been driven much further west by adverse winds, he might have passed Cornwall altogether, entering the Bristol Channel and the Irish Sea, or worse, foundered among the Scilly Isles.

Notably, John Leland also mentions Mousehole on his journeys, even then noting its picturesque quality: 'Mowsehole ys a praty fyschar town yn the west part of Montesbay lyying hard by the shoore, and hath no savegarde for shyppes but a forced pere. Also yn the bey be est the same towne ys a good roode for shyppes cauled Guaves Lake.'[1] Had Albizzi been forced to stop, he might have found good anchorage at Guaves Lake, perhaps in trying conditions, although not at Mousehole itself since it is a dry harbour at low tide (see above); no 'savegarde' if driven before a storm.

South Coast Ports

John Leland understandably waxed lyrical about Falmouth: 'Falemuth ys a havyng very notable and famose, and yn a maner the most principale of al Britayne. For the chanel of the entre hath a space of ii myles ynto the land xiii fadum of depes, wich communely ys cawlled Carryk Rood (The Carrick Roads) bycawse yt ys a sure herboro for the greatest shyppes that travayle be the ocean.'[2] He goes on:

> On the very north shore of the creeke towards the havyn's mowth ys a poor fischar village cawled S. Mausa (St Mawes), alias La Vousa, and nygh to this village toward the same haven ys a fortelet lately buylded by the contery for the defens of the haven ... In the west syde of the haven is a creeke that floweth up from the haven's mowth ynto the land above iiimyles, at the very hedd of the which standeth a prety towne cawled Peryn (Penrhyn), of marchandyse, and vytayle market.

Falmouth was the principal deepwater anchorage in Cornwall, and its use is a story of maritime continuity. In Leland's day Falmouth harbour was worth protecting with castles; even today it is one of the Royal Navy's principal anchorages. Guarding it from the 1540s was the Henrician castle of St Mawes, one of a state-of-the-art chain with a twin at nearby Pendennis.[3]

Falmouth and St Mawes impressed all visitors. In August 1662 they were visited on the same day by Dutch artist and possible spy William Schellinks, who wrote of Falmouth in his diary: 'Besides its great width and convenience, this harbour is also remarkable for another thing, namely that it provides this uncommon facility that 100 ships of 100–1000 tons can lie there at anchor so that the top of the masts of one cannot be seen from any other etc.'[4] He drew Falmouth, with St Mawes Castle for future reference, and showed careening of some large vessels going on in the shallows.

Falmouth, Cornwall: The Carrick Roads, deepwater anchorage for everything from pleasure craft to the Royal Navy's 16,000-ton RFA *Lyme Bay* (L3007) at far left. The same anchorage would warrant building both St Mawes and Pendennis castles in the 1540s (2008).

Fowey is ascribed a defensible wall on the coastal side, was gated and was noted as a haven by Leland,[5] but its creek (Fowey on one side, Polruan on the other) and boatyard are said to be restricted by the tides. Elsewhere, however, Leland clearly investigated further, and Fowey piqued his interest, to our benefit:

> But a smaul fischar town. The glorie of Fawey rose by the warres in King Edward the first and the thirde and Henry the v. day, partely by feates of warre, partely by piracie, and so waxing riche fell al to marchaundice: and their shippes went to al nations.
>
> The shippes of Fawey sayling to Rye and Winchelsey about Edward the 3. Tyme wold vale no bonet being required, wherapon Rhy and Winchelsey men and they fought, where Fawey men had victory, and therapon bare their armes mixt with the armes of Rhy and Winchelsey ...

> The French-men diverse tymes assailed this towne and last most notably about Henry the vj tyme ... In Edwarde the 4 day 2 stronge towers made a little beneath the toun, one on each syde of the haven and a chayne to be drawen over.
>
> At the est syde of the haven's mowth of Fowey stondeth a towr for the defens thereof, and a chapel of St Savyor a lytle above the same. Ny by the said towr standith a fysschar village cawled Porthruan (Polruan).
>
> When warre in Edward the 4 dayes seasid bytwene the French men and Englisch the men of Fawey used to pray kept their shippes and assailed the Frenchmen in the sea again King Edwardes commaundment; whereupon the capitaines of the shippes of Fawey were taken and sent to London, and Dertemouth men commaunded to fetche their shippes away...[6]

Fowey in the fifteenth century seems to have had a problem with strangers, and not just those of Rye and Winchelsea. Foreigners there encountered rough treatment in the early 1480s, and on his brief accession the uncrowned boy-king Edward V (directed by his uncle, later Richard III) set up courts of enquiry to address violent vandalism against foreign ships – the *Nicholas* out of 'Landregave' (Brittany) and the *Peter* out of 'Fonterrabia' (Spain),

Polruan, Cornwall, across the river mouth from the Fowey bank. The east-bank blockhouse is at far right. Photo by Walton Hudson (1959).

both despoiled in the harbour by 'men of Fowey.'[7] At the same time one Picis de Neto had £200 of goods taken by men of Fowey, repaid by the king.[8]

Fowey in fact does have some deepwater anchorages within its confines, and until modern times could support some very large vessels indeed. Schellinks drew Fowey when he visited in August 1662 and noted in his diary 'the good harbour which is deep and protected by the surrounding hills'.[9] He went on to say that it compared closely with Dartmouth and that there were stories of mariners anchoring at Fowey who thought they had arrived at Dartmouth. Schellinks' drawing (see colour plates) shows the town and the harbour in panorama – Penleath Point in the middle – and both blockhouses on either bank, between which a chain could be strung, although no actual village of Polruan appears to exist. At the far left (west) of his drawing and elevated well above sea level is what he calls 'an old platform', shown as a ruined two-cell building lacking its front wall, but on it are mounted two cannons covering the approaches to the harbour.

Fowey, Cornwall: Old Town Quay (left). The pair of large ships at anchor give an indication of the available draft at the headland, Penleath Point (25 ft in 1973). The nearer vessel is the *Ampleforth*, 6,327 tons. Photo by Walton Hudson (pre-12 August 1959).[10]

South Coast Ports

The fifteenth and sixteenth centuries at Fowey encompass all the major threats to merchandise in supplying England and Wales, even adding strife between one home port and another: foreign raiding, reprisal raids, new fortification, and the breaking of treaties with concomitant punishment. It is as if England's fluctuating maritime fortunes in the medieval era were concentrated in one place.

Lostwithiel[11] is an interesting early example of industrial pollution according to Leland, who says that marine access was spoiled by the discharge of debris into the creek from tin mining, a hazard he notes in relation to several small havens along the Cornish coast. Meeting the River Tamar and the 'simple fisshar towne cawled Mylbrooke',[12] which warranted no further comment, Leland, like the modern traveller at this point, left Cornwall.

South Devon

Plymouth warrants a considerable mention by Leland, who says: 'The mouth of the gulph wherein the shippes of Plymouth lyith is waullid on eche side and chainid over in tyme of necessite. On the southwest side of this mouth is a block house: and on a rokky hille hard by it is a stronge castel,' and: 'there is a goodly rode for great shippes betwixt the haven mouthe and this (Schilleston) creeke.'[13]

When William Schellinks visited Plymouth in August 1662, he said that the town 'has only recently grown by and by from a poor fishers' village to such a very populous and large town that it may be compared to a city. Its harbour is so large and convenient that a large ship may, without lowering its sails, sail right into the bay, where there is a good and safe anchorage, protected by two forts against all interference.'[14]

Plymouth began the fifteenth century being pummelled by a Breton fleet, the town abandoned to its fiery fate by the terrified inhabitants.[15] Perhaps unsurprisingly, like Fowey it bore a grudge, and in 1483 there was an instruction to the people of Plymouth to deliver two French ships they had confiscated, the *Couronne* and

Plymouth, South Devon, waterfront toward Mill Bay from Plymouth Hoe. Photo by Walton Hudson (*c.* 1960).

the *Daulphyn*, both out of Dieppe, together with their guns and their livery, to two local captains who were to use them for two voyages.[16]

John Leland says of Dartmouth: 'There is only a bay fillid by fluddes with salt water, driving at the ebbe 2 miles, that devideth Ardenes from Dertmouth Town: and over this bay is a stone causey and 2 flatte bridges.'[17] He continues: 'The toune of Dertmouth lyith in lenght on a very rokky hille on the haven side, about half a mile from the very mouth of it, and extendith in lenghth aboute a quarter of a mile, there be good marchaunt men in the towne: and to this haven long good shippes.'

Those 'good shippes' belonging to Dartmouth were sorely tested in 1403 when the French plundered the town but came a cropper when they were challenged by the Devonian townsfolk, not least the women, who caused significant casualties among the attackers, including the death of their leader. The language barrier between French and Devonian English was said to have worsened matters, which is perhaps surprising as men of Dartmouth regularly sailed to Bordeaux for wine and did so throughout the fifteenth century. In any case, the people of Dartmouth were rewarded by the king for their stout defence. Between 1480 and 1495 the town constructed Dartmouth Castle, one of the first to deploy cannon near the waterline to assault approaching ships.[18] They built it to wrap around St Petrox church, which was already in the mid-fifteenth century noted as the Dartmouth seamark in the *seebuch* of Karl Koppmann. The castle has none of the eye-catching platforms of Henry VIII's later fortifications but nevertheless represented a considerable innovation. Its juxtaposition with St Petrox left no one under any illusion as to its prominence from seaward.

William Schellinks recorded the defences in 1662, describing Dartmouth as 'a small harbour or seaside town, a port protected by two forts which lie on either side of the harbour at the foot of the hill. This place has shipping from all parts and is frequented by merchants.'[19]

Nearby was Leyland's 'praty towne of fischar men caullid Brixham; and this towne is a member of the privilege of Dartmouth, and hath a peere by it'.[20] Further on, at the mouth of the River Exe, stood Topsham. This was the late medieval port for Exeter, further upriver. Leland describes it: 'Apsham

Dartmouth, South Devon: view out from Kingswear to the open sea. Dartmouth Castle, St Petrox church and Battery Point to centre right, covering the approaches. Photo by Walton Hudson (*c.* 1960).

(Topsham) a praty tounlet on the shore a 4 miles upper in the haven. Heere is the great trade and rode for shippes that usith this haven: and especially for the shippes and marchant mennes goodes of Excester. Men of Excester contende to make the haven cum up to Excester self. At this tyme shippes cum no farther up but to Apsham.'[21]

Leland was clearly aware of contemporary efforts to make a harbour at Exeter to bring the merchandise closer and unload where it could be stored more securely, Topsham being a half-way house with which Exeter had become frustrated. Such a move would be to the detriment of Topsham. Exmouth itself, where there were boats already, was perhaps not suitable, being only 'a fisschar tounelet a litle withyn the haven mouth'. Exeter finally built a new quay in 1564, and added a large crane, making the most of its haven. It encountered silting problems from the outset and the crane had to be rebuilt around 1625. It made little difference to accessibility and cargoes evidently remained limited; in July 1662 Schellinks visited and noted 'a quay where ships of (only) 20 tons come in from down-river. Three miles down on this side of the river is Topsham, where the seagoing ships tie up and load and discharge, and over the river, 8 miles distant at its mouth, is Starcross, where the ships first anchor.'[22]

East of Exeter and Topsham lies the rocky Jurassic Coast, where there were few small harbours and many a rocky approach. Fifteenth-century seamarks here were few because the whole coast could by and large be kept at a safe distance.

Dorset

Respite might also be found at Lyme Regis, known just as Lyme at the end of the medieval period. It received its charter in 1284 from Edward I, who used its harbour as a base of operations. Although here Leland's notes are incomplete, he says of it around 1545 that it 'hath good shippes, and usith fishing and marchauntice. Merchauntes of Morleys (Morlaix) in Britaine (Brittany) much haunt this town. Ther is no haven at Lime: but a quarter of a mile by west southwest the toun is a great and ... (in the sea for succour of shippes)'.[23] In this last, broken sentence, Leland may have been describing the Cobb, a massive stone breakwater and harbour arm, today a well-known tourist attraction, immortalised in John Fowles' 1969 novel *The French Lieutenant's Woman*. Leland's note that Breton merchants from Morlaix frequented the town is an unusual observation for him. With a drying harbour it may have been an observation that meant Bretons from Morlaix regularly visited after landing elsewhere or anchoring outside. They could certainly not leave large vessels within the harbour. By the time of Edward V (1483), there was already a customs house at Lyme Regis.[24]

Lyme Regis, Dorset: the drying harbour, looking inland from the Cobb (2008).

Seas of Plenty

The Cobb was dominant by the time Schellinks visited in September 1662. He described it succinctly as 'a man-made breakwater of heavy stones and piles, which serves as a harbour for ships'.[25]

East of Lyme Regis, Burton Bradstock and Bridport were well-known during the fifteenth century for making sailcloth and ropes of flax and hemp, natural resources long imported into England by the north Italian galleys, and against whom the Dorset makers had to compete. Bridport, lying at one end of the geological marvel that is Chesil Bank, battled constantly against nature's sifting and sorting of its mounds of shingle. The harbour required frequent repairs, so much so that by 1444 episcopal indulgences were sought for those who took their part and helped dig it out.

Adjacent to the painfully exposed promontory and harbour of Portland (raided and burned by the French in 1404 and 1405 and strengthened under Henry VIII by the addition of an artillery castle) lies much of Chesil Bank, 40 feet high in places but sheltering beyond it a safe salt lagoon – 'The Fleet' – for the few who could access it with local knowledge. Beyond this, later stone quarries and a harbour removed Portland's medieval predecessor. East and north lay the haven of Weymouth, where Leland writes of its suburb Milton, or Melcombe Regis (where the Black Death first came ashore in 1349): 'Ther is a tounlet on the hither side of the haven of Waymouth caullid Miltoun (Melcombe) ... This toun, as is evidently seene, hathe beene far bigger than it is now. The cause of this is layid onto the French men that yn tymes of warre rasid this towne for lak of defence.'[26] Of Weymouth itself, he mentions that 'ther is a kay and warf for shippes'.[27] It seems unlikely that Melcombe remained depopulated from the Black Death, given the relative recovery of most other locations, and Leland's attribution of its decay principally to French raiding, gleaned from local hearsay, seems very plausible. Like Lyme Regis, Weymouth contained a customs house.[28]

At nearby Lulworth, beloved in modern times as a holiday destination, Leland recorded 'a lytle fisshar toun caullid Lilleworth, ... wher is a gut or creke out of the se into the land, and is a socour for smaul shippes'.[29] Thus the instantly recognisable Lulworth Cove makes an appearance. The shelter it might offer is clear, but that was restricted by its size.

In the lee of the shoreline formed by the Isle of Purbeck, modern Swanage remains the most peaceful family seaside destination. To its south lay St Aldhelm's Head, a dangerous, rocky promontory surmounted by a chapel, another one of the very few medieval beacons or lighthouses still in existence here. In the sixteenth century Leland noted 'a fisher town caullid Sandwiche and ther is a peere and a litle fresch'.[30] There is still a small pier and slipway from which a lifeboat launches, although Swanage Bay is among England's most benign bodies of water. In the fifteenth century it exported Purbeck marble to London for the most skilled marblers in the capital, who fashioned church monuments and grave slabs that were distributed to churches and monasteries across the country. Some was also sought on the continent.

Poole harbour is among the largest deepwater harbours in the world. In the late medieval period it was well known but not a major port, others nearby such as Southampton and Portsmouth having better inland connections. It was disastrously raided and sacked in 1405 by the Spanish, led by the well-known pirate Gutierrez Diaz de Gamez, leading to an extensive rebuilding programme. At the site known as 'the Foundry' on Thames Street, archaeologists uncovered the pre-raid quayside, of stone and timber piles; it continued to be used in some form until at least 1564, when the town was in steep decline, with documents remarking on rubbish being dumped down its slipway in preceding years. In the infilling that extended beyond the pre-1405 quayside, the excavations retrieved scores of newly made and reclaimed waterlogged ships' timbers, some in the process of being reworked before they were buried in the construction for the new wharf. Here was evidence of a boatyard where boats were built, repaired and perhaps even broken up before the destruction of the attack in 1405.[31]

The sheer size of Poole harbour impressed contemporaries, including Leland:

> Pole is no town of auncient occupying in marchantdise: but rather of old tyme a poore fisshar village ... It is in recent times much encreasid with fair building and use of marchaundise. It standith almost as an isle in the haven and hangith by north est to the mayne land by the space almost of a flite shot ... The key for the shippes standith south est ... If a man should round aboute cumpace the water withyn the mouth of Poole Haven it wold stretch welle toward 20 miles.[32]

Like Lyme Regis and Weymouth, Poole warranted the presence of a customs house from at least 1433, when it became a wool-staple port. Poole was probably the destination of a

Poole, Dorset, harbour with Brownsea Island (far left); view north from Studland (2023).

fifteenth-century Basque wreck, discovered in the 1970s and known as the Studland Bay wreck, which was carrying Spanish lustreware. In general the town's archaeology includes French and German pottery imports.[33] Henry VIII built an artillery blockhouse on Brownsea Island within the harbour, but Leland makes no mention of it.

Hampshire

On the southern side of the New Forest lies the picturesque estuary of the River Beaulieu. Here Beaulieu Abbey had maintained as many as three ships of its own from at least the thirteenth century, exporting corn and buying in herring from Yarmouth (where it owned land), salt from Poitou and wine from Gascony.[34] On the river nearby lies Buckler's Hard, where slipways would eventually hold a dozen or more new ships from Nelson's navy, including combatants at Trafalgar. The fifteenth- and sixteenth-century facilities would have been very rudimentary, but Beaulieu Abbey's vessels were seagoing examples, crossing Biscay and going to 'northern parts' also, so considerable wharfage might be seen as normal, even if more extensive boatyard facilities were only embryonic under the Cistercian monastic regime.

Much has rightly been written on the foreign trade of Southampton.[35] It was, alongside London, Sandwich and Bristol, the most important port of medieval England. For our purposes let us begin with Leland's description of the port facilities:

> the old town of Hampton was brent in tyme of warre, spoyled and rasyd by French pyrates. This was the cause that the inhabitauntes there translated themselves to a more commodious place and began with the kings licens and help to build Newhampton and to waulle yt yn defence of the enemies.[36]

On the marine-side of the strong fourteenth-century defences he adds:

> ... not far beyond it is a fair gate called the Water gate: without which is a fair square key forsid with piles into the haven water for shippes to resort to. The west gate is strong, and even without it is a large key for shippes, as there is without the water gate.[37]

There had been a crane on the town quay since around 1410, paid for by private means, when the quay was renewed just outside the Watergate. The crane, or its successor, can still be discerned on the end of the quay as a tiny, spidery doodle on John Speed's generic map of Southampton from around 1610. Once the financier had been recompensed, the crane was supposed to pay for itself, and to keep it in top condition its continued suitability and good repair had to be demonstrated to any merchant who asked for its credentials. Henry VI in 1447 noted that Southampton was full of merchants and seamen from overseas with huge quantities of merchandise. He may have been stating the obvious, but the town clearly had the Crown's full attention.

In the 1540s Leyland goes on: 'The bredth of the mouth or entery of Southampton haven is by estimation a 2 myles from shore to shore. At the west point of it is a stronge castelle a late buildid caullid Caldshore, commonly Cawshot (Calshot).'[38]

Calshot Castle is another Henrician artillery fortlet, but here is described in more glowing terms, perhaps as it was brand-new in Leland's day. It was one of four fortifications to cover the Solent with those at Hurst, Cowes and Yarmouth. The spit of land on which Calshot is constructed was previously an unadorned natural windbreak near which the Venetian state fleet was encouraged to lie at anchor during its stays. The Florentine captain Albizzi also mentioned it in his 1429 diary:

The West Gate (inner face), Southampton, Hampshire, noted as 'strong' by Leland. Through here in 1415 marched the army destined for Agincourt (2023).

> On Saturday morning at 3 am we found ourselves off the Isle of Wight, and the wind turned to the south and east (i.e. a full headwind in the Spithead), so we had to change our plans and return to our berth about 8 miles from Southampton, opposite the Isle of Wight, which is called Calshore [sic].[39]

Michael of Rhodes and Karl Koppmann also note Calshot in their contemporary passage notes. However, the Venetians had stopped their annual state voyage a full decade before the castle was built. At low tide the lagoon is a muddy morass, and it was for mooring here that the Venetians were bidden by their Signory to bring their own ropes rather than rely on local ones which had lain out on the mud for who knew how long. Leland goes on:

> The haven shorith up 7 miles on the west side tyl it cummith up to Hampton toun standing on the other side: and here by estimation the trajectus (crossing) is a mile from land to land.[40]

This was the best deepwater anchorage in southern England, sheltered from attack and storms. A 600-ton galley could ride out most storms at anchor along the deepwater channel edge with impunity.

Calshot Castle also impressed Schellinks, who visited Southampton in September 1662. He drew the castle and noted for his drawing that he sailed past 'Calshot castle, which lies on a spit of land, and is at high tide completely surrounded by water'.[41] They fired their cannon in salute. Schellinks' drawing, depicting Southampton Water looking towards the Isle of Wight shows the castle at high tide, when Calshot Spit was, to all intents and purposes, non-existent. It is a view not possible today as the spit has been much enlarged and surmounted by numerous buildings. The castle remains an impressive structure nonetheless, and in a commanding position.

A string of wealthy and influential men sought to aggrandise Southampton, none more so than William Soper, sometime clerk of the king's ships, and Southampton's mayor, who was well known for his hospitality. He lived right next to the Watergate, which he rebuilt by 1433 and was an influential and energetic merchant. He also entertained Italian merchants at his rural New Forest manor, probably near Marchwood and Hythe on the west side of Southampton Water, where he would have had personal control of much timber – oak, ash and elm for repairs and long, straight firs for masts. Even today storms still uproot good fir masts there, each as straight as an arrow. Soper entertained the Florentine Albizzi during a church festival on his first visit in 1430, dining with the captain and going hunting, also later ensuring that he was shown far inland to tour Italian interests at Farnham, Guildford and Kingston-upon-Thames.[42] It was a far cry from one of his successors as mayor, John Payne Senior, who in 1463 was removed from office by Edward IV for his anti-Italian sabre-rattling.[43] While the senior mariners enjoyed some singular entertainment, the oarsmen, when not carousing, would often be put up at places like 'Edwardstow', or St Edward's Place, which was the Cistercian Abbey of St Mary and St Edward, Netley, just south of Southampton, still said at the Dissolution to be of 'great relief and comforte' to mariners both English and foreign.[44]

The relative ease with which one might traverse the long approach to Southampton is made clear by events in 1403, when a French fleet landed on the Isle of Wight, raided the coast and demanded tribute from the Crown for the island. Naturally this was refused, but the venture only foundered when the overweening French sailed west to Dartmouth and attacked that town (see above), where they were soundly trounced.[45]

Leland lists the various creeks that feed into Southampton Water, drawing attention in particular to the River Hamble and 'Hamelle haven, wherein is a very faire rode for greate shippes'.

Southampton was an expensive port to maintain. Its inhabitants and institutions were expected to contribute to keep the defences in good repair, and each monarch successively added to available funds, including Henry VIII, even as the upkeep began to slip. The defences needed constant attention and this uniquely exposed port resorted to one of the most extensive early batteries of cannon anywhere, with plenty in reserve at its armoury.

Southampton Water, Hampshire: the vast saltwater lagoon behind Calshot Spit, near where the north Italian galleys anchored and tethered. Calshot Castle is at far right where the spit still terminates, although now much built up (2023).

Southampton, Hampshire: God's House Tower – the civic armoury (2023). A 1490 fire here was blamed on the Venetians, but it was extinguished, and the matter died down.[46]

As the modern home of the Royal Navy, adjacent Portsmouth enjoys an especial place in the national psyche. However, even before Henry VIII the town enjoyed singular attention from the Crown and it is here that some of the earliest royal men-of-war were berthed – furthermore, it was the home port (and original wreck site) of the *Mary Rose*, which sank in 1545. John Leland says of it:

> There is at this point of the haven Portesmuth toun, and a great round tourre almost doble in quantite and strenkith to that that is on the west side of the haven right agayn it: and here is a mighty chaine of iren to draw from tourre to towre ... About a quarter of a mile above this tower is a great dok for shippes, and yn this dok lyith yet part of the rybbes of the *Henry Grace of Dieu*, one of the biggest shippes that hathe beene made in human memory.[47]

The *Henry Grace à Dieu*, once in the purview of Southampton's William Soper and the pride of Henry V's navy, in modern times can still be seen at low tide breaking the surface through the mud of the Hamble, where it was eventually allowed to rest.

Leland goes on to relate just how well Portsmouth was defended in his day, with multiple cannon in many towers and defensible gates and provisioned for wartime. One notable example was Henry V's construction of a tower in 1418 to protect his ships and the area round about. To this Henry VIII added Southsea Castle, an artillery fort. The king's fleet at the start of the fifteenth century – for keeping the sea – was relatively small, apparently comprising three carracks, two great ships, four barges and six balingers, crewed by three carpenters, twelve masters, 896 marines and sixty-five boys and pages. They may not have been awfully effective, since in 1418 they needed safe conduct from the Thames to Southampton due to French numbers assembled in the Channel.[48]

Ship and lighter on a St Christopher wall painting of 1440 at St Peter's Church, Shorewell, Isle of Wight (2023).

As to the town's mercantile credentials, Leland notes at the end of our period that 'the town of Portesmuth is bare and little occupied in time of pece'. This is echoed by Schellinks, who noted after his visit that 'Portsmouth is a small but strong and famous town, one of the arsenals of England'. Anyone who has departed these shores past aircraft carriers, destroyers and frigates cannot but agree wholeheartedly.

East of Portsmouth there is many a small creek and navigable mudflat protected from the winds of the English Channel, and harbours at places such as Chichester and Langstone were very much locally serviceable. Buried in silt north of Hayling Island was found a medieval wooden harpoon tip, testament to local fishing for flatfish or other large fish. It was probably too slender to be a whaling harpoon.[49]

Isle of Wight

Although it had a proud history of its own shipbuilding, direct imports into the Isle of Wight during the fifteenth and sixteenth centuries were comparatively few. The separation between the island's historic havens and the mainland meant that it received most goods through coasting, largely by locals who knew its very complex tides. In the period covered by this book, Cowes was the main point of entry. Few other places had proper berths for ships of any size, nor was the island infrastructure sufficiently advanced for distribution purposes. Cowes fed directly into the principal settlement, Newtown. There was no journey made by John Leland or any near contemporaries. Schellinks visited in September 1662 and stayed mainly in Newport, noting a dearth of inns when he went inland; he only found one at Shorewell (possibly The Crown), and otherwise had to make do with sleeping on a haystack.[50]

At Quarr Abbey on the north coast, a short ride from Cowes, a mariner visiting before 1536 would find a welcome from the Cistercian monks there, not dissimilar to the reception at

South Coast Ports

Southampton's Netley Abbey. Quarr had long had maritime links, maintaining a string of its own ships throughout the fourteenth century as wine carriers, and it is recorded as being instrumental in organising the defence of the island against French attacks. Being so well disposed to visiting mariners briefly seemed to count well with the king's commissioners but, like Netley, Quarr was dissolved in 1536.[51]

The wreck-strewn and cliff-fringed south coast of the island has few safe landing places; beside Cowes on the north coast, only Yarmouth on the west coast and Bembridge/St Helens on the east coast presented a reasonable prospect. Yarmouth, at the west end of the Solent, had long been a place where English fleets gathered before getting underway for France, but the medieval harbour was very small, much smaller than its enlarged modern successor. In the 1540s it acquired a Henrician artillery blockhouse, where the modern car ferry now docks. Not far away stand the Needles, one of the most enduring and photographed seamarks, mentioned by all of Michael of Rhodes, Luca di Albizzi and Karl Koppmann. However, the Needles were once larger and more numerous than today – and probably more impressive too. A particularly 'needle-like' stack – a tall, thin chalk shaft – quite unlike the rest and known as 'Lot's wife' collapsed in 1764.

Of equal importance, if not spectacle, was the church of St Helen at the settlement of the same name on the north side of Bembridge harbour on the east side of the island, looking out onto Spithead. Here the church was a prominent seamark, noted by Michael of Rhodes and Karl Koppmann, and from it visiting ships could judge their distance and anchor safely just offshore at a distance from rocks and ledges, a short lighter journey away from a warm welcome at Quarr Abbey.[52]

In 1488 the Venetians gathered their Flanders galleys off St Helen's after calling at Antwerp. Preparing to enter Southampton Water, they were challenged by three English ships. The Venetians closed the range and, although the galleys announced their friendly intent, the English forcibly boarded them anyway and a desperate fight ensued. Doubtless the Venetians had their bows strung or their arbalests loaded, since eighteen Englishmen were killed; the rest then pursued the Venetians right up to Southampton. A diplomatic protest from Venice went all the way up to King Henry VII, but the Bishop of Winchester was left to arbitrate, not least since the Venetian captain died – whether of wounds received is unclear.[53]

St Helen's church was built very close to the beach and by the mid-sixteenth century the sea was undermining its foundations. In the time of Elizabeth I it was reported that one could see right through the church from its wave-truncated chancel to its western tower door. Its building stone was considered sanctified and visiting mariners habitually stole blocks, 'holy stones', from

St Helen's parish church tower, Isle of Wight, the nave and chancel lost between the mid-sixteenth century and 1703 (2023).

the ruins to scrub their deck planking, hopefully bestowing divine protection upon their vessels. In 1703 the body of the church was demolished, leaving only the tower remains buttressed in a vast block of brickwork, whitewashed to maintain the structure's value as an ongoing seamark. That brick buttress, a judicious heritage-inspired stone apron and a Second World War concrete pillbox today sandwich the beleaguered tower, washed twice a day by the waves.

The island always remained exposed, and French raids were common. In 1545 a particularly nasty one hit Bonchurch, now part of Ventnor, well out of reach of any new Henrician fortlets. The French commander was killed and his body buried in the churchyard at Bonchurch, although it was later returned to France.

St Boniface Old Church, Bonchurch, Isle of Wight – erstwhile burial place of an unfortunate French raider (2023).

7

CHANNEL COAST PORTS

She drove in the dark to leeward,
She struck – not a reef or a rock
But the combs of a smother of sand: night drew her
Dead to the Kentish Knock[1]

Gerard Manley Hopkins,
'The wreck of the *Deutchland*'

Sussex

Hastings was and remains a fishing town. Along with Romney, Hythe, Dover and Sandwich it was one of the original Cinque Ports, a confederation of ports and towns in the south-east that grew to include over forty members. The tall, clapboarded net sheds on its shingle beach are listed buildings and some of them date back to the sixteenth century. It is highly likely that others since rotted away predated even these. However, nothing remains of the original harbour, having been washed away by the sea even before Leland's time. An attempt to build a new one in the time of Elizabeth I met the same fate. With no haven in which to shelter, the fishing boats of Hastings' fleet have for generations been winched up the shingle. A 1566 census at

Hastings notes that 146 out of 280 households in the town were engaged in fishing.[2]

Winchelsea grew rich on the wine trade but had to relocate to survive as Old Winchelsea was destroyed by storms at the end of the thirteenth century. New Winchelsea was built, prospered again, but then began to struggle against the powers of the sea in a long process of degradation which saw its share of the Gascon wine trade dwindle through the fifteenth century to a point where it was barely viable in the middle of the sixteenth century. Up to 1491 it could provide what the Cinque Ports asked of it, but thereafter it struggled to provide ships even to the Crown. Many of its medieval mercantile wine cellars still survive under more recent buildings and several are listed. Despite its heyday having long passed, it still imported many hundreds of tuns of wine, principally from France, and it remained a tempting (if rather overripe) fruit for foreign raiders. It was also a favoured port for pilgrims heading to Santiago de Compostela.

Geophysical prospection by archaeologists has begun to indicate just how extensive Winchelsea's docks and harbour once were. Lying well below the strong walled defences of the town, they are long since filled in and silted up, now turned over to farmland. In 1513 a tower was built on an old shingle spit to mark the Winchelsea anchorage and that of nearby Rye, and in the 1540s was much enlarged to become Henry VIII's Winchelsea Castle, better known today as Camber Castle. Like modern Winchelsea, the castle is landlocked by the silted deposits of the sea. The town was always vulnerable, and its history indicates a constant need for the considerable defences that surrounded it, as Leland indicates:

> ... it was twise enterid by enemies, first by Frenchmen, that did much hurt in the toune, and secondarily by the Spaniardes,

that enterid by night Fairly (Fairlight) aboute the middle way betwixt Winchelsey and Hastings ... At this invasion the towne of Winchelsey was sore spoyled, and scant syns cam ynto the pristine state of welth. For the commune voyce is that at that tyme were xx aldermen yn the toune marchauntes of good substaunce.[3]

In 1548, an Act of Parliament that proposed prohibiting the dumping of ballast noted that it was 'too little, several centuries too late'.[4] New Winchelsea, itself a reinvention of Old Winchelsea, had seemingly already passed the baton to nearby Rye.

Rye and Winchelsea shared the same marine inlet, but at Rye, which saw its importance wax just as Winchelsea waned, silting has also stranded the town, now 2 miles from the sea although in the late medieval period the sea flowed right up to its walls. At that time its strong fishing fleet supplied fish to the table at the royal court. Rye still has a harbour, but it is some way from the

Once a stone's throw from the harbour, St Thomas' Church, Winchelsea, East Sussex, contains the burials of two English admirals (2019).

town. William Schellinks in April 1663 described it as 'a small seaside town in Kent (Sussex)' with 'a good harbour'. There he stayed 'with the postmaster at the Mermaid, a good inn'.[5] The harbour today is less commodious, but the Mermaid remains a good inn.

Just like New Winchelsea, Rye was and is well fortified – it too had been badly mauled by French raiders during the fourteenth century. Its town gates have few parallels for strength along the south coast, but they are also clearly out-workings of civic pride. Built to keep out the raiding French, the town fathers were probably seriously affronted when attacked by men of Fowey.[6]

In its battles against encroaching silts and sands, the original Rye Harbour, with a strong fishing fleet and a cross-Channel passenger service to France, remained somewhat restricted. Into the Elizabethan period a great majority of vessels using it were under 50 tons, the town being insufficiently wealthy to improve the dwindling access for much bigger ships. Its main workaday trade was with France and Spain's Biscayan ports for wine and salt, very much worth protecting with its strong castle and town defences.[7]

At nearby Camber Sands there is today a wide and sandy beach, which on more than one occasion had to suffice for vessels that could not make Rye's town dock when driven by adverse winds; then it was known as the port of Camber, Chamara or 'Camber-before-Rye'. It boasted a broad and relatively deep basin which from the early fifteenth century was used by the Venetian State's Flanders galleys as a rallying point to await their compatriots as they loaded up at Southampton and Sandwich.[8] There are salty lagoons behind the beach today – the last vestiges of the silted channel that led to both Rye and Winchelsea – but these no longer link to anything and are cut off from sea access by huge sea defences. Their erstwhile mutual protector, Camber Castle, stands alone in green fields.

Rye, East Sussex: a stoutly defended harbour town, now stranded 2 miles from the sea. Town gate (2019).

Kent

Dungeness ('Dinginesse' to Karl Koppmann in the fifteenth century), despite its windswept desert conditions and wildfowl idyll, was and is a wholly unsafe stretch of coast, best avoided, accumulating massive bands and spits of constantly shifting shingle. Beyond its shoreline the currents are alarmingly swift and strong. Just inland at Lydd, the most outlying market town to jut out on solid geology, the once seafaring town sports All Saints Church where among its graves lie those of several shipwrecked mariners. Even in Leland's day, however, Lydd's days on the coast were well behind her, being a mile from the sea even then, although its inhabitants could still row out.[9] At Dengemarsh, near Lydd, there is archaeological evidence for butchery of stranded whales, one of the less common fruits of the sea.[10]

Of Romney, just north of Dungeness and one of the original Cinque Ports, Leland says, 'Rumney is one of the v portes, and hath bene a metely good haven, yn so much that withyn remembrance of men shyppes have cum hard up to the towne, and cast ancres yn one of the chyrch yards (perhaps St Clement?). The se is now a ii myles fro the towne, so sore thereby now decayed.'[11]

Today Romney Marsh is characterised by its tiny villages and 'stranded' maritime churches that once served half a dozen communities of mariners and boatyards. Old Romney is mentioned in the passage notes of Michael of Rhodes in the early to mid-fifteenth century (as Romaneo), and St Dunstan's Snargate, even further inland, has a fine wall painting of a carrack, testament to the area's former reliance on maritime trades.

All Saints Church, Lydd, Kent. Its 134-foot tower was a prominent seamark behind shifting 'Dinginesse' (2019).

Seas of Plenty

A shifting sea of shingle under big skies characterises Dungeness, and stranded Lydd, Kent (2014).

Wall painting *c.* 1500 of a great ship – a carrack – in the church of St Dunstan, Snargate, Romney Marsh, Kent (2014).

Channel Coast Ports

Clearly the woes that beset so many of the small south and east coast ports in the later fifteenth and early sixteenth centuries ruined Romney's reliance on the fruits of the sea as well. In the generations before Leland wrote, the sea had done its worst along a huge stretch of coastline. The fifteenth century opened with a particularly nasty storm surge that coincided with a high tide in 1404, inundating large portions of the Kent coast and devastating the continental coastline too for many miles.[12]

Just beyond the verdant patch of land reclaimed from the sea is Hythe, another of the original Cinque Ports. It once had a small, sheltered harbour, but coastal erosion and the deposit of shingle and sand mean that nothing remains of its former glory. The strand today is of shingle and sand, punctuated by lines of timber groynes that slow the continued advance of the sea.

Leland says that 'Hithe hath bene a very great towne yn length' but was 'clene destroied' and laments 'bankinge of woose and great casting up of shyngel' in front of the place. He does, however, note that nevertheless in his day something survived: 'The haven is a prety rode and liith meatly strayt for passage owt of Boleyn (Boulogne). Yt croketh yn so by the shore a long, and is so bakked fro the mayn se with casting of shinggil, that smaul shippes may cum up a larg myle toward Folkestan as yn a sure gut.'[13]

As Leland hints, records show that during the time of Henry VIII, although the port was already in steep decline and would never fully recover, there was still regular passenger traffic to France. Hythe was also used to supply the garrison at Calais. A little later, in a list of town boats in 1566, the town had seven 'crayers' of up to 40 tons involved in sea fishing and trade. Everything else was smaller and used only for fishing.[14] The smaller boats at Hythe (so-called shotters and tramellers) were referred to as 'stade boats' and were winched up onto the beach by way of capstans or the aforementioned 'horses'. Nearby Henry VIII built Sandgate Castle, another of his artillery forts and yet another victim of the sea it once guarded, lost to the pounding of the waves since the sixteenth century.

Folkestone was in some difficulty at the end of our period, as Leland notes: 'Folchestan ys a v miles fro Dovar, and be al gesse stondeth very directly apon Boleyn ... The towne shore be al likelihood is mervelusly sore wasted with the violens of the se.'[15] He goes on to list monuments and buildings lost to the marine onslaught. Folkestone still held its own somewhat in the time of Henry VIII, in 1528 sending twenty boats, in a fleet with Romney and Hythe, round into the North Sea after cod and herring, a trip some Hythe boats of up to 40 tons had been making as far up as Scarborough since at least 1412.[16]

Dover had been known as the key to England long before the fifteenth century. Directly facing the French, no English port was better defended, although all trace of the medieval harbour has long been subsumed into its modern successor. In his description of the castle Leland notes the port facilities, together with the age and pedigree of Dover as a survivor of Roman times: 'Ther hath bene a haven yn tyme past, (with much made-ground). Ther hath be fownd also peces of cabelles and anchores, and Itinerarium Antonini cawleth hyt by the name of a havon. The towne on the front toward rhe se hath bene right strongly walled and embateled, and almost al the residew; but now yt is partly fawlen downe, and broken downe.'[17]

He goes on to mention in respect of the port and Dover Castle: 'On the toppe of the hye clive between the towne and the peere remayneth yet, abowt a flyte shot up ynto the land fro the very brymme of the se clyffe, a ruine of a towr, the which hath bene as a pharos or a mark to shyppes on the se...' These were the well-known ruins of a Roman lighthouse that stands within the enceinte of Dover Castle, its purpose well understood but not employed in Leland's day, nor probably within living memory given its ruined state even then. Nevertheless, Dover was always important, and from here ran the most regular service to and from France. It remained the principal port for travelling individuals and small parties heading for north-western France and the surrounding duchies. Many an exile and miscreant, 'abjuring the realm' as punishment for misdeeds, chose to leave by the Dover passage.

Before its castle was built in 1540 little was notable about Deal, on 'a flat shore and very open to the se'.[18] However, it is that Henrician coastal castle which is the key to the town since its shore lay directly opposite the Downs, a safe, offshore deepwater anchorage where an entire fleet could ride at anchor and await favourable winds in the hands of skilled masters. At the end of our

The Roman 'pharos' at Dover Castle, Kent, notable but long since a ruin by Leland's day (2014).

period, the castle, along with its flanking sister castles at the more commodious Walmer to the south and Sandown to the north (the last of these three subsequently destroyed), eventually ensured that no enemy fleet could enjoy such shelter.

In fact the Downs, while offering a good anchorage in some winds, could be a perfidious mistress if the winds changed, and nearby on the Kent coast lurks Goodwin Sands, one of the most treacherous stretches of water anywhere. This 12-mile-long sandbar, much of which is always submerged, and which shifts and changes shape, is a deathtrap for shipping and is one of the most densely packed shipping graveyards in the world. The slim difference between high water and a favourable wind and low water and an adverse breeze could spell disaster for the unwary.

Nearby Sandwich was a major late medieval Cinque Port, frequented by foreign fleets. In the 1540s, when those fleets had largely departed, John Leland described it thus:

> Sandwic, on the farther side of the river of Sture, is meatly well walled where the town stondeth most in jeopardy of enemies. The residew of the town is dichid and mudde waulled. Ther be in the town iiii principal gates, iii paroche chyrches, of the which sum suppose that St Marye's was sumtyme a nunnery. Ther is a place of Whit freres, and an hospital withowt the town first ordened for maryners decesid and hurt. Ther is a place where the monkes of Christ Chirch did resort when they were lords of the towne.
>
> The caryke that was sonke yn the haven yn Pope Paulus tyme did much hurt to the haven, and gether a great banke. The grounde self from Sandwiche to the haven, and inward to the land is caullid Sanded Bay.[19]

Notably, Leland states that 'now Sandwich be not celebrated by cause of Goodwin Sandes and the decay of the haven'.[20] Not all

Channel Coast Ports

Deal Castle, Kent, under construction in 1540, looks out on the Downs, an anchorage which might favour an enemy fleet. It was arguably the strongest of Henry VIII's artillery shore forts and remains the best-preserved (2014).

the casualties of Goodwin Sands were flesh and blood; clearly at the end of the medieval period this sailors' *bête noire* presented an insurmountable obstacle to trade for Sandwich, previously one of

Sandwich, Kent: much had to be rebuilt after the disastrous French attack of 1457 (2014).

England's principal trading gateways and beloved of the Florentines and Genoese. In another turn of bad luck, its fourteenth-century walls, ditches and fortified gates proved insufficient to protect it from some 4,000 French raiders from Honfleur in a fleet of as many as sixty ships in 1457, leading to the burning of the town, although it was slowly rebuilt.[21]

Leland's reference to a carrack being sunk, whether accidentally or deliberately, indicates some unwelcome silting, and dates this probably to the time of Pope Paul II (1464–71). Sandwich's days as a great medieval port were by then numbered. In 1469 the local authority endeavoured to clear the main channel of obstructions, including fish weirs, and in 1485 every man of Sandwich was required to take a hand in cleaning it out once more. When the Florentine state galleys ceased their annual journeys to Sandwich in 1477 the writing was on the wall; the vessels frequenting the town shrank year after year thereafter. Even late in the day, when its population had plummeted by three-quarters, Sandwich's former popularity was not lost on pirates who still plied the waters of the English Channel, and in 1536 attacked a Sandwich 'crayer' off Hythe and 'broke both his topmasts'.[22]

8

LONDON, EAST ANGLIA AND THE NORTH-EAST

When the port's cleared and the coast out of sight,
And ships are few, each on its proper course,
With no occasion for approach or discourse
                                    Robert Graves, 'Quayside'

It is regrettable that among John Leland's journeys, with few exceptions, his travels across England do not take in East Anglia. He has left us virtually nothing of Norfolk, Suffolk, Essex or Cambridgeshire. William Worcestre's journey too began at Norwich and headed west, away from the North Sea. William Schellinks in 1661–63 is a different matter; he travelled north from London, where he was based, and stayed in Norfolk a while. Although later than the specific period covered by this book, his study nevertheless predates by some margin any modern developments to the ports he visited, and his keen observations, whether as a professional artist or a possible spy, are invaluable.

London
Without doubt Leland knew London and the Thames well. However, it did not lie within his remit to describe it in his notes.

London, East Anglia and the North-East

Although the River Thames might look timeless, London in the fifteenth and early sixteenth centuries bore little resemblance to the modern metropolis. There are few contemporary descriptions for a marine approach.[1]

Having avoided the Kentish Knock and any other threatening sandbars, the vessel heading for London would note the church of St Mary at Reculver on the north Kent coast, with its twin towers (and originally spires too) atop the bluffs. It is a prominent seamark which dominates Herne Bay even today, although the body of the church was demolished in 1803.[2] Thereafter the estuary begins to narrow, after passing the Swale and the sparsely populated Isle of Sheppey.

The land is low-lying at the confluence of the Thames and the Medway, the latter still undeveloped in maritime terms during Leland's time but destined to become a centre of shipbuilding before the end of the sixteenth century. To local mariners this was 'Sea-reach', the start of the Thames. Further in, at Lower Hope Point, lay the village of Cliff or Bishop's Clive. There stood beacons which were lit if approaching vessels failed to announce themselves appropriately or appeared openly hostile.

Gravesend marshes continued the low-lying ground, out of which poked Chalk Church (St Mary) on rising ground. Gravesend Reach hereabouts lay at the top of the floodtide, where a variety of vessels would gather, anchored during the ebb. Eventually Henry VIII would have a blockhouse built at this spot. Here the water is turbid and brackish, mingling North Sea saltwater and freshwater from the Thames. All would get under way at the onset of the next flood. On occasions the visiting Venetian galleys went no further than Gravesend, allowing the watermen (who held a monopoly thereabouts) to offload cargoes and take them upstream at less than 6*d* per covered barge and more than 2*d* for each uncovered. This was 'the long ferry'. At such a time the Venetian oarsmen might have given thanks for their arrival at SS Peter and

Paul, Milton, St Mary's Chalk or St Clement, Thurrock, over on the north bank, where the Thames could be forded at low tide. If so, their stay might fall disappointingly short of the Metropolis and the accustomed wharf-side market for their seaman's portion. Sometimes, when London was particularly restive, foreign ships would stop well short of the capital; this happened in 1449, when the Venetians ordered their galleys to go no further than Gravesend and let the lighters do the rest, preferring to go on to Southampton or Sandwich instead.[3] In 1453, the atmosphere in the capital was so febrile they not only chose to go to Southampton and Sandwich instead but sent their London-bound goods overland from there.[4]

Past Greenhithe on the Kentish side lay Erith with its boatyard (where several of Henry VIII's ships were built) and further boatbuilding at Woolwich, then on past Barking, with Barking Abbey conspicuous, and Blackwall. Some larger vessels unloaded

The distinctive towers of St Mary's Church, Reculver, Kent, once supported spires (2014).

London, East Anglia and the North-East

bulk cargos at Erith to reduce their draught and progress further upstream.[5] Only as they rounded the last bend in the river after Greenwich would London hove into view in all its late medieval splendour and ordure. However, although there were many stairs or jetties serving individual properties and streets on either side, they were largely for foot traffic and hand luggage only. Around them the watermen would gather; there was always insufficient riparian wharfage to comfortably land all the incoming goods, and the sheer numbers arriving made for a constant riverine traffic jam midstream, where the navigable channel did not dry out.

The Dutch artist-cum-spy Willem Schellinks arrived in 1661, when nothing much had changed in this respect. He wrote in his diary on 14 August: 'Past this bend in the river, one comes within sight of the city of London, with its suburbs Redriff (Rotherhithe) on the left and Ratcliff on the right, extending three miles along the river up to London Bridge. There was a great throng of all kinds of craft...'

Boats were parked, gunwale to gunwale, four vessels or more wide across, and unloading was by lighters managed by Thames watermen who jealously guarded their taxi trade and ferry service, crossing and recrossing the river many times daily when the tide was high enough. This was the 'Pool' of London, which stretched, as Schellinks notes, for 3 miles up to London Bridge, the only bridge crossing that existed. It was resplendent with its nineteen narrow arches and just a single drawbridge in the central arch, through which a taller vessel might pass, guiding its mast as if threading a needle. Larger vessels went no further, and it was left to the lighters and the watermen to do the rest. East of London Bridge, here at the Pool, goods were landed mostly at Billingsgate, then the premier portside market in the country. For lighters taking goods upstream, the much smaller Queenhithe market beckoned west of the bridge, and it was left to the watermen to shoot the dangerous tidal race between the 7-metre-wide cutwaters as the Thames ebbed and flowed, squeezing through the narrow arches or 'sterlings'. Just downriver, the congested mid-stream marina of the Pool looked on.

Private moorings stood below Thames Street for the Hanse traders and their wealthy neighbours. There stood the Easterling Hall, in the time of Henry VIII decorated with wall panels painted by Hans Holbein the Younger (one of which can be seen on the cover of this book). The neighbours also maintained their own private wharves along the Thames in St Dunstan's parish, between the Tower and Billingsgate. Each wharf lay at the foot of its owner's plot, named after the family in possession: Asslyns Wharf, Passekese Wharf, Horser's Quay, Porter's Quay. The names were updated as the properties changed hands.[6]

At Billingsgate the customs men awaited the cargo manifests and saw to it that duties were paid on incoming goods – occasions when they were bypassed were serious breaches of the law, such as the bale of Bokeram that was secretly unloaded on a stormy night in 1432 at Billingsgate without payment of customs.[7] The Heydox crane could perhaps deal with heavier materials or load and unload directly from specific ships by arrangement. It might also

HMS *Belfast* (11,500 tons) now lies where the Italian galleys once unloaded at the Pool of London. The (then brand-new) Shard lies beyond in Southwark, its top shrouded in mist (2015).

be used to aid repairs, although a visit downstream to Erith might be required if something major like a new mast was needed.

Upriver, Queenhithe gradually waned until it dealt exclusively with river traffic up the Thames, ceding its handling of inward cargoes and the capital's own voracious consumption to Billingsgate and smaller south-bank wharfs like Rotherhithe.

Fortunate incomers might mingle with the royal barge, which regularly plied the Thames, accompanied by a small flotilla, between the royal residences of Richmond and Greenwich, the Tower, Westminster and Baynard's Castle. The royal barge was a magnificent affair and was regularly used by both Queen Elizabeth of York (wife of Henry VII) and her son, Henry VIII. Powered by twenty-one rowers, with a second 'great boat' of eight rowers regularly accompanying it carrying courtiers, since the days of Edward IV its crew had been resplendent in a uniform of blue and purplish red (murrey), embroidered with two roses, the bargemaster additionally wearing a black gown of chamlet (a wool-and-silk mix).[8] This was perhaps the original 'claret and blue'.

Essex

Overland links from Essex to London were considerable, and this familiarity gave rise to the county's relative dearth of independent ports that might trade with foreign merchants and establish their own business, except perhaps Colchester. Essex became a favourite country retreat of London merchants, and its widespread examples of very fine timber-framed housing are testament to the London money which filtered out along good road connections to fund many relaxed lifestyles. In the fifteenth century the port of Tilbury on the Thames was considered to be an outlier of London, with ships departing London congregating here to await others and form safe Channel convoys. All ships heading for London passed Tilbury, although at this date it had yet to acquire the fort and defences associated with it from the later sixteenth century.

The coast here includes countless small tidal creeks and mudflats which militate against easy and regular boat journeys by all but smaller, flat-bottomed craft such as coasting barges. The local salt industry had also given way to imports in volume from continental sources. Along Walton-on-the-Naze, the shifting sands can quickly render even local knowledge out of date and this coast generally boasts few good harbours. While the county had numerous small fishing villages around the coast, none were major centres; one exception is Harwich, already a long-lived Essex port with a good harbour. In the medieval period it was a walled town (because it was vulnerable from the sea), and in 1340 the fleet of Edward III set off from its port to fight the French. Later, Henry VIII built a blockhouse here to protect the anchorage. Colchester appears on a mid-sixteenth century list of ports, accessible up a long channel of the River Colne via Hythe, but it struggled with weirs and other unsanctioned encumbrances throughout the medieval period and was comparatively restricted.

Suffolk

Like Essex, Suffolk's medieval wealth was built on a good return on its wool exports, which shows itself in some extraordinary timber-framed towns and villages, such as Lavenham. Already, however, the worst erosion processes in England had accounted for the total loss of the wealthy port town of Dunwich because of massive storms between 1286 and 1364. However, when it came to Suffolk's imports, it was more likely to get much of what it needed through either London to its south-west or through Yarmouth and Norwich to the north. There were exceptions, some of which have been the subject of detailed studies.

William Schellinks said of the riverine frontage at Ipswich in October 1662: 'The quay is a large place, where ships arrive from the sea from Harwich 6 miles up with the tide; large colliers go with every high and low tide up and down the river, for tuppence one can go by them.'[9]

Ipswich, up the River Orwell, was encouraged to take up arms against pirates in 1398. The principal town and port of the county, and already a very old settlement with a town quay at the start of the fifteenth century, Ipswich grew steadily for a further generation but experienced a slump during the 1450s and 60s when its local trade in French wines suffered greatly after the English loss of Bordeaux. At the same time, its cloth exports declined. It enjoyed greater stability towards the end of the century as English carriers began to import more wine, and trade with Spain also increased.[10]

Lowestoft was principally a fishing port that often benefited from the silting troubles of Yarmouth further up the coast, together with not a little rivalry as more southerly fishing fleets moved north to take herring off the coast there.[11] Southwold always battled with the onshore winds and tides which, by the end of the sixteenth century, had choked its harbour with shingle. Although this was eventually cut back, in the seventeenth century the town was virtually destroyed by fire. At nearby Aldborough there are two sea-facing watchtowers, admittedly later in date than our period, but which may have had forerunners from which to monitor and guide shipping. These later towers were used by rival salvage teams.

Norfolk
Yarmouth and Norwich are mentioned together here because, like York and Hull, one was the principal market for goods entering at the other. Norwich, famously described as 'a fine city', had been a market centre since late Saxon times, but particularly since the Normans moved the principal East Anglian bishopric there in the eleventh century. By the fifteenth century the city was pre-eminent in East Anglia and its access to the North Sea via the rivers Wensum and Yare, out through Yarmouth, meant its links to the Low Countries were arguably second to none. Extensive archaeological excavations since the 1980s betoken a city that in the fifteenth century was cosmopolitan in outlook, with a wide

variety of continental products for sale at its markets. The river was navigable right up to Norwich and its wharves, locally known as 'staithes', were accessible by small craft all the way into the city.[12] A disastrous urban fire in 1507 sealed a cellar deposit in Pottergate which indicates an extensive variety of mainly Rhenish and Netherlandish ceramics that graced urban tables, with few parallels excavated anywhere.[13] Inland, monasteries as far away as the Cistercians at Combe Abbey in Warwickshire maintained their own staithes at Norwich; Beaulieu Abbey had an estate there too. At Yarmouth the fishmongers of landlocked Coventry, 150 miles distant, moored their own fishing boat, while other boat owners in the port were members of Coventry's Holy Trinity Guild. Yarmouth battled constantly with its shifting sands, and its fishermen had to fight off predatory southern fleets hunting the migratory shoals of herring off its coast.

William Schellinks visited both in October 1662 and had this to say of Norwich: 'Coneysford Street is one English mile long along the water, where the wharves are, where the ships coming up from Yarmouth load and discharge, bringing fish and coal a journey of 30 miles because of the twists and turns of the river. Regular ferry boats from Norwich to Yarmouth sail daily, mostly in the evening. The fare is 12d.' Of Yarmouth he writes: '[It] has a good harbour and is well known because of its fishing industry and shipping … the quay is as long as the town and the streets along the river, where a large number of all kinds of ships lie along the wall.'[14]

The port of Yarmouth boasted defensive walls by 1390. A tollhouse survives from which the borough had overseen the town's business for much of the fourteenth century, and archaeological excavations have regularly uncovered timber piles and other fragments from the medieval quayside along the bank of the River Yare since the late nineteenth century. However, despite the town's pre-eminence in the herring industry and its annual herring fair, overseen by bailiffs from the Cinque Ports as arbiters,

London, East Anglia and the North-East

it suffered from the silting of five successive havens for shipping, three of them within the period of this book's concern alone.

Schellinks noted one drawback which was probably unchanged from the fifteenth century:

> On the 14 October we went to look at the quay, but because of a heavy mist, there was a very bad smell there ... mainly because of the vile odour of the new herrings, which were being smoked at all the warehouses, as it is now the end of the year and the fishing season. The stench is so bad that somebody who is not used to it would become ill.

One tends to forget that England's past was generally a lot smellier than the present.

North of Yarmouth, Lucas Wagenhaer's 1585 map notes Winterton-on-Sea as the next seamark. This is almost certainly because the church tower here, at Holy Trinity and All Saints, can be seen from far out to sea and can see far out in turn; built between 1415 and 1430, and 135 feet tall, it is one of the highest in Norfolk. The village itself was a fishing community where boats were drawn up onto the beach. Northwards again and Wagenhaer rightly notes Cromer as a seamark, undoubtedly referring to the church of SS Peter and Paul and its fourteenth-century tower, claimed to be the tallest parish church tower in Norfolk. Again, its height and proximity to the beach means it can be seen a long way off and, like Winterton, the tower may have had a light burning at a window as a marker. Both Cromer and Winterton subsequently acquired modern lighthouses.

At Cley-next-the-Sea was another small fishing village which imported a modicum of goods from the nearby continent, some at least by coasting. However, its fishermen achieved great acclaim and not a little notoriety when in 1406, in the middle of a truce with Scotland, they sparked an international incident by capturing the heir to the Scots kingdom and the Earl of Orkney and handing them over to Henry IV, who promptly imprisoned both in the Tower. Their accompanying bishop, probably in another ship, managed to escape to tell the tale.[15] The medieval portside facilities were lost in the seventeenth century when the approaches silted up, leaving the later village stranded some way inland.

At King's Lynn, and from Elizabethan times, just after the end of our period, there survives a five-storey brick watchtower (Clifton House on Queen Street) from which the return of ships could be monitored. Presumably it could also be used to mount a lantern as a beacon, although it is known that the tower of the medieval Franciscan friary church (Greyfriars) was a seamark at which to steer on the approach up the Great Ouse, as recorded by Sir William Dugdale in the mid-seventeenth century. This is probably one good reason why the tower survived the Dissolution of the Monasteries.

After the pre-eminent *kontor* at London (the Steelyard), Lynn contained a smaller Hanseatic factory, this one frequented particularly by merchants of Bremen and Danzig.[16] Although the riverine approach has changed course, the late medieval wharf can be picked out in the surviving building line close to the river, where a complete rarity – a Hanseatic warehouse – still stands on a side-street running towards it. There were two harbourside markets at Lynn, both founded by bishops of Norwich.

The men of Norfolk seem to have garnered a reputation for themselves from the start of the fifteenth century. In 1400, Lynn fishermen captured a Scots fleet off Aberdeen who then went on to ravage the Orkneys; a few years later, the fishermen of Cley-next-the-Sea changed the course of Anglo-Scottish relations with their capture of the future James I of Scotland. In 1467 merchants of Lynn and Bristol murdered the Danish governor of Iceland, leading to considerable reprisals.[17] After the Treaty of Utrecht in 1474, the Hanse set up a new steelyard at Lynn.

The fifteenth-century *seebuch* of Karl Koppmann is as comprehensive on the east coast as it is on the south. His list of

London, East Anglia and the North-East

seamarks and harbours is extensive – although the Low German spellings take some getting used to. Moving south to north by county, here is his itinerary along the coast:

County	Harbour/haven	Modern name	Seamark	Modern name
Essex	Herwyk	Harwich		
Suffolk	Orferde	Orford	*Unde Orfferde is en grot casteil mit velen tornen*	Orford Castle
	Orfferdnesse	Orford Ness		
Norfolk	Jerremude	(Great) Yarmouth		
	Wintertun	Winterton-on-Sea	(See below)	
	Cramers	Cromer		
	Blackene	Blakeney		
	Wyles	Wells-next-the-sea		
	Linden	(King's) Lynn		
Lincolnshire	Bustene	Boston		
Yorkshire			Vlamberger hovede	Flamborough Head
	Hummer	Humber		

The detail given by Koppmann is sometimes greater than that of Michael of Rhodes for the south coast. Witness his entry for Winterton-on-Sea in Norfolk:

> 15. Item from Happisburgh to Winterton is 3 miles (not modern miles). Happisburgh stands up a nice high cliff half a mile long. From Happisburgh to Winterton there are many sand dunes by the beach and that land stretches to and from Winterton southeast and northwest and is an empty beach so that one can beach a ship there.

16. Item Winterton is a considerable village that lies on the seashore, and there stands a tall tower and two narrow ways in, where one should enter by the south and leave east-south-east towards the sea.[18]

While the East and West Midlands lie a long way from Lynn, the town remained the principal eastern port for incoming goods as far inland as the likes of Warwickshire (up the River Nene, then

King's Lynn, Norfolk: the tower of the Greyfriars, a seamark on which to steer (2020).

along the east–west road, tellingly called 'the Portway'), but the town benefitted greatly from a wide variety of major inland fairs at which goods could be sold. As well as annual fairs at Lynn and Boston (Lincolnshire), there were similar ones to be found at Stamford, Northampton and St Ives, and a huge one every September at Stourbridge near Cambridge. Although in the late fifteenth century Lynn was very much in decline (from its wool and grain port heyday in the thirteenth and fourteenth centuries), it remained, thanks to the Hanse, a principal point of importation for many luxury goods.[19]

A long customs accounts list of imports through Lynn in 1503–04 has few parallels and is worth noting here. It picks out furs, cloth, featherbeds, lamps, copper kettles, drinking glasses, tankards, knives, scissors, baskets, straw hats, musical instruments, hops, sugar, fish, grindstones, bricks, tiles, carpets, tapestries, frying pans, playing cards, paper, vinegar and mirrors. Also known to be imported at the time are millstones, leather goods, brass, furniture, flax, spectacles, hair, cork, onions, paving tiles and purses.[20] This was partly the result of the wide interests of the Hanse but it also owes plenty to the entrepreneurs of Lynn, whose enterprising Baltic merchants were ensconced in Rostock, Wismar, Stralsund, Danzig and Scania by the early years of the fifteenth century.

William Schellinks, visiting in October 1662, stayed at Lynn longer than at most of his stopovers. He described it as Old Linne, Linnum Regis and Lynn.

> It has a very good harbour, the River Great Ouse flows into the sea there, forming an inlet. There is much trade and business in this place because of the situation. On St Margaret's church, standing on the crossing of the church is the lantern, having a gallery from which one has a very fine view over the town, the harbour and the countryside around ... In the afternoon we went to look at the town [from the Council Chamber] and at

the common guard, went up some stairs to a platform which is built there to look over the river and harbour out to sea for incoming and outgoing ships. We saw 16 ships come in from Wells[-next-the-sea], a small seaside hamlet, and go out from Wells over to Iceland to load saltfish and bring it over.

Clearly the English late medieval penchant for stockfish (air-dried cod, an Icelandic speciality) had not waned.[21]

The tides off north Norfolk turn and race rapidly, limiting the use of many inlets and creeks. Coastal villages like Wells and Cley, which did thrive, usually did so by fishing and some coasting, both of which relied upon good local knowledge of the ever-changing sailing conditions. Few foreign importers would choose to eschew the principal ports at Lynn and Yarmouth to get their valuable goods ashore.

Lincolnshire

Shifting sands and wide beaches massively complicate approaches to long stretches of Lincolnshire's coastline. Between the Wash and Skegness lies Gibraltar Point, a huge area of salt marshes, shifting sands and mudflats that have stifled many port ventures. A number of incipient port facilities have been snuffed out hereabouts. Further along, Spurn Head encloses yet more sandbanks.

However, one very successful Lincolnshire port does stand out on this coast. The town of Boston, which also bore the medieval name of St Botolph's, contains several remains relating to the town's heyday as a port of importation and particularly to the presence of the Hanseatic League. Like nearby Lynn, Boston had seen better days as a place of export but the Hanse kept it going. Leland wrote of his visit:

> The staple and the stiliard houses yet there remayne: but the stiliard is little or nothing at alle occupied. ... merchauntes

of the stiliard cumming by all partes by est were wont greatly to haunt Boston: and the gray freres toke them yn a manor for founders of their house and many Esterlinges were buried there. The Esterlinges kept a great house and course of marchanundice at Boston ontylle such tyme that one Humfrey Litlebyri, marchaunt of Boston, did kille one of the Esterlinges there about Edward the 4 dayes; ... so that the laste the Esterlinges left their course of marchaundise to Boston, and syns the towne sore decayed.[22]

Of Boston's celebrated 'stump', the church of St Botolph, Leland notes that it was a seamark, not only from Lincolnshire's flatlands, but also from out to sea, just like the Greyfriars tower at Lynn.[23] He adds that although the sea lies 6 miles distant, the town remained a port and 'dyverse good shipps and other vessels ryde there'[24] in his own time. In fact, Boston would enjoy another heyday in the seventeenth century. The nasty episode of a local merchant killing a Hanseatic rival in the mid- or late fifteenth century was far from uncommon, and such spats occur in contemporary chronicles. It should not be forgotten that for a large part of the fifteenth century England was beset by the Wars of the Roses, with all the deep-seated hatreds and resentments that involved. Trying to steer a course through this difficult period while remaining aloof would have been very challenging for even the most diplomatic merchant. Perhaps best known is the murder of Ansel Adornes, a Florentine merchant from Bruges who was murdered in Scotland in 1483 while serving as an advisor to James III. His marble effigy and tomb, in Bruges' Jerusalem Church, is a rare surviving example of a fifteenth-century merchant's sepulchre.

At the end of the hostilities between England and the Hanse in 1474, the Treaty of Utrecht provided for the Hanseatic League, who insisted upon the gift (not lease) from the Crown of their former steelyards in London, Boston and Lynn. When their trade dwindled, that property did too.

On a more minor note, Leland wrote of Wainfleet that 'it hath beene a very godde toune ... Shippeletes cam in recent times up to the schole. The haven now decayeth.'[25] This is another example of the economic slump that was setting in along the east coast in the 1540s, just as it was in many parts of England at the time.[26]

Yorkshire

Yorkshire's shoreline, like so many stretches of coastline further south, is treacherous. There are several small havens which are fine for fishing boats — and later for coalers, engaged in coasting trade in and out of Newcastle — but these relied entirely upon local knowledge. Many of those havens, such as the achingly beautiful Robin Hood's Bay and Staithes, while providing space for small boats to tie up, have steep, constricted landward exits and to seaward are too shallow or even dry at low tide. As a result, even a high-tide approach in a vessel with the shallowest draught is at best inadvisable and at worst an invitation to strand. Coaling ports would later emerge, granting access to coal barges in a coasting trade. In modern times, these rocky stretches of coastline have given rise to a concentration of RNLI stations.

John Leland's report from York is quite extensive, yet he mentions nothing about the city's trade or mercantile life other than to note the Ouse and Fosse running through it, describing the portion of the city to each bank separately.[27] The absence of detail is disappointing since the city was home to its own Merchant Adventurers Company, a merchants' guild in existence since 1357–61 and incorporated by royal charter in 1430. It is some recompense that Leland gives a little relevant information about Kingston upon Hull, past which all York shipping had to pass to reach the North Sea: 'The first great increasing of the towne was by passing for fisch into Iseland, from whens they had the hole trade of stoke fisch into England, and partly other fisch. In Richard the secundes days the towne waxed very rich.

York, North Yorkshire: The Merchant Adventurers' Hall; their trading guild was incorporated in 1430 (2022).

From the mouth of Hulle river upper ynto the Haven ther ys no waulle, but evry marchant hath his staires even to the north gate. (In Trinity Church) ... the lowest chapelle is caullid the Mariners Chapelle.'[28]

Even as Leland was writing, royal engineers were beginning to fortify Hull by building a long wall with three state-of-the-art Henrician blockhouses on the riverbank opposite the town. This way, the town's riverine anchorage could be better protected by sweeping cannon fire and the north side of the town could be covered more effectively.

Bigger ships arriving at Hull during the fifteenth century were mostly those serving Hanseatic merchants supplying the north of England, which London could not sensibly do. Their range of merchandise was bewildering, encompassing everything from staple foodstuffs to musical instruments and gaming tables, accommodating the whole spectrum of society, from the ordinary man to the supremely wealthy.[29]

The Merchant Adventurers Company of York, which survives today, records that its principal imports were salt, fish, iron, wine, spices, dried fruit and medical products. The extent of imported luxuries is seemingly ignored; perhaps they were embarrassed by their attachment to 'fripperies'. Their motto, 'God grant us all prosperity', seems perhaps a fitting sunshade under which all merchants might shelter.

Leland next stops at Heddon, which 'hathe beene a fair haven toun: it standeth a mile and more withyn the creke, that cummith out of Humbre ynto it. The sea crekes parting aboute the sayde toun did insulate it, and shippis lay aboute the toun; but now men cum to it by 3 bridges, where it is evident to see that sum places where the shippes lay be overgrowen with flagges and reads; and the haven is very sorely decayed.'[30] Perhaps Heddon was a victim of the slump which followed the withdrawal of the Hanse from England, just as he described at Boston. In any case, Leland's observation of an overgrown dock full of flowering irises and reeds is a rare digression into the changing landscape of the national economic downturn he was witnessing.

For all the strength of its imposing castle, Scarborough's port facilities were in a poor way. Leland says of it: 'At the est ende of the toun on the one point of the bosom of the se, where the harborow for shippes is, stondeth an exceeding goodly larg and stronge castelle on a stupe rok ... At the south est point of Scarburgh toun by the shore is a bulwark, now yn ruine by the se rage, made by Richard III, that lay a while at Scardeburg castle. The peere whereby socour is made for shippes is now sore decayed, and that almost yn the middle of it.'[31]

Nearby Patrington warrants another almost cursory note as Leland calls it 'a toun of no market yet having an havenet'.[32] He does not try to explain the conundrum. At the picturesque

Scarborough, North Yorkshire, a 'harborow for shippes', full of fishing boats with steamers beyond. Photo by Walton Hudson (1958).

Robin Hood's Bay Leland writes of 'a fischer toune of 20 bootes caullid Robyn Hudds Bay, a dok or bosom of a mile yn length'.[33] This is a rare indication of a fleet size.

Whitby, meanwhile, boasts 'an havenet holp with a peere and a great fischar toune'.[34] Any development of the harbour had perhaps been held back by the famous steepness of the land approach, which is no great help to any imports destined for the interior. The abbey there would certainly have been supplied by the harbour. However, in one glimmer of hope in an otherwise somewhat decayed north-eastern coastal vista, efforts were being made in the 1540s to build up Whitby: 'a new key and port is yn making of stone fallen down yn the rokkes thereby.'

Durham and Northumberland

Excavations in Hartlepool, County Durham have turned up old dock structures dating to the thirteenth century along Southgate, and the town is known to have reached its zenith in the late fourteenth and early fifteenth centuries. There has been little evidence, however, for dockside buildings. Although it handled some of Newcastle's coal exports, the economic impetus which propelled Hartlepool was the conflict with Scotland in the fourteenth century. By the sixteenth century the town was in decline, the haven decayed. Leland merely lists it as a market town in County Durham.[35]

Noting the 'Picte wall' (Hadrian's Wall), Leland ignores any port facilities at Newcastle-upon-Tyne, instead writing of former monastic input into the town and notable local gentry.[36] He mentions that the benefactors themselves, members of the Greyfriars, were originally 'marchauntes of the same toun', that some were Scots and that they originally pursued a life of 'marchaundice'. Elsewhere he stresses the quality of the town's merchants and their work to edify it, building what he considered the strongest town defences anywhere in England, useful against the Scots. He even rated these defences against much of what he knew of European towns.[37]

9

SATING APPETITES

Where we went in the small ship the seaweed
Parted and gave to us the murmuring shore
And we made feast and in our secret need
Devoured the very plates Aeneas bore
      Allen Tate, 'The Mediterranean' (1932)

We saw earlier how the exhortation to cherish merchandise accompanied a shopping list of documented contemporary trade into England from abroad. Archaeology regularly retrieves similar evidence, not just for the rare and exquisite Venetian glass, Limoges enamels, Italian maiolicas and Spanish lustrewares in our great museums, but for the 99 per cent of imports into England and Wales between 1400 and 1540 that were either raw materials or organic matter, usually mundane and often perishable. Such products remain arguably more important than any luxury goods and apparent fripperies.

 Good environmental sampling strategies on excavations confirm that the English and Welsh appetite for foreign foodstuffs was considerable. Careful retrieval makes for a growing body of imported material in national and regional museums and archives, some published and some not. The documented variety of imports and excavation data are increasingly in accord.[1] Monastic drains are a rich source of macroscopic and microscopic environmental data, as are those of castles, together with urban cesspits from a dozen towns and cities, particularly if discrete and well dated.

It is to many of the monasteries that we must turn for the most consistent evidence, because they were the best chroniclers and recorders of their purchases, records of which survive in some cases.[2] They are also ostensibly 'closed' societies, so potentially least exposed to imports and ideas – certainly monastic orders were cocooned to various degrees from secular society. However, they also associated certain foodstuffs with their liturgical calendar; for example, figs and raisins figure strongly in Lenten servings, and fish was served on Fridays. Winchester kitchen accounts show the use of 180–225 lbs of figs and raisins at a time, with similar mixes needed by the abbeys and priories at Sibton, Selby, Abingdon and Peterborough. Geography was clearly no issue, and a variety of inland markets, north and south, had plentiful stocks.

The accounts of Durham Cathedral Priory are sufficiently discerning to distinguish between orders for figs from Malaga and figs from Seville, although it is not always clear where they bought them. For the cellarer at Bolton Priory in Lancashire, his many purchases, of rice, sugar, raisins, almonds, figs, pepper, saffron, cumin, mace and cloves, were made at St Botolph's Fair in Boston, Lincolnshire. Brought from the Mediterranean, principally by the Venetians, they are as likely to have come in on Hanseatic ships from Bruges markets as they are to have come directly from the Venetians unloading at the Pool of London or at Southampton.

Monks from Battle Abbey in East Sussex travelled to London markets for regular purchases of dates, exotic fruits, nuts and spices. Meanwhile, the Abbot of Winchester went to St Giles' Fair, where he bought almonds and almond milk from a north Italian merchant, probably imported through Southampton.

It is thus the records of monastic refectories and guesthouses which provide the most widespread evidence for the prevalence of fine dining, doing so through a plethora of account books and through environmental samples taken from a variety of enclosed monastic drains and discrete rubbish pits.

In Leicestershire even the lowliest of monastic houses, such as Gracedieu (Augustinian) nunnery, was well known for its regular hosting of local ladies, including their patrons, and made purchases of almonds and raisins (as likely as not Spanish or Portuguese imports) for their kitchen.[3] We do not know where they got them – as nuns they were generally not allowed to leave their premises, sending servants out instead – but it is unlikely their servants had to go far, probably just to the weekly or even daily market at Leicester itself.

If the records of the celebrated *Trinity* of Bristol are typical, carriage of these exotic and perishable foodstuffs were not limited to Mediterranean carriers – who were certainly instrumental – but extended to more and more English carriers as time went on. After receiving licence to trade out of Bordeaux in 1464, the *Trinity* carried hundreds of tuns of wine, oil, fruit, wax and sugar through the 1460s and 1470s. Its individual cargoes were in the names of some ninety-nine shippers, so widespread was the interest in the luxury foodstuffs trade.[4] This multiplicity of shippers for one cargo also tells us how the financial risk of loss at sea could be minimised by spreading it among many merchants.

Even with regular orders, no supplies could be guaranteed. There is a possibility that spice stocks may have run low across the kingdom in the summer months before the Venetian state fleet arrived off either London or Southampton, as an expectant annual hubbub at Rotherhithe suggests great anticipation. In 1467, by the end of September, there was a severe shortage of olive oil across the country, a fact which even reached the ears of the Pope.[5]

If the average rural farmworker, 'peasant' perhaps, rarely saw anything imported, it was probably less to do with his class than with his rural existence. It was into the town markets that imports eventually found their way in vast quantities, driven not just by the corporate demand of more than 800 (supposedly) cloistered monasteries and nunneries across the country and the communities within them (each based upon twelve, twenty-four or thirty-six monks or nuns plus attendants and lay brethren), along with their guests, but also the hundreds of noble and gentry households that vied with each other to showcase a fancy table that outshone all others. It was supremely important to provide hospitality appropriate to the station of one's guests, reflecting the so-called 'chain of being'.

These were not dinner parties between nuclear families or good friends as we might understand today. It has been calculated that throughout the fifteenth and early sixteenth centuries the average gentry household numbered about seventy persons, while those of the nobility and bishops were more than double that, at around 160.[6] Dukes, earls and bishops, with their families, staff, servants and hangers-on, put on celebrations which, for dinner alone, could strip an area of everything that flew in the air, swam in the rivers or scuttled across the fields locally for weeks on end.[7] Cellars were drunk dry, pantries emptied and the spice cupboards scraped clean when the relatives came to dinner. God help the noble who was required to entertain royalty! One example is that of Edward, 3rd Duke of Buckingham who in 1508 held Stafford Castle (Staffordshire), Maxstoke Castle (Warwickshire), Writtle (Essex), Tonbridge Castle (Kent), Thornbury Castle (Gloucestershire), a house at Queenhithe in London and another at Bletchingley (Surrey). On 6 January that year, at the end of the Christmas festivities at Thornbury Castle, 519 people sat down for lunch, 319 of them guests. Later that day, 400 sat down for dinner, of whom 279 were guests.[8] This huge percentage of guests is persistent, hovering around 44–50 per cent. Edward of Buckingham was already known for his hospitality and had some years before entertained the ambassadors of the Duke of Burgundy, so this was not an isolated case – noble and gentle households, always conscious of their image and seeking to reflect their station, drove the economy and England's desire for luxuries, and the largesse was clearly extended to large numbers of people. In a six-month period in 1503–04 the duke's household across three properties consumed 52,000 lbs of beef, around 25,000 lbs of mutton and 1,400 lbs of pork as their staple. One can only imagine what wonderful platters presented the food and how the table was set.

Generally, each port had its own sphere of influence and the further inland one looks the more that influence recedes. By that measure, Southampton dominated Hampshire and parts of surrounding counties in all things, not least wine, but also sent commodities to the Midlands, with woad and wine reaching Coventry and some goods travelling as far as Derby.[9] A good example of how even the most detached consumer could manage to get what he or she needed 'locally' is Humphrey, 1st Duke of Buckingham, whose household accounts survive and are published for his homes at Maxstoke Castle (Warwickshire) and Writtle (Essex) for the years 1452–53.[10] While his steward was buying wine mainly from London, he was also getting it through a Bristol wine merchant (up the Fosse Way) and via Bewdley in Worcestershire, where he also got iron ingots, probably from Bayonne through Bristol.

The records show that for Maxstoke Castle his staff were seeking wine, herring and spices in London, spices, fruits, corn and cattle from Coventry, oats from Coleshill (Warwickshire), wine from Bewdley (Worcestershire), bar iron from Bristol and fish from Lichfield, Torksey and Stockwith (Lincolnshire). For Writtle, meanwhile, they were in London shopping for wine and fish, at Chelmsford looking for all sorts of things and at Maldon for fish or corn from Holderness (Yorkshire) and Sheringham (Norfolk), and sea coal from Newcastle-upon-Tyne. It was a pattern following ease of purchase, existing carriage routes and availability. There was little which had to be especially sought out by the household.

If these seem the preserve of the very wealthy, then it may be noted that even in a gentle household affected monetarily by the loss of its head, the household of the widow Alice de Bryene in Acton, Suffolk kept many spices in store, comparable with that of the Duke of Buckingham, and both red and white wines were served at table, along with home-brewed ale.[11]

Gascony and Beyond: The Wine Trade

A great pleasure to all estates and degrees, great riches and by the might of such shipping, great defence for all this land.
Froissart on the Gascon wine trade, 1399

Always England's nearest neighbour, France was the source of a considerable proportion of the huge quantities of wine consumed by the noble and the aspirant Englishman alike. It was a trade which largely emanated from the western parts of France, controlled and administered by England, principally Aquitaine, and a portion of it in what is still known as Gascony.

The Gascon wine trade was key to the region, and although France always fought hard to wrest control from England, that small portion of what eventually became France owed considerable allegiance to this island. Convinced of the importance of the trade to the continent and the lighter taxation that the English levied, in 1399 the chronicler Froissart surmised that Bordeaux and its important southern Basque neighbour, Bayonne, 'will never turn French, for they cannot live in their danger, nor they cannot suffer the extortion and restrictions of the Frenchmen; for under us they live unfettered and free, and if the French should be Lords over them, they should be taxed and tailed and retailed two or three times a year, to which they are unaccustomed, which would be hard for them to begin'.[12] He was wrong, of course, but the trade was indeed peculiarly English, despite the regular depredations of war until Bordeaux finally fell to France in 1453. Such was England's thirst that the trade continued despite the change of ownership, although from that date onwards licences had to be bought and paid for to carry on the trade, ship by ship, merchant by merchant. Royal restrictions were imposed in 1462 as England quarrelled with France again and again, and there was little improvement until the mid-1470s.

Even at the peak of military operations between England and France, the wine flowed in prodigious quantities and in relatively unexpected quarters, not least since England controlled Gascony. Rymer's *Foedera* records that in January 1418 Henry V ordered his brother to deliver 100 tuns of wine to the servants of the Duke of Bourbon, who had been captured at the battle of Agincourt in 1415 and was at that time shut up in Windsor Castle. Later, in the continuing aftermath of the same battle, Henry VI issued safe-conduct passes to the servants of the captive Duke of Orleans in 1426 so that they could bring sixty pipes of wine to their master, who was laid up at Bolingbroke Castle as the king's hostage.[13]

Gascon wine imports into England peaked in the late 1440s, just as French pressure on Gascony redoubled. In 1448–49 alone, 13,000 tuns came in from all sources and through all ports, with the largest share arriving through Southampton. In 1446–48 there came 11,000 tuns from French vineyards. The wine fleets were mainly English, although vessels of Bayonne also carried a considerable burden. Strangely Bordeaux itself was not a seafaring city and provided few ships for its own exports – it hardly needed to. Of the English traders, the accounts of the constable of Bordeaux record mainly English ships from thirty-five English and Welsh ports from Newcastle to Milford Haven. Vessels out of Dartmouth were the most numerous, although many of them were probably loaded with wine for south-west England, or even for Ireland. It is likely that much longer overland journeys from there would spoil the hard-won cargo and, in any case, were likely to compete with the produce through other ports further east, such as Southampton, where a great deal came in, or Winchelsea, whose star was waning rapidly in the later fifteenth century.

In 1409–10, from December to March, more than 200 wine-laden ships left Bordeaux. There were twenty-seven out of Dartmouth, thirteen from London, eleven from Hull, nine from Bristol, nine from Fowey and nine from Plymouth. There was variety in all this, however. Bristol also landed Gascon wine in ships from Bayonne, Lynn, St Jean de Luz and La Rochelle, probably among many others, such as monastic-owned ships from the Cistercian abbeys of Beaulieu (Hampshire), Quarr (Isle of Wight) and Combe (Warwickshire via Norfolk), to name but three.

Generally, the ships of the wine fleets travelled in convoy to avoid pirates. They arrived in vintage season or early spring and then returned home in December or March. Although the passage could be most perilous at this time of year, dwindling stocks at home needed to be replenished and the demand for the new vintage grew as old stocks began to turn. A ship returning south from unloading a late summer cargo on the south coast could in theory get to Spain and load dried fruit and fresh oranges from a December harvest and have it back in England before Christmas. The voyage generally took about ten days, but the entire expedition about two months, of which a month or so was spent in port while the master haggled over prices, unloaded and loaded, and made repairs to the ships.

The greatest evidence for the national thirst and consumption beyond the well-documented royal court is monastic records. Many monasteries had cellarers, whose job included checking in wine, storing it properly and maintaining the supply.

At Coventry's Carthusian priory of St Anne, founded in 1385, the wine supply began as an annual tun from Bristol in 1457 (when Gascony had already been lost and its wine came in under French licence). The Carthusians were a restrained and silent order known for their austerity. However, this first tun was augmented by a second annually from 1461–62, accompanied by two further tuns annually from London. Given Anglo-French tit-for-tat bans on wine and French goods in 1462, it is uncertain that this tun could be found at any English port; perhaps it came in via a third, non-French port. The restrictions mean that it was an empty gift for a while, being impossible to fulfil, as the plummeting tonnages imported suggest. For Gascon wine there was little hope until an Anglo-French treaty in 1475. From 1494, the Carthusians at Coventry saw a fifth tun added to their quota from Bristol.[14] A tun contained some 256 gallons, and there were only ever a maximum of twelve quire monks at St Anne's; unless they sold some or all of it, that amounts to 1,280 gallons annually, or 106 gallons annually per monk. It is often said that wine (or beer) was universally drunk instead of poor-quality water, but at St Anne's at least some of the quire monks had their own wells and cisterns in their individual cell gardens. There is no indication of the exact origin of St Anne's wine, but Gascony is as likely a place as any (except in those restricted years after 1462). There is less indication of the monks' state of inebriation.

Across in Valle Crucis in north Wales, the Cistercian abbots, who lived in sumptuous quarters (long lapsed from their austere heyday in the twelfth and thirteenth centuries), were famed for their hospitality, just as at Netley and Quarr abbeys were among foreign sailors. The fifteenth-century bard Guttyn Owain praised their munificence, noting that their table was often spread with four meat courses on silver dishes, accompanied by 'sparkling claret'.[15] Also Cistercian, and also in north Wales, Abbott Thomas Pennant at Basingwerk Abbey kept a fine table and a fine cellar. So many guests stayed there that they were fed in two sittings and had a choice of wines from Aragon, Castille and Brittany[16]. Many were probably pilgrims, going to and from nearby Holywell and the more distant Bardsey Island. At both houses the wine probably came in via Chester. This may represent a considerable relaxation of what had once been a very prescriptive monastic rule, but it shows that even the most isolated monastic establishments, who enjoyed a clean water supply, had unimpeded access to fine wines in the fifteenth century. This was true even if they were exceptionally cloistered, either by dint of their rule (as Carthusians and – initially at least – Cistercians chose to be) or due to geographical isolation; only an exact selection eluded them, dictated as it was by trade restrictions, at least when it came to Gascon fare.

Wines, perhaps more than most other foodstuffs, are easily spoiled. When Jean II of France was captive in England (1356–59), 19 per cent of wine for his court-in-exile at Hertford Castle was spoiled.[17] Some was certainly for court consumption – and each barrel was tested to prove that forty-six were spoiled – but at least 300 tuns from the king's cellar was used to pay other suppliers, such as his furrier in London.

The drop in the wine trade that accompanied England's exit from Normandy in the late 1440s and the fall of Bordeaux to the French in 1453 was remarkable. From its 1446–48 zenith, imports dropped dramatically. Trade restrictions from 1462 tightened it further, to a nadir of 3,411 tuns in 1469–71, before a modest recovery to little more than half of its late 1440s peak.[18] England's perennial quarrels with France made its links with other sources of viticulture even more valuable – Spain and Portugal, the Rhineland and notably the Aegean.

Archaeologically wine does not survive so much as wine cellars among structural remains, and many if not most cellars – which usually survive only up to the spring of their collapsed vaults unless under a standing historic building – are merely cool, subterranean or half-sunken cellars or undercrofts, storage spaces that cannot be distinguished on the basis of what they once stored since they could and did store just about anything. London, Southampton, Northampton, Norwich, Winchelsea, Chester, Coventry – many medieval towns contain numerous surviving examples.

It is surely the humble barrels in which the wine initially arrived and was transported overland that indicated the thousands of 'tuns' consumed throughout the land each year. But this too is problematic since the wooden staves and even the iron hoops rot and rust in less-than-perfect conditions if not reused. And it is certain that many were reused, in their thousands. A barrel which stored wine as it lay supported on curved stays could ideally become a receptacle of other materials, especially if liquid or semi-liquid. Many a domestic water butt surely began life as a wine barrel, and they also became favourites of dyers and tanners, attested by their discovery in archaeological contexts set into the ground in riverbank and other waterside locations, as far inland as Green Street, Northampton (1981) and Minster Pool, Lichfield, Staffordshire (2008); at both sites they were clustered together half a dozen at a time as vats for washing and steeping hides and cloth. Elsewhere, sunken barrels at the end of their lives could be used as latrines.

Alongside the construction of the city wall at the Cheylesmore, Coventry between the fourteenth and sixteenth centuries, one barrel was sawn off, set into the ground and used as a mortar-mixer's pan, still containing a depth of sticky lime putty which had preserved the wood, offsetting the natural corrosive acids of the clay geology.[19] One may ask how one might know these were wine barrels reused and not just purpose-made items produced by a skilled local cooper. The answer in each case is that one, some or many may indeed be just that: local creations. But documents show that empty barrels were indeed widely sought after for secondary purposes and were easily available and inexpensive, such as in the building accounts of Kirby Muxloe Castle in Leicestershire, where in 1482 builders' mates (not coopers) were paid regular expenses for: '3 barelles ... 4 barrell hedes' and for 'hopyng and cottyng

6 barells for water and mortar to be put therein'. Also, they purchased '4 heryng barelles for putting mortar and water in'.[20]

The many uses of a humble barrel mostly involve holding liquids, and they were reused and resold until they gave out. A cry of 'eat more fish' or 'come on, drink up' – born of a need to sell the barrel to the builders next door – might not be as preposterous as it might sound.

Wines from Further Afield

> *Cokes and here knaves crieden 'hote pies, hote!*
> *Gode gris and gees gowe dyne, gowe!'*
> *Taverners until hem, told the same,*
> *'Whyte wyn of Oseye and red wyn of Gascoigne,*
> *Of the Ryne and of the Rochel the roste to defye'*
> William Langland, *The Vision of Piers Plowman*[21]

William Langland is believed to have been writing near Malvern, Worcestershire. Even rural England had a hearty thirst and a discerning palate for wines from far-flung places: Portugal, Gascony, the Rhine and La Rochelle, as Langland mentions. However, his palette may have been a conservative one. The variety was certainly not that of country folk forced to drink wine because the water was so poor, which is a common statement which misses the point; indeed, there was great taste at work here.

The Florentines often brought Spanish and other Mediterranean wines to England in large quantities, but it was the Venetians who monopolised the trade in sweet Aegean and eastern Mediterranean wines, for which England had a particular penchant. Known generically as Malmsey (a word derived from the placename 'Monemvasia' in the Peloponnese of southern Greece), this dark, sweet wine was in fact brought principally from Candia in Crete.

A publican tapping a wine barrel on a misericord at St Lawrence's Church, Ludlow, Shropshire (2012).

Alongside Malmsey came Candia and Rumney. The former was a Cretan wine, taking its name from the Cretan port, over which trade Venice had a monopoly. The second owed its name to its origin in Romania. Sweet wine was also brought from Portugal in appreciable quantities.[22] At the beginning of the fifteenth century there was a penchant in the royal household for sweet wines. Henry IV in 1400 spent considerable sums for his household's consumption of sweet Spanish wine, 'Romeney' and 'Malvesyn'.[23] Occasionally we have a brief reference to the convivial surroundings of consumption. In 1480, payment was made for wine (unspecified) brought for the king's council meeting at The Cardinal's Hat outside Newgate – an informal place for such an august body.[24]

The growing and eventually widespread appeal of wine, particularly sweet wine, should not be underestimated. It was far from being the preserve of a privileged few, or only the gentry and nobility. Thus we find that Edward IV, on his return from exile in Bruges in 1471, bought two casks of red wine for a group of Londoners as thanks for sticking up for him at Mile End, while later in 1480 he paid a huge £273 to a goldsmith for the eighty butts of Malmsey he had brought for the royal army against the Scots.[25] One can imagine that the army drank every last drop.

During 1441, Venetian merchants based at Southampton landed wine valued at £1,700 from a carrack docked there, while Venetian carracks brought their Malmsey there in the ensuing years even without specific end purchasers pre-agreed, so popular was this sweet nectar.[26]

Foreigners staying in England, for whatever reason, sated their thirst on imported wine, in some cases wine probably from their own countries. Witness under Henry V the large quantities of wine sent to Pontefract for use by the captive dukes of Orleans and Bourbon, both taken prisoner at Agincourt in 1415 and held hostage for many years.[27] Earlier that year, the king's chief butler paid for wines bought for the use of 'diverse embassies' seeking the release of Agincourt prisoners as well as the prisoners themselves, all held in various places. Arriving at the same time as another embassy – from the Duke of Brittany, who was residing at the London Dominican friary – they all shared in vast amounts of wine, which had to be transported all over the country.[28]

Silks, Velvets and Furs

Dress was an important element with which to express wealth and status. The right apparel in the right company has always got a person noticed. In the fifteenth and early sixteenth centuries this meant silks and furs – but restricted by so-called sumptuary laws that ensured only the appropriate people in society wore the best materials. Silk lay mainly in the hands of those who had traded with the Middle East, importing Islamic and Cathay-inspired silks, before looking to their own production as relations with the east deteriorated. That meant mainly Italy – Venice, Florence, and Genoa – and France.[29]

There was demand for Venetian silks throughout the fifteenth century, and in 1491 there were as many as forty looms there, its exports greatly helped by its existing maritime links. From 1410 onwards its velvets and silks ceased to be affected by its own size restrictions. Genoa became a huge producer, its factories supporting over 2,300 silk weavers with a highly specialised output in 1531, particularly a type of velvet known as 'terciopolo', or 'triple pile'. The Genoese traded extensively north with Geneva but also with Spain and Flanders (and thence into England). Florentine silks in the fifteenth century included brocades, damasks, velvets and taffetas. They were exported extensively to England and to Bruges, as well as being exported eastwards back to Islamic countries whence the technology had come, such as Syria and its capital, Damascus, the origin of 'damask'. In 1427 there were between forty-five and fifty silk factories in Florence, and they set up another at Lyons, consolidating their western European overland exports to complement their maritime journeys. Early in the fifteenth century the two Flanders galleys carried crimson velvet along with other colours like azure, damask, crimson damask, damask of various colours braded with gold, and black damask.[30] The demand rarely let up.

Fur was a problem in that, like silk, it was also heavily restricted by sumptuary laws. Demand increased as these laws were relaxed, particularly for north European squirrel pelts. These were principally from what today is Russia, Finland and surrounding areas of Scandinavia, shipped out in prodigious quantities by the Hanseatic League, notably at Danzig, Sigtuna and the Hanseatic *kontor* at Novgorod (the latter closed by the Muscovites from 1494 to 1514; although it reopened in the latter year, it languished). Excavations in 2010 on the former line of Much Park Street, Coventry uncovered the workshop of a pinner *circa* 1524 who seems to have had a skinner living adjacent. In a rubbish pit in his yard were the leg and foot bones of numerous squirrels but no other parts of the skeleton, indicating that he was working with pelts, probably imported from the northernmost reaches of Europe and Scandinavia. As an indication of how many were needed in this trade, the captive King of France, Jean II, when incarcerated at Hertford in 1359 ordered a suit of clothes which consumed 300 furs for the corselet, 366 for the coat, and 686 grey-backed furs for the rest. At Easter he also ordered special robes for which 1,578 minivers were required, plus a cloak of 1,972 more.[31] Of course not all furs were quite so expensive, but the variety imported was very wide indeed. Records show that Hanseatic ships in Boston were importing deerskins, otter pelts, beaver pelts, rabbit skins, lambskins and even bearskins.[32]

Metal and Timber

To make and to add embellishment to the finest dress, needles and pins were needed from a pinner. His copper wire was drawn in carefully measured widths out of thicker, heated copper bars. More than 60 per cent of England's copper through the fifteenth and sixteenth centuries was imported from Prussia, Bohemia and Poland, again mostly by the Danzigers of the Hanseatic League. The Hanse added more from central Sweden to bring to these shores. The Bohemian trade involved riverine traffic down the Vistula to Danzig and such a long journey was hazardous. It probably went on the same barges that brought huge quantities of timber softwood, which was consumed voraciously in England. Generally, all softwood for major building projects (especially wainscotting) and for building ships came from what is now Poland and its interior, which still holds the European continent's last great primeval forest. England's east coast ports generally landed the material, particularly Danzig's close ally Lynn. When it reached England, the Bohemian and Baltic copper would be combined with Cornish and Devonian tin to make bronze and other copper-based alloys. Tin was the one metal these islands were not short on, and it was exported in large quantities, although even this came under pressure when in 1513 the Portuguese began importing tin from India.

Sating Appetites

Gold and silver were always the most precious metals. Gold was to be found in Devon and Cornwall, but never in sufficient quantities, so the Portuguese trade in gold from across the Sahara was always important after their capture of Ceuta on the Mediterranean coast of Africa. When the Portuguese sailed down the Atlantic coast of Africa (the Gold Coast), setting up a fort at Mina and seeking to cut out the trans-Saharan Berbers, England took notice and tried to follow suit under Edward IV. However, a sharp rebuff from the papacy, which had officially backed Portugal as its preferred contractor in such matters of exploration, brought England's embryonic efforts to a swift end. Perennially short of bullion, which it generally bought at Bruges in return for wool, Edward's court was left with his beautiful new gold coinage and a devalued currency. The gold shortage was never fully rectified.

Silver was more abundant in the coinage but no less sought after. The Devon and Cornwall mines which mined silver also produced some as an offshoot from tin-mining as lead mines did in parts of Derbyshire. In the middle of the fourteenth century these belonged to the Crown, specifically Edward the Black Prince, who let them out on long leases to merchants of the Hanseatic League. Consignments of English silver made the headlines, such as the account of William, Marquis of Suffolk, official receiver of the tax for gold and silver in Devon and Cornwall, who in 1447 recorded 8 kilograms of pure silver originating from the mines there.[33]

Swedish iron, or osmund as we have come to know it, was as important an import as French iron. Although undistinguished, and delivered by the Hanse in bulk, osmund arrived in ready-smelted cakes from places in Uppland like Österbybrük, where cottage industries from the late medieval period smelted ore from the mines near Dannemöra and other places around Lake Mälaren into 'sows' (bars). It was then shifted along sleigh routes during the snowy Swedish winter and sent out via markets and Baltic trading centres at Sigtuna, Vädstena and Visby on the east-coast island of Gotland for shipping as soon as the Baltic spring thaw set in. Mining in central and eastern Sweden, for both home and foreign markets, became a major factor in the kingdom's growth and urbanisation in the fifteenth and sixteenth centuries.[34]

Also from Sweden, particularly the southern coastal town of Trelleborg, and from Eidsborg in Norway, came huge quantities of schist, used for sharpening all manner of iron and steel blades. These honestones, which could be shipped ready-made or unfinished as ships' ballast, have been found all over England and made their way even to the centre of the country, being found in excavations across Northamptonshire and Warwickshire.[35]

England did have several medieval production centres where iron was mined and smelted, such as the Weald of Kent and Sussex, Northamptonshire and the Forest of Dean in Gloucestershire. However, these were mostly local concerns and did not have huge distribution networks nor massive open quarries. England required extraneous sources to supplement these for construction programmes and manufacturing, and largely this meant France, Spain and Sweden.

There can be few more 'finished' (and thus expensive) iron imports from the continent in the fifteenth and sixteenth centuries than arms and weaponry. Although English cities, notably Bristol, gained a reputation for developments in early cannon, much of the know-how was continental in origin. In the early years of his reign, Henry VI employed foreign artisans in this respect – so-called *Gunnemeysters* – named as Gokyn Gunner, Walter Lokyer, Walter Hermanson and Gerard van Ewe, said to be from Germany.[36]

Spices

Drugs and spices were usually supplied by London-based Lombards, who used the Venetian galleys as carriers. Their accounts read as a shopping list for the Middle East and Mediterranean, most of the contents being sourced across the Middle East and beyond by Venetian merchants in Cairo, Alexandria, Beirut and Aleppo: sugar, ginger, pepper, mace, aniseed, cloves, honey, lemon preserve, frankincense, rose conserve, chamomile flowers, paper, sealing wax, ink, scammony, sandalwood, nuts olive oil, camphor, aloes, agaric, rhubarb, spikenard, balm wax, mastic, diachylon, electuaries, baby oil, claret powder, polypody, candy, labdanum, rose essence, fennel, saffron, absinthe, gilliflowers, gums, prunes, violet essence, senna.[37]

Throughout the fifteenth century the Venetians brought a huge list of spices to our shores and their relative lightness meant they were superabundant aboard their galleys, even in the chests of the seaman's portion. Witness the rower who carried pepper and ginger for one of his fellow rowers, plus a little silk too. Almost every spice imaginable was carried by the Venetians.

It has been said in the past that the Venetians were the only importers of spices, and while they enjoyed a great majority of the trade, others were involved, as the same Middle Eastern ports visited by the Venetians also produced silks, in which the Florentines had considerable interest. The Venetians nonetheless guarded their existing routes and contacts closely, and other carriers were left to eye them covetously until Portugal broke the monopoly by reaching India via the Cape of Good Hope. The loss of their spice (near-) monopoly was a blow from which Venice never fully recovered.

A good example of a shopping list of spices (and related fruits) comes from the household accounts of Humphrey, 1st Duke of Buckingham in 1452–53. His accounts deal with two of his properties, Maxstoke Castle in Warwickshire and Writtle in Essex.[38] In that year he bought his specialist spices and fruits from London and Coventry: pepper, ginger, almonds, rice, dates, sugar, sugar of cassis, cloves, mace, red sandalwood/saundrez (red food colouring), saffron, aniseed, raisins (currants), wax, wax moulds, wicks, turnsole (purple food colouring), alkenet (red food colouring), blaunchpowder (for sprinkling on food) and figs.

Ceramics

Ceramics are a bellwether for archaeologists since pottery is ubiquitous on most excavations. In terms of land-based excavation, any imported pottery found is necessarily viewed as being at the end of its traded life, and its numbers are therefore at their most dispersed, not just by distance from market but also by gradual breakage and losses at different times, which whittles away an assemblage until it is gone.

Shipwrecks are a valuable source of imported pottery, or at least pottery that is being carried (but not necessarily traded) across the sea; all ships would have carried a few ceramics for the use of the crew, since most ships contained a small galley, often built of brick and tile, for cooking. While some mariners might prefer pewter or treen for their durability, pottery is not uncommon.[39]

Excavated sunken cargos of this date are vanishingly rare. Where found, they carry no indication of where they were bound or for whom. Such a cargo might have been intended to be coasted around to another port or loaded onto carts and transported 100 miles or more inland before sale, again to an unknown number of purchasers. Thus, in the absence of written records, an excavated wreck can only be said to indicate the eventual country of destination for the cargo as well as its origin. Even then, the ship might have been blown off course when it sank. The further from shore an excavated wreck lies, the less certain its intended destination. The evidence is usually equivocal.

Pottery was probably not often a principal cargo, simply because even in the late medieval period it was not a very expensive commodity and did not travel particularly well. Prices remained relatively low and local substitutes in terms of function were often available. It was usually the curiosity or rarity value of a ceramic which made it stand out; it would have been difficult to justify its carriage by charging a price much higher than that of local alternatives unless the piece was very distinctive.

Sating Appetites

Port-based excavations can be a useful indicator of trade connections with other countries over a longer period. Thus, Southampton's ceramic assemblages contain a background of imported pottery throughout the medieval period, as do those of many sites in London. One celebrated assemblage from Southampton in the period 1486–97 comes from the cellars of Roger Machado, Henry VII's senior customs receiver and herald. He was a key member of several embassies to the continent.[40] In addition he entertained the king's ambassadors at his home, the excavation of which produced Valencian lustrewares, Italian maiolica, Rhenish stonewares and Venetian glass, now on show in Southampton's museums. These were the markets closest to the landing places, the break-of-bulk points, where the best, the specific, the personally requested and the pieces used as bribes all end up in local cupboards, after which a more representative dispersal begins to take place in the hinterland beyond the port. Thus, anything chosen to serve entirely local consumers, happenstance purchases, unloading accidents and sometimes even impounded goods – for duties unpaid – can account for such materials never leaving their port of arrival. These are also among the places where overseas merchants usually either chose to live or were forced to reside thanks to punitive and restrictive laws during xenophobic governmental campaigns that were never even thinly disguised. They therefore may relate to the personal use by resident foreign merchants, or even the foreign crews during their stay in port if they weren't required to remain on board when the turnaround was of short duration.

At the heart of London's south bank, opposite the Tower, lay the Rotherhithe and Southwark wharves where the Venetian state galleys usually unloaded their much-anticipated annual cargoes. Here stood a row of handsome, moated high-houses, inlets, docks and tidal mills, known from excavation.[41] A steady process of Thameside land reclamation took place here, a constant churn of infilling and renewal of waterfront wharfage, and behind each new revetment (most made of imported Baltic timber) were dumped quantities of rubbish belonging to the wealthy owners of these prestige properties, packed down to create new quays as the old ones wore out, swept daily by the tides and the wash of passing boats, bumped and scraped by innumerable keels and gunwales as they rode alongside at anchor.

Some of the properties here had their own inlets and docks directly off the Thames. The exceedingly well-appointed house of Sir John Fastolf opposite the Tower was probably attended by his own ship, the *Bon Aventure*, purchased in Calais in 1441.

Picked out from the dumping here, and through reclamation of the banks, archaeologists have identified Rhenish/German stoneware of every type, Dutch red earthenware, Saintonge ware, Valencian lustreware, Spanish green-glazed wares, South Netherlands maiolica, Martincamp stonewares, Beauvais wares and Montelupo slipwares. Nearby lay pits containing Middle Eastern Islamic glass vessels. In all, it is a mélange of Italian, Spanish French and Rhenish types reflecting the sophisticated and eclectic tastes of the metropolis generally and the uppermost echelons who were able to indulge the latest fashions. For a site to be considered genuinely high-status, it needs to have evidence of vessels of every material at the table or in the kitchen, whether precious or base, from gold and silver through bronze, pewter and glass to pottery and treen.[42]

The lavish former Thameside home of Edward III at Rotherhithe was, for all of the period of this book, owned by the Cluniac monks of St Saviour's Abbey, very close by in Bermondsey.[43] Here we know little of the riparian property, which is believed to have been rented out, but it is true to say that excavations at nearby Bermondsey Abbey itself have produced a wide variety of imported wares from both northern Europe and the Mediterranean. It would be foolish to imagine that their principal

Thameside property at Rotherhithe did not enable them to pick and choose what was imported for their guesthouse and refectory; after all, it looked directly out onto the principal wharves used by the foremost foreign shippers. In fact, it is possible that foreign shippers may have been tenants there.

The practice of allowing individual crew to import items personally as, essentially, hand luggage resulted in the Venetian state fleet restricting the allowance to preserve the principal cargo capacity and help trim their galleys at sea. The Flanders galley rowers were each allowed a full chest measuring 3 feet 8 inches long by 18 inches wide and 18 inches high. These might account for a multiplicity of odd items, including ceramics, which could, and probably did, find a ready market at the quayside as part of the seaman's portion. It is unclear what kind of money an entrepreneurial rower or mariner might make from a box of handpicked foreign bric-a-brac sold from the wharf, but it was evidently a thriving trade for Venetian crews when Richard II officially licensed the practice in 1399, also allowing 10-gallon barrels of wine in individual ownership to be carried on board and sold on disembarkation in this way. Rowers were forbidden to carry tin, lead or copper for sale, so as not to upset local exchange, but we know of one sailor on a Flanders galley who carried pepper, ginger and gold-embroidered cloth on a colleague's behalf in 1443.[44] How much made it to their final ports of destination and how much was sold en route in French or Spanish ports is impossible to know – with 170-odd rowers in each galley, one might expect plenty in each. Equally such personal hoards, perhaps simple or basic on embarkation in Venice, might be enriched en route for onward sale in Southampton or London or Sluys, so long as the merchandise fitted into their permitted hand luggage at each stop.

The regular occurrence of chafing dishes (supportive pedestal bowls for holding hot charcoal) in the archaeological record is worthy of note. When east coast ports began importing Dutch redwares in the early sixteenth century, particularly distinctive chafing dishes for keeping food warm at table, their popularity across England grew rapidly. So notable was it that it soon became one of the few ceramic forms which regularly warranted a mention on its own in sixteenth-century inventories.[45]

Such a full selection as seen at Southwark and Rotherhithe rarely occurs outside London, but it is notable that most types can be found in some provincial towns and cities across the country, if not all on the same site. At times the range is surprising, with examples found as far from the ports and the capital as it is possible to get, and not necessarily in association with the finest private properties.[46] Rather it seems to be a characteristic where fine dining might be expected from a host, be they secular or religious, who had a reputation for generous hospitality (or wished to garner one). It was noted some time ago that in the later fifteenth century there emerged an 'urban mercantile and artisan elite, dependent upon international trade'.[47] A trend towards this can be seen in probate inventories, but, as will be seen below, it extended to religious houses and religious guilds, which one might call 'centres of excellence' where a visitor might expect to be wined and dined in a manner which was in keeping with secular expectations. Certainly, while one might never be surprised to encounter spirituality and liturgy in abundance at a house of Benedictines, Cistercians or (especially) Carthusians, it might not be so common to expect to find there a more secular dose of worldly goods pursuant upon an atmosphere of fine dining.

For the purely secular, at Pottergate, Norwich, a cellar contained the contents of a house burned down in 1507 wherein one-third of all the pottery comprised Raeren ware and related Rhenish stonewares, despite the fire only happening perhaps twenty-five years after their initial introduction and spread into

Sating Appetites

England's interior. This alone is not so unique, but alongside these finds were tin-glazed earthenwares from Italy, fashionable maiolica altar vases from the southern Netherlands and Dutch redwares from the kitchen, which came in at east coast ports by the boatload. This was not just changing dining habits but a statement of secular consumer taste.

At Coventry, known from documents to be taking its principal bulk imports from Bristol (wine), Southampton (woad and alum) and Yarmouth (fish), there is no comparable secular site so far published, but rather a variety of sites and monastic houses denoting a similar taste for fine dining. At the Benedictine cathedral priory, excavations found evidence for a range of Rhenish stonewares for drinking at table, with wines served in Martincamp flasks while food courses employed Saintonge chafing dishes. This was the monastic site that hosted three Lancastrian parliaments and later the Christmas court of Edward IV. Meanwhile, just outside the city walls, among the purportedly otherworldly Carthusians some 6 per cent of their

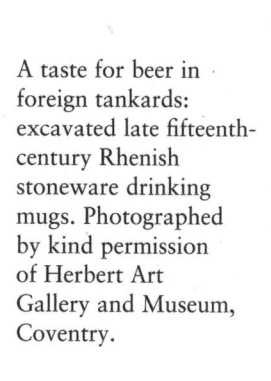

A taste for beer in foreign tankards: excavated late fifteenth-century Rhenish stoneware drinking mugs. Photographed by kind permission of Herbert Art Gallery and Museum, Coventry.

cell-derived ceramics (i.e. for their personal use only) in the period *circa* 1475–1539 were imports, mainly Rhenish stonewares, but in claustral areas excavated, both reflecting outside influence and projecting their way of life to visitors, or giving the visitor more of what they expected to see, the occurrence of imported pottery almost doubled (11 per cent), once more comprising drinking cups and flagons, usually thought of as beer mugs and Martincamp stoneware flasks holding wine. Also, from the Charterhouse comes part of a pre-Dissolution stove tile, copying the best interior décor the continent had to offer, perhaps following the lead of Cardinal Wolsey's house around 1530. The Charterhouse assemblages are similar in wares, type and purpose to the city's secular sites and show no bias but rather a cosmopolitan table.

At Much Park Street, Coventry, only 200 metres from the Charterhouse, the excavated pinner's workshop, home to one John Garton, produced almost no imported drinking cups or flagons around 1524, suggesting that he did his drinking elsewhere – perhaps not unexpectedly away from his workshop where he spent his day – but he was fully conversant with the use of the chafing dish at his dining table.[48]

Another 150 metres from Short Street, in 1533, right at the end of this book's primary period of study, a select feast for a small group held by the Holy Trinity Guild included claret from Gascony, Malmsey from Greece or Crete and Muscadell from Greece, along with sack, sugar, cloves, mace, currants, dates, prunes and oranges.[49] Census records at that time show that there were only a few foreigners in the city, or at least those who chose to be classed as resident: two Dutch (Easterlings), three Irish, one Welsh, one French and three Danes. The muster rolls of the same period also record two Bretons.[50] By comparison, in Exeter in the same period there were between forty and fifty foreigners, and at far-flung Totnes (closer to the coast) 20 per cent of the population was foreign. However, some of these may have been mariners, not merchants, merely kicking their heels until a favourable wind allowed them to leave.

It is perhaps evidence for 'closed' societies using imported ceramics that most reflects a widespread liking for foreign pottery. This bears greater scrutiny. By this term, 'closed', one considers monastic refectories or guilds and societies whose meetings were not open to the public. It is in this way that one may be faced with the pre-Dissolution assemblage of imports excavated at Cell 8 of Mount Grace Priory in North Yorkshire. As a Carthusian foundation, if their monastic rule were followed to the letter, dining ought to be spartan and simple, reflecting their avowed poverty. The above examples at Coventry Charterhouse show that this was not so, and foreign wares were everywhere, with little to distinguish their preparation of food and drink from that of less restricted monastic orders, so Mount Grace should not be a surprise – except perhaps for its relative isolation in rural North Yorkshire when compared to the city. In Cell 8 at Mount Grace, the widespread use of imported pottery may have amounted to the gift of materials by a benefactor, with monks simply making use of the donation, unconcerned by the origin of the ceramics and unaware of how trendy they were.[51]

Decorative tablewares in a Carthusian setting might perhaps be surprising. With only limited access to the outside world, the supply of such material by a benefactor is quite likely, but it was an artisanal flourish and an expense that may have been wasted on them as consumers. Such apparently 'closed' societies and groups may have been very similar in their outlook, since they were often linked by episcopal visitations or convocations of their own principals – abbots, priors, etc., whose exposure to the outside world was either limited or controlled by their rules. Thus an archbishop, visiting monasteries of different orders in turn, might give the same gift to each, or a group of convening abbots might share the same communal experience in attractive surroundings, such as all the heads of all the Black Monk houses (Benedictines, Cluniacs) who routinely met at St Andrew's Priory, Northampton every three years, except for in the 1490s and between 1504 and 1516.

Some senior monks simply could not avoid being in a secular limelight, even if they tried. Coventry Cathedral's Benedictine prior had a permanent seat in parliament, not least since his office held military responsibilities to the king for centuries. Prior Richard Crosby presided over the Coventry parliament in his own Benedictine cathedral priory in 1403 (the so-called Unlearned Parliament), while one of his successors, Prior John Shotteswell, hosted two sessions of parliament, in 1456 and 1459 (for the Lancastrian Henry VI). On the latter occasion Henry visited the Charterhouse too. In 1467, Prior Deram provided his house's hospitality for both Edward IV and his queen for their Christmas court, which would need to be on a lavish scale. Only four years later the pro-Lancastrian Earl of Warwick (Warwick the Kingmaker) garrisoned the city against the royal field army of Edward IV, encamped round about. He refused to come out to fight while Edward refused to lay siege and so withdrew. Both were aware of the city's strengths from personal experience. The matter was settled at the battles of Barnet and Tewkesbury within a short space of time and Edward's second reign began.

Viewed in this context, excavated altar vases in South Netherlands maiolica might have made their way into the churches of both Coventry's Carthusians and Carmelites (200 metres apart but a world away in outlook), Mount Grace's Carthusians, and that of the Cluniacs of St Saviour, Bermondsey.[52] Others share these types, performing similar functions from one monastery to another. They constitute status possessions, pure points of beauty, perhaps for displaying flowers, but may also be found in secular surroundings of good taste such as at Norwich's Pottergate. Such cosmopolitan tastes do throw into question just how cloistered these apparently cloistered lives really were when they shared good taste with the wholly worldly.

Monastic meetings between the heads of houses were regular but not common; but when they did happen, they were notable events where undoubtedly materials as well as ideas were shared. There was a quadrennial meeting of all Carthusian priors in Grenoble in the French Alps, a journey of no small undertaking; likewise, Cistercians were required to send representatives to their own quadrennial chapter at Cîteaux in Burgundy, France. During the Great Schism in the church (*circa* 1377–1417), adherents of the Pope in Avignon could continue to travel to Grenoble while those who followed the Roman Pope were forced to go all the way to Seitz in Austria, steering clear of Avignon-aligned lands.

Sometimes the different orders mixed too, just as all the Black monks met triennially at Northampton, with very few exceptions indeed during the period of this book. In this way practices and usages, so long as such things did not transcend their monastic rule, could transfer with them. For instance, the abbots of seventeen Cistercian monasteries in the Midlands met in Coventry to discuss the finances of their order in March and April 1479 as guests of the Franciscans at the Greyfriars;[53] those not attending met separately in smaller groups at London and Salisbury, again in very un-Cistercian urban surroundings. Not only do ideas travel through this arrangement, but new surroundings are admired, brotherly monastic orders are compared, and shared tastes or items in their houses are openly sought out.

Even some ordinary monks were not as cloistered as one might imagine. The Irish Franciscan friar Simon Simeonis (or FitzSimon), writing of his 1322 journey to the Holy Land, stayed in very secular surroundings most of the time, although being a mendicant friar this was not viewed as so much of a hardship as it might have been for a travelling Cistercian (possibly) or a Carthusian (certainly).

For Lazarus of Padway and his companion John, travelling in 1471, the twists and turns of their journey, brought about by war and politics, did not include listed stays in any monastic environments, though they named several cities in which they stayed along the way to Cîteaux. Padway's admission that they relaxed and had a bit of fun in Bruges merely reinforces the likelihood that they led an almost secular life during their tortuous journey. Every monastery and friary had its monastic officials who routinely dealt with the outside world (*procurators*) and regularly had to travel within it. Their exposure to continental tastes and apparent luxury was unavoidable. And so, even in the least likely of surroundings, things, foodstuffs and new ideas all spread unchecked.

Glass

In 1483, Felix Fabri, staying in Venice for the second time while on pilgrimage to the Holy Land, went on a daytrip:

> On the 7th, which is the feast of the translation of St. Peter, we went in a boat out of Venice to the island of Murano, and heard the Dominican service in the church ... and then we crossed over to the furnaces of the glassworkers, in which glass vessels of divers forms are wrought with the most exquisite art – for there are no such workers in glass anywhere else in the world. They make costly vases of crystal, and other wondrous things are to be seen there. After we had seen all these we went back in our boat to our inn at Venice.

The Murano glassworkers clearly already enjoyed a strong reputation. Archaeologically such glass is, by its very nature, dreadfully fragile. It rarely survives in good condition and records of its discovery are few and far between, mostly outweighed by Rhenish copies. Since its fragility also meant that it did not travel well, items seldom turn up in the archaeological record. However, one such example was retrieved from a late fifteenth- or early sixteenth-century grave in the nave of Coventry Charterhouse in 1987.[54] It was a clear glass goblet roughly 95 millimetres across at the rim and decorated with opaque white spiral trails and dots – so-called '*lattimo*' – and mould-blown ribs. Why such a valuable vessel was buried with a benefactor in the nave of the Charterhouse is unclear, although its owner may have been close to the supply chain since at least two of the original benefactors to the Charterhouse were (or were related to) customs officials in the business of wool export at Boston. However, like most excavated glass of that date, the goblet was in poor condition after 450 years in hard, acidic clay.

Fine Arts and Music

Foreign fine artists and specialist designers were present throughout the period of this book, against a backdrop of regular xenophobic outbursts. However, since they were usually employed by the nobility or the wealthy, and engaged in creative enrichment that benefited their patrons directly, their presence, if not overlooked, was seemingly more than merely tolerated. For instance, at Warwick in 1454, the German artist Christian Colborne was painting the (now lost) reredos of the fabulous Beauchamp Chapel, and the brass effigy and weepers of the tomb of Earl Richard Beauchamp therein were gilded, polished and brushed by Bartholomew Lambespring, 'Docheman'.[55] Colborne would later be naturalised under Edward IV, but in the 1480s he was one of a number of foreign craftsmen and painters working in the Royal Wardrobe and for the College of Heralds. In fact, Bruges painters had been painting noble portraits in England since at least the 1440s and even Hans Memling had an altarpiece ordered from him by Sir John Donne in 1480, now in the National Gallery. In early Tudor London there was a flourishing Flemish artists' colony in Bermondsey, among an estimated 16,000 Flemish families living here in the sixteenth century.[56]

Musical instruments may seem like a niche import, but such items were commonly brought in by Hanse merchants, not least through Hull and Lynn. In fact, there is plenty of evidence for the widespread presence of professional musicians in the fifteenth century, from civic bands of street entertainers (so-called 'waits') to key players, such as the urban lutenists and lyrists paid to attend the Duke of Buckingham's feasts at Maxstoke Priory, Warwickshire through the reign of Henry VI.[57] There is widespread evidence for the import of instruments by the Hanse; lutes, bundles of strings, and even a pair of small harpsichords came into Hull aboard the *Trinity* out of Danzig in 1483.[58] The same Danzig ship also brought in almost 3,000 bowstaves, meaning that it is not impossible that this one cargo supplied the

St Mary's Church, Warwick, Warwickshire: Richard Beauchamp's brass effigy, gilded and polished by Bart Lambespring, Dutchman, 1454 (2013).

A musician playing a hurdy-gurdy, such as were imported by the Hanse – Beverley Minster, North Yorkshire (1989).

archers who fought for one side or the other in the decisive battle of Bosworth in 1485.

War Booty

Any attempt to list all imports into England is doomed to failure. Each ship carried something different. A good example of this is the amount and variety of war booty taken on scores of forays into the continent to make war on our neighbours. Gold, silver and precious stones were always sought after as trophies, as were arms, armour and the finest horses, many of which could be ransomed back. At the battle of Poitiers in 1356, Edward the Black Prince took a magnificent gold-and-silver table-centre in the form of the French ship of state and displayed it before his defeated enemy,

Jean II, at an after-battle banquet in his own camp. Anything which could be carried on horseback, in a cart or on the troop transport could and did make the journey without customs declarations.

A perfect example of the incalculable meeting the unexpected took place in 1544 when an English fleet under Henry VIII raided Boulogne. The French harbour was ransacked and a huge copper ball, part of some harbour enhancement, was ripped from its pier. It was brought back intact and placed atop the tower of the parish church in Naseby, Northamptonshire, where it perched for more than 200 years, its head-on-shoulders appearance from a distance lending it a gigantic anthropomorphic aspect, almost as far from the sea as it is possible to get. Its silhouette became known as 'the old man of Naseby' and it would have looked out over Naseby battlefield on a fateful summer's day in 1645 as England's parliamentary democracy took a leap forward. Eventually it was taken down or fell off and was melted down for its raw materials. The driver on the A14 passing Naseby church today would have no idea it had ever existed.[59]

10

A PERMANENT HEAVY SWELL

So great is the malignity of these rascals ...
they evince immense hatred towards foreigners
Sebastian Giustinian, Richmond, 5 May 1517

Xenophobia

As far as resentment towards foreigners is concerned, *The Libelle of Englysshe Polycye* was the tip of the iceberg. Indeed, it boiled below the surface for the entire period of this book. Tensions during times of worsening trade could and easily did turn into open xenophobia: probably, to modern eyes, unalloyed racism. Often it took very little to spark trouble. Casual, explosive violence against foreigners was never far beneath medieval England's Christian veneer. The cry of 'they are taking our jobs' or 'the trading terms aren't fair' echoed around the ports, with irate crowds choosing to ignore that English merchants were working hard to secure their own favourable terms across the sea.

Language barriers, divergent ideas of propriety, different sexual mores in the ports – each could play a part in sparking off trouble or ending cordial negotiations. Even as the Venetians had sent their very first state-sponsored fleet to Southampton in 1319, trouble flared after a quarrel which resulted in deaths, injuries and looting, prompting an early Venetian moratorium.

We have seen in preceding chapters how on many occasions foreign ships were attacked, robbed and sunk or confiscated, many cargoes being spoiled by English vessels out to do mischief. Anti-Italian feeling in the 1450s and 1460s was considerable, while anti-Hanse feeling in the 1460s and early 1470s compounded issues. The Crown under Edward IV tried to steer a 'neutral' course (if there can be such a thing), aware of the huge financial support that foreign traders had given the house of York in its struggles with the house of Lancaster, but equally trying to take a 'protectionist' stance on English trade and English livelihoods. It was a narrow fence on which to sit.

It has been written that English xenophobia was 'commercially based and London-led, greater tolerance being given even over the River Thames in Southwark'.[1] But that is to simplify the issue, gleaning too much information exclusively from historical documents, which so often focus on London. The problems were widespread – some of the worst anti-Italian parliaments were held in Coventry – and were likely to come to a head wherever language barriers existed, or future or ongoing trade terms and privileges were under discussion, complicated by the fluctuating fortunes of a fifteenth-century England whose regions and populace were variously affected by civil war, rebellion, factionalism and even natural disaster.

London was in fact highly cosmopolitan, with subsidy records of 1441 suggesting that one in twenty in the city were foreign, with as many living in the suburbs in addition to that. Moreover, it is estimated that as many as 10 per cent of England's population beyond London was foreign-born.[2] This at a time when the country was trying directly, without even the semblance of fairness, to address the issues raised in the *Libelle* through legislation and restrictive registrations such as the imposition of sales caps, to be returned twice yearly to the Exchequer. However, in the fifteenth and early sixteenth centuries it must be borne in mind that a 'Walssheman' and an 'Irissheman' might also be considered foreigners by many, and even their presence would draw comment in an era of growing census and subsidy records. Many of England's own merchants traded overseas, and similar comment may be made of merchants of Bristol, Southampton, Norwich, Coventry, York, Winchester and a host of smaller towns, both coastal and landlocked, from Chipping Campden in the sleepy but immensely wealthy Cotswolds to Beverley in the wide expanses of Yorkshire. In most of these, for most of the time, 'aliens' were considered to stand apart, and in census and merchant rolls alike their nationality is usually carefully recorded. Coventry's statute merchant roll, for instance, carefully records the names of those who were accorded civic trading privileges and admitted to a prestigious guild, admittance being no more than a sweetener to all deals thereafter – a warm civic embrace which sought some reciprocity. It certainly wasn't altruism.

Foreign traders in London, with some exceptions among the more powerful and influential, were usually required to lodge with approved hosts whose returns were sent twice yearly to the Exchequer, the so-called 'Views of Hosts'. Fees were usually extracted, and movements monitored in a manner redolent of a police state. Stays were restricted, usually to a period of inbound cargo unloading, sales, purchases, and return cargo loading, all under the unpredictable vagaries of English duty fees. It was not uncommon for a stay to be capped at forty days. It was perhaps akin to handing over one's passport at a hotel, but with an added feeling of menace if the pendulum of the current financial climate was swinging against one's dealings. The baseline restrictions were written into law in 1439, at a time when Italians were coming under extreme English suspicion. Though at that time Hanseatic traders were exempt from the legislation, they too were reeled in under different subsidy collections in 1449.[3]

Whether they were just stubborn or inured to the reception they might get, the Neapolitans sent their first state galleys to England and Flanders at the height of anti-Italian opposition in 1451–52. Their specific reception is unlikely to have been much different to that of any other Italians – surly at best. For the Florentines, the English reception was dreadful. In the years 1448–55, relations were so bad that they declined to send any state galleys at all. After a brief resumption, matters deteriorated so badly that in 1457 most Italian merchants (Venetians, Florentines, Genoese, Lucchese) abandoned London for Winchester due to anti-Italian xenophobia and, because of the reorganisation, the Florentines once more sent no state galleys that year.[4] These were the last years of the anti-Italian government of Henry VI. Its days were numbered, and under Edward IV things would improve – a little. The Genoese, meanwhile, came in for punishment under Richard III, and in 1484 news of his restrictions on their trade reached Pope Sixtus IV. They were to sell all their merchandise within one year and depart, anything unsold being forfeit.[5]

As has been seen, the issues in London, however widespread, meant very little if one's ship was under attack when apparently safely at anchor or tied up at Plymouth or Ilfracombe, or when it was targeted by the so-called 'men of Fowey'. Witness the number of times that 'men of Fowey' enhanced a growing reputation as vagabonds, despoiling a succession of vessels moored in their harbour despite their apparent safety. Or how they sent ships to harry Winchelsea and Sandwich as if their victims were not their countrymen. Cornwall was often restive, never more than in the 1490s when disputes about the royal tin monopoly boiled over (along with the rebellion against Henry VII by Perkin Warbeck, a Yorkist claimant to his throne), with the Portuguese trying to import tin from India and the Venetians merely nodding knowingly, spreading rumours. Cornwall does seem to have garnered its own reputation, not least Fowey. The Cornish broke

A Permanent Heavy Swell

into open revolt before the end of the century, and were brutally put down by Henry VII at the battle of Blackheath.

When England later concluded a peace treaty with France, in 1510, the wording was chosen to be helpful to Italian traders, but even then only begrudgingly. The terms set out 'that all merchants, *even Venetians, Florentines or Genoese*, may come freely and securely to the Kingdom of England by sea and fresh water, armed for the safety of their persons, property, goods, ships and effects'.

Simmering resentment against the foreigners did just that: simmer. But what was arguably the worst case of open xenophobic violence was carefully premeditated in 1517 in the heart of the capital and scandalised even the Venetians, at whom so much casual violence was often directed.[6] On this occasion, however, they themselves were largely unmolested observers who lay low, probably in an attitude of self-preservation.

On the night of 1 May, about 2,000 London apprentices went to the French and Flemish quarters of the city, sacked the houses of foreigners and wounded many of them, although none were reported killed. Then they sacked the house of the French king's secretary, who escaped by the skin of his teeth by shinning up into the belfry of an adjoining church. Unperturbed, the mob moved on to the houses of Florentines (whose state fleet had disappeared from English waters a whole generation before), Lucchese and Genoese, hurling insults and abuse but held back by the inhabitants' successful defence. From there they proceeded to the Spanish embassy, where they dealt out similar taunts, curiously sparing the Venetians.

Acting on behalf of the Crown, Cardinal Wolsey was forced to bring in troops but found himself shut out of London by the rebels, whose blood was up, and who overpowered the city authorities to facilitate a mass jailbreak. Even the wives and mistresses of the apprentices joined in, venting their venom and hatred of foreigners. Forced entry into the city was eventually made when the Earl of

Surrey and the dukes of Norfolk and Buckingham arrived with reinforcements. They ringed the city with 15,000 troops and artillery, raised gibbets and hanged between sixty and seventy of the ringleaders, who were then drawn and quartered for good measure. A further 400 were spared only at the intervention of Queen Katherine of Aragon, backed up by Wolsey, but they were publicly humiliated and pleaded for mercy before it was granted. It turned out that the riot had been instigated by a couple of clerics who had stirred up a crusading spirit against all foreigners over Easter. Anyone already disaffected had taken little persuading.

After the event, the unscathed Venetian secretary in England, Nicolo Sagudino, made light of it, saying that 'the mischief done was not very great' but that 'it was horrible to pass near the city gates, where nothing but gibbets and the quarters of these offenders were exhibited'. The plan had been to kill all foreigners – thousands of them. Had it succeeded, this was little short of ethnic cleansing, to coin a modern, matter-of-fact term for an old, barbaric solution. Racism, it seems, was never far from the surface.

Of course, this prevailing current of anger and reprisal was not without its more enlightened detractors. To be sure, not everyone was xenophobic, at least openly. When John Payne Snr, mayor of Southampton, was a little too racist towards the Italians in 1463, threatening to bring trade to a halt, the king had him removed from office.[7] In 1483, a statute of the realm stated that England's own brand of furniture-making would benefit from the residence of foreigners. However, in a seemingly practical nod to their more voluble xenophobic cohort, even a real thirst for continental design and ideas could not stop them from adding that foreign-born furniture craftsmen could only take on Englishmen as apprentices, an ordinance regularly reprised during Henry VIII's reign.[8] In a similar vein, Edward IV, while taking regular swipes at Italian carriers, licensed two naturalised Italians to bring in twenty craftsmen to teach English dyers in new methods of dyeing and finishing cloth.⁹ By such methods did the Renaissance catch on in England. Various statutes regularly sought to restrict carrying to English shippers, particularly disadvantaging the Italians but arriving at a middle road which did not alienate the industrious and generally helpful continentals and, just as importantly, did not reduce home support for the king and parliament.

There was, at times, no immediately obvious reason why a particular group should be singled out for rough handling, not least when it was meted out by locals who hardly stood to benefit in the way specific merchants might. During Edward IV's brief exile in 1471, and with Henry VI precariously back on the throne under the Earl of Warwick's guidance, a Kentish mob charged into London's southern suburbs and attacked Dutch and Flemish beerhouses.[10] While the Dutch and Flemings might have connections with the exiled Edward IV's friendly host, his brother-in-law the Duke of Burgundy, no one would really be inconvenienced (sore heads apart) other than the very Kentishmen and Londoners who regularly drank at those beerhouses. It was ill-directed and pointless rabble-rousing by the ringleaders, trying to show their support for the newly re-adepted Henry VI but merely hurting their own communities.

Violence could be casual or pre-meditated, but it was often sudden and explosive; it was sometimes state sponsored. There was hardly a decade in which casual and fatal violence was not visited upon shipping in English and 'international' waters (such a modern distinction did not exist at the time). One such dire occasion came in 1380 when a Cornish vessel out of Fowey was captured by Flemings. They killed the entire crew but for one small boy, who hid below decks and raised the alarm by shouting as they reached port.[11] English mariners could be just as bold; in 1400, fishing boats out of Lynn captured Scottish ships off Aberdeen together with their admiral, Sir Robert Logan, taking him back to Lynn as a prize. This is not to even mention the men of Cley's capture of the Scottish heir.[12]

The fifteenth century opened with a carefully and secretly prepared attack on England by a Breton force. On 10 August 1403, sailors from Brittany fell upon Plymouth without warning. Unable to mount a defence in time, the populace fled the town, which was promptly sacked and torched by the Bretons who carried away whatever they could, without a fight. The Crown, 'not so much grieved at the losse as ashamed at the disgrace', fitted out a fleet which returned the favour, taking forty ships of all sizes, seizing iron, oil, tallow and 1,000 tuns of La Rochelle wine. They went on to burn the ships before landing and torching Penmarc'h and St Mathieu, which lie at the end of the shortest sea route directly south from Plymouth to Brittany and where prominent medieval lighthouses would help position an enemy fleet without the need for a friendly pilot.

Not content, however, the vengeful force pushed inland for some miles, wasting the region (the wealthy *Presqu'isle de Pemarc'h*) in a prolonged act of revenge.[13] Then, of course, unwilling to lie down and take it, the Bretons returned and sacked Portland in 1404 and again in 1405. It was a sorry pattern of punishment and reprisal that went on throughout the fifteenth century, observed at Fowey and Sandwich in 1457. Perhaps the men of Fowey never forgot these earlier slights, leading to its reputation as a very risky anchorage towards the end of the century. Perhaps coincidentally, 1457 was the year that Italian merchants abandoned London because of the strength of feeling against them.

Local resentment aside, there were even rivalries between different trading nations with seemingly equal rights that boiled over without provocation. Peaceful anchorages in a seemingly friendly English port could turn nasty very quickly. In February 1496, in the middle of Southampton Water, two Venetian merchants had their ships boarded by French vessels and were held to ransom. A third Venetian, the son of a nobleman, was shot through the thigh in the initial struggle. All three were only released on payment of a ransom.[14]

In 1492, violence was once again perpetrated with official sanction. In one of the regular Crown appropriations of merchant vessels, Henry VII took the opportunity to vent his fury on the Venetians for a long-festering dispute over the trade in sweet wine. The king rather petulantly seized the Venetian state galleys themselves, to use for an expedition against France. The story goes that, unfortunately, unskilled in their handling, their surrogate English masters made a mess of it and crashed the galleys into the harbour works at Calais.[15] However, it takes only the merest leap of faith to suggest that the inexpert handling may have been a deliberate manoeuvre, using the vessels, each carrying at least 10 tons when merely in ballast, as marine battering rams.

During the early sixteenth century, England's disputes with France, Britanny and Spain simply went on and on. Tit-for-tat raiding and attacks on shipping were rife – and sanctioned by the Crown. The Venetians corresponded on many aspects of these, and their archives are rich in evidence of England's disregard for its neighbours, with sailors from these shores on one occasion landing in western Britanny and burning twenty-six villages. That is awfully precise. Thankfully, the record notes that early warning meant that the villages had been abandoned ahead of the landing and only property was damaged.

Raiding probably never stopped, just abated for a while during poor weather or when one country or another was distracted by internal issues. Such internal strife was inevitably blamed on outside influence from those neighbours, however, and on it went. Well into the 1540s, John Leland, on his travels around England and Wales, noted of the far-flung Scilly Isles: 'Few men be glad to inhabit these islettes, for al the plenty, for robbers by the sea that take their cattail of force. These robbers be French men and Spaniardes.'[16]

Piracy

Piracy (if it was to be separated from violent xenophobia) was a constant problem, across every sea that concerns this book, from the Baltic to the Mediterranean.[17] Pirates came from the Adriatic (known as Uskoks), from Malta, even from Florence; there were Turkish and Moorish corsairs, not to mention English, French and Dutch seamen marauding across the seas. None bore any scruples to speak of and all represented a threat to decent traders and trading nations, even their own. At the end of the fourteenth century an organised group of pirates called the Vitalienbruder openly worked for the Danes to pressurise the Hanseatic cities in the Baltic. Their leaders were gorily executed to bring their activities to an end.

Perhaps most difficult to comprehend in the English view of the high seas was the xenophobic element. Casual violence encountered at sea was usually described as piracy, but 'they' were doing what 'we' were doing and raiding each other's coasts was part of that. More recent stories by the likes of Robert Louis Stevenson, and tales of individuals smuggling against the power of the state, have led to piracy being seen very much as an economic choice, somehow righting old wrongs and restoring wealth to those who had none. In the fifteenth and sixteenth centuries, however, it was more about international waters presenting 'fair game', a place where old scores could be settled. For no reason other than that the victims were nasty foreigners – not *us* – traders could be despoiled of their goods and sometimes their ships too, with apparent impunity – or chased into their harbours and their homes plundered. The same level of violence dealt out to English ships and traders by foreigners was regularly visited upon foreign ships and traders by English sailors, sometimes in response, sometimes pre-emptively. In 1407, Henry Pay and a small fleet of fifteen ships out of the Cinque Ports took 120 French ships lying at anchor, seizing their cargoes of iron, salt, cloth, olive oil and wine of La Rochelle.[18] How 120 were sailed or handled by fifteen is unclear. A few short years later, in 1411, two English admirals on a seakeeping exercise had a particularly successful sweep, taking many French pirates out of the equation, but in doing so attracted condemnation at home – because they removed a good reason for English raiding.[19]

Of course, sailors could and did defend themselves, with varied results. The Venetians were instructed by the Signory, their governing body, to keep their bows strung and their arrows at hand as they entered port. When in port no one was to sell, pawn or even carry ashore any weapons – which had the dual intention of reducing the risk of killing or wounding ashore but also making certain that no weapons, so vital to defence at sea, would be lost.[20]

On their last visit to England and Flanders, perhaps mindful of the febrile situation in those two countries and on the lookout for pirates, Florence's state-backed Medici galleys were heavily overloaded with alum for a market which was in desperate need of the mordaunt, so much so that they had to offload some to another galley in Cadiz. In fact, the level of overloading was so severe that they were forced to leave some 1,100 sacks on the quayside there.

No one was immune to piracy, and the only reasonable defence against it was to travel in convoy. However, this was not a guarantee of safety. In 1473, a Florentine state galley was taken by pirates off Gravelines while on its way from Sluys to Southampton. On another occasion, Henry VI was embarrassed into paying £40 in recompense to the Lady Isabella de Lallyng, of the ducal house of Burgundy, who was captured at sea by an English ship seemingly on a whim – red faces all round.[21] In 1458, a Genoa-born pirate captured two English ships off Malta. The Genoese generally were blamed, and English ports seized all Genoese merchants in England (this coming a year after they had already decamped from London to Southampton in fear of their lives). Too keen on trade to protest much, the Genoese let it blow over and trade went on.[22]

Shipwreck

> ... *a shrieking northerly gale strikes them head-on and lifts the waves up skywards. Oars are splintered, then the prow swings round, she presents her side to the waves and a crashing mountain of water seeks them out ... A southwesterly wind dashes three ships against the lurking rocks which the Italians call the Altars, forming a monstrous spine in the midst of the sea...*
>
> Vergil, *Aeneid*, I[23]

The ultimate fear from time immemorial was shipwreck, as Vergil described for Aeneas' fleet of Trojan refugees in the Mediterranean in the first century BC. Even then the most fearsome rocks had garnered evocative names that sent shivers down a mariner's spine. Off Land's End the Wolf Rocks, still so called, are already marked as such on Lucas Wagenhaer's 1585 map. In the mid-fifteenth century, while the portolan of Michael of Rhodes is strangely clear of rocky dangers, Karl Koppmann's *seebuch* contains many, some of which bear the same fearsome names today: *Wolffs staen* is but one. There he records *Idensteyn* (Eddystone Rocks, off Plymouth – now with their famous lighthouse), *Hillensteyn* (unknown), *sunte Edemunde staen* (St Edmund's Rock) and *Koe unde de ander dat Kalff* (Cow and Calf Rocks, between Newquay and St Ives, Cornwall).

Koppmann also records, almost poetically, Saint Nicholas' Deep and Saint Andrew's Deep, parts of the navigable sea where only the saints and the will of God come between life and death. They are named after the patron saint of seafarers, Nicholas, and the patron saint of fishermen, Andrew. Koppmann was painfully aware that only fools venture on the seas while taking its moods for granted. Often pleasant, sometimes benign, the sea can change locally in a very short time, a fact which was not lost on any late medieval mariners who plied the Baltic, Mediterranean,

Atlantic, North or Irish Seas. For those who were familiar with all of them, the variety of moods would have filled them with dread. The English Channel was (and remains) a graveyard. Good navigation was a must. Poor navigation could mean certain death.

For the unlucky ones whose skills were not up to scratch, or whose ship was in a poor state, a turn in the weather could mean disaster and certain death. Generally, sailors were not taught to swim and did not wish to entertain false hopes as most sinkings took place in weather that generally precluded survival. The ability to swim was a personal choice and happenstance based on upbringing. Many believed that if lost at sea it was better to simply surrender to one's inevitable fate – or, more properly, the will of God.

Stories of shipwreck had circulated from distant antiquity. Most late medieval Europeans would have known of St Paul's shipwreck on the island of Malta[24] or in the Old Testament the storm endured by the unlucky Jonah's ship.[25] Principal would have been the New Testament Gospel story of Christ calming a storm on the Sea of Galilee when his disciples cowered in the boat fearing for their lives. It was proof, as it were, that God's grace (or St Nicholas) could save them from maritime disaster if their prayers were sufficient.[26] Some, with links to places of learning such as monasteries, may have heard of Aeneas or even Odysseus. In any case the tales of maritime woe, even from the distant past, were consistently terrifying.

Throughout the medieval period more lives were lost, and cargoes destroyed, and such stories, real and imagined, multiplied amongst the general populace and mariners alike. They needed no embellishment in the telling. Around 1170 David, brother of the Jewish poet, philosopher and physician Simon Maimonides, travelled from Egypt to 'Aydhab in the Sudan, where he found little that he could buy. Writing to his brother before he took ship to the Malabar coast of India, he encouraged him and invoked his God: 'Do not worry. He who saved me from the desert will save me while at sea.' He was never heard of again.[27]

Miscalculations could have dire consequences, even (and in some ways especially) within sight of land, as the Brother Felix Fabri attested on his first pilgrimage to the Holy Land aboard a Venetian galley in 1480:

> When day broke and the galley was loosed from the mooring-posts, as they were violently directing her head towards the wind, the helm or rudder struck upon the rocks and broke under water; and the ship was within a little of striking her beak-head upon the rocks which ran out from the shore, in which case the whole galley would have broken up and we should have perished. Wherefore, a loud shout was raised, and people came running from the city to help us. As the rudder was broken, we could not sail, but brought back our galley into the harbour to the place where she lay before.

Repairs were completed by means of a 'free diver' over the side, armed with ordinary hand tools.

Accidents on board were common. Fabri, as a regular pilgrim and therefore frequent traveller, perhaps encountered more than his fair share, and they could be sudden, unlooked-for and deadly, as he found on his eventful first pilgrimage of 1480: 'While they were hoisting the mizen-mast, by the carelessness of one of the sailors, it fell down again, and striking another sailor, killed him on the spot. My Lord Bishop of Le Mans stood close to this dangerous falling spar, and I was by his side with many others, and we were all within a very little of being struck by it and killed. As for the dead man, they wrapped him in a sheet, tied a bag full of stones to his feet, and threw him into the sea.'

A Permanent Heavy Swell

Later during the same journey, disaster struck again:

In that port (Paphos on Cyprus) we bought necessary stores, left it hurriedly, and were carried along the coast without making any progress. Besides this another great misfortune befell us that same night, while the officers of the ship were engaged in managing the sails and tackling of the galley, when suddenly a block fell from the masthead, which struck and killed our best officer. There was great lamentation in the galley at this man's death, as there was none so well liked on board to take his place.

Later, on his second pilgrimage in 1483, and again in a galley out of Venice, Fabri recalled another storm and a breakage which almost cost them the ship. As the storm blew stronger the crew wanted to change tack and began adjusting the sail when it broke loose and fell onto the oars on one side. When the wind filled the untethered sail it tangled with the oars, and the ship heeled over, dipping both sail and spar in the water and threatening to capsize the galley. It was righted only after much effort.

Clearly while many consider the effects of the sea upon the hull of a ship, these two accidents and a sailing incident show that wear and tear up in the masts and rigging were also a constant problem, and not easily remedied while the ship was at sea. Only slick handling at sea, regular inspection and a programme of replacing worn parts and fraying ropes might reduce the constant risk.

Stories of fortunate survivors kept the mystique of the sea circulating, along with the last resort of religious faith. The Mediterranean storm weathered by Ranulf, 6th Earl of Chester in 1220 as he returned from Crusade in Egypt would have struck a particular chord since he survived to tell his tale of sheer terror, buoyed up through the storm – in Heaven's eyes – by the sure and steadfast prayers of his supportive Cistercian monks back

A 10-metre wreck emerges from the harbour mud where it settled: Guilvinec, Finisterre (29), France (2010).

home.[28] Many a coastal church or chapel, or simply a chantry altar, was dedicated to St Nicholas, to whom mariners would pray for deliverance. Often the church was the first place on land a ship's master would go, to give thanks for his ship's safe arrival; there the pre-eminent place for a fresco of St Nicholas or St Christopher, patron saint of all travellers, was usually on the north wall, right opposite a church's entrance and the first sight for the grateful traveller upon entry.

Medieval art and wall paintings depicting ships at sea and ships in distress are relatively common.[29] Sailors are often shown sporting looks of abject terror, not least when illustrating those biblical scenes mentioned above.

The regular state sailings by the north Italian city states included wrecks almost as regularly, despite their familiarity with the sea's moods and their consistent observance of the calendar. The Florentine state-sponsored fleet to England lost one of its principal galleys crossing the Bay of Biscay early in 1459,[30] while

St Peter's Church, Shorewell, Isle of Wight: a single-masted ship of 1440 on a wider St Christopher polychrome wall painting, opposite the entrance. Every traveller arriving was encouraged to give thanks (2023).

the Venetians' more numerous sailings over a longer period – and including many stops and some detours – ended in disaster on several occasions, notably in 1495, when that year's four-strong galley fleet was reduced by half, including the loss of the flagship.[31]

Some dreadful eventualities simply could not be anticipated. In 1406, four ships out of Lynn on the Bordeaux wine run were swallowed up in a whirlpool which had appeared in the Bay of Biscay.[32] The description includes a 'vertiginous' sea, seemingly capturing the way in which a vessel might be sucked down into a vortex. In 1480, Felix Fabri encountered another whirlpool, seemingly well known thereabouts, off Corfu:

> After a tedious voyage ... we came to a part of the sea, where the galley could make no headway, nor could it be moved by the oars to the right nor to the left but hove-to, because beneath it was the whirlpool called the 'Abyss,' or opening into the earth, which there sucks up a great part of the sea, and where

the waters sink down into that Abyss. For this reason the waters stand still above it, awaiting their descent into the Abyss; and at low tide the water swirls around, and whatever swims upon it is in danger of being dragged down. Ships would be swallowed up if the steersmen did not avoid it. So in this place we were hove-to (unable to make progress), and our sailors tried with much shouting and hard work to row the galley away from this gulf, but in vain. When the people of Corcyra saw this – for we were within sight of both the island and Corfu town – they came to our aid with two small galleys.

The two small galleys acted as tugs and, with all three vessels fully under oars, towed them away until they could make their own headway back into port. Corfu was very much Venetian territory, so not unfamiliar waters to the captain and crew.

There were numerous occasions when prompt action around English coasts only just saved both ship and cargo. In 1519 the Venetian Flanders galleys urgently put into 'Porto Camera' (Camber-before-Rye) as the deteriorating weather prevented them from reaching Southampton.[33] Florentine ships were already sheltering in harbour at Ribadeo in 1429 when the fourteen-strong Portuguese royal fleet of the Infanta Isabella, on its way to Flanders for her marriage to Duke Philip the Good, was scattered and reduced to five, which had to hastily put in twice (at Vivero then Ribadeo) or face destruction.[34] This same storm accounted for several Biscayan ships.[35] The weather was and is no respecter of persons. Sometimes even the ports and harbours were not quite the havens they seemed, as in 1403 when there occurred what John Capgrave described as a 'great inundation of the sea' between Calais and Kent, drenching many towns in Kent, Flanders, Holland and Zeeland.[36] It seems that an exceptionally high tide there combined with other climatic factors moving southwards; such coastal disasters have been regular occurrences before and since.

Camber Sands, East Sussex, once an inlet to both Rye and Winchelsea: in 1519 the Venetian Flanders galleys were forced to put in here, unable to make Southampton in torrid weather (2019).

One contemporary observation of a shipwreck comes from the fastidious monastic traveller and chronicler William Worcestre, who recounted the story of the cog *Anne* out of Bristol, skippered by the Bristolian merchant Robert Sturmy, a successful businessman who, for whatever reason, seems to have swapped merchandise for 160 pilgrims and sailed to Jerusalem via Seville and Jaffa for his first such voyage in July 1446. On the return leg, a sudden storm sprang up on the night of 23 December 1446 off the southern Peloponnese. They were driven onto the rocks of Methoni, where the ship broke up and the entire Bristolian crew of thirty-seven perished, their passing marked by a new chapel erected there by a local bishop.[37] The date is interesting since it suggests that the 160 pilgrims, once safely delivered to the Holy Land, then stayed on to come back by another ship; they warrant no further mention. That alone might suggest that Sturmy's fateful return leg saw him carrying a more regular cargo from the east.

Be they concerned with Santiago de Compostela, Rome or the Holy Land, pilgrims were not passengers normally carried by merchants, although a regular 'service' did run out of Bristol alongside that town's mercantile concerns. Indeed, the Venetians forbade their state fleet from stopping at Santiago since it represented a big distraction from their normal run. One notable exception, for an important English guest, occurred in August 1408 when Richard Beauchamp, Earl of Warwick was assigned one of their Beirut galleys to take him to Jaffa on his way to the Holy Land with his retinue. He must have paid a very high fee, since he booked both the outward and return leg, to the exclusion of all merchandise in either direction, and he was assigned the stern cabin, the galley and the sailing master's armoury on board, all to be otherwise kept clear and unencumbered. On arrival at Jaffa, the boat was to go on to Acre for safety and then return to Jaffa to pick the earl up again. The whole pilgrimage, from disembarkation to pick-up, was allowed a maximum of only ten days.[38] This was the route that Brother Felix Fabri would later take.

Of course, it was not just the direct routes to England from the home ports of trading partners which were dangerous. It was noted that even as the Portuguese attempted to break the Venetian spice monopoly, their ambassadors, acting as commercial spies, wrote that only seventy-two of their 104 ships returned from the first expedition to India. Nineteen were known to have sunk, with the fate of the remaining thirteen being unknown.[39]

In 1510, word reached Venetians at Palermo in Sicily that a Biscayan ship out of England had been wrecked off Ivica (Croatia) carrying English cloth, about half of which was lost.[40] Notably a ship out of Southampton was said to have passed the same spot without incident on the day before with a similar cargo owned by the Genoese and Ragusans. The fact that both were observed shows that Venetian lookouts or spies were everywhere, feeding back information on the fortunes of rival shipping to the Signory back in Venice.

One particularly notable storm, responsible for both wreck and extreme inconvenience, struck in January 1497. King Philip of Castille and Queen Juana, sister of Katharine of Aragon, embarked aboard their flagship, one of thirteen in their flotilla, on 7 January at Arnemuiden in the Netherlands but did not leave harbour until the full moon three days later. Bound for Spain, they stood off Southampton two days later when a violent storm sprang up. They made good headway on the 13th, probably in the eye of the storm, but the next day a violent west-south-westerly drove them towards the English coast. Two days later, unable to make any progress, they stopped at Portland in Dorset with two other ships. The rest of the flotilla was scattered, four reaching safety at Plymouth, another three Dartmouth, while the last three foundered. A generation later locals still recalled the event, such that it was reported to the antiquary John Leland, who was writing around 1545: 'Sum say that part of Philippe King of Castelle navie was driven toward the mouth of this water (he reports the River Arme), wher is no haven, but periculus rokkes.'[41] That would be the Eddystone Rocks. With the contingent that reached Plymouth was the Venetian ambassador, Quirini, who first recounted the tale.[42] He and his compatriots were not impressed with Cornwall, where no one understood the language of the locals. This had been a notable concern among travellers since ancient times, as in Homer's *Odyssey* – 'So he wandered with his ships, among strangely spoken men'[43] – and Shakespeare's first words among castaways in *Twelfth Night* – 'What is this place?' There were, of course, no signs or placards anywhere. One's first words to an uncomprehending local could seal one's fate.

Apparently, the storm of 1497 was the worst January weather seen in living memory. It was noted that the royal party themselves had a lucky escape when their ship capsized but righted itself. When news of their arrival reached the court, Henry VII extended all hospitality to his royal guests close to London. King Philip was at Richmond while Queen Juana stayed at Romford, totally at odds with her husband, whom she constantly suspected of serial adultery. Their flagship was taken from Portland to Falmouth to be repaired and the two royals left the London area and made their separate ways there, Philip stopping at Reading due to illness and the queen going via Exeter. All the while Quirini was stuck in Plymouth or nearby Falmouth, hating it and pouring out invective against his unintelligible hosts. The party were all together again at Falmouth on 30 March but due to another storm were unable to put out until 23 April. It had been a difficult stay for all, Falmouth apparently being poorly provisioned – at least so far as a royal court was concerned – and expensive. So far from London, it was simply provincial in its outlook, unused to royal visitors. Cornwall was also simmering on the edge of rebellion against Henry VII, so the foreign royal presence was probably viewed with great suspicion as a Crown ruse. The enmity between king and queen continued unabated throughout, leading to Quirini later describing the queen as 'mad, miserly, and jealous' and driven to distraction by suspicion of her husband;[44] unsurprisingly, she has come down to us as 'Mad Joan'. The party eventually reached Coruña on 26 April.

While many stops en route to and from England were to pick up merchandise, others were signally to ensure that ships were in the best condition for the journey that still lay ahead. In the late fifteenth century English ships entering the Mediterranean would stop at Huelva in southern Spain, where they would be hauled up via horses – ground-anchored winches – onto the beach to have their hulls routinely careened and caulked. When the Biscay crossing was expected to see the worst of the weather they might encounter, Venetian galleys stopped at south-eastern Spanish ports to buy tarpaulins and hatch covers to protect their below-deck cargos, which might be ruined by salt spray and overtopping the gunwales.

It is inescapable, however, that many ships were lost at sea because they were old, worn out and simply unseaworthy. It has been calculated that even in the comparatively late period of 1625–28, for which good records exist, 130 English vessels were lost each year.[45] To be clear, that represented one-third of all England's ships over 100 tons. Even as late as the eighteenth century the East India Company lost 10 per cent per year – a massive, wasteful turnover and loss of lives. Such debilitating losses were probably perfectly normal – and surpassed – in the fifteenth century.

One might expect no more than twenty to thirty years' regular service from a good ship before the sea claimed it in some way. Even half-rotten hulks, leaking like sieves, continued to sail and ships which would have been withdrawn from service by more enlightened masters continued to ply local waters until the inevitable happened. If discretion did get the better of a more scrupulous owner, the whole might yet have a resale value for others to address its problems or be sold off to a boatyard for its parts to keep others afloat.

The experiences of Brother Felix Fabri are notable, simply because he wrote them down at length. He is effusive about the effects of being caught in one nighttime storm:

> Storms are endurable by day, but at night they are too cruel, especially when they are violent, like this one: it was very fierce and very dark except for flashes of lightning. So fierce was the wind kept tossing and rolling the galley about, that no one could lie in his berth, much less sit, and least of all stand. We had to hang on to the pillars supporting the upper deck, or else crouch beside our luggage-chests, hanging on to them to stay still – sometimes both they and the men clinging to them would get tossed about. The galley heaves so violently and unpredictably that it up-ends everything – even things which were hanging up against the bulkheads came off their hooks and fell down.

In such conditions, there was no staying dry. 'Although the ship was everywhere dressed with pitch and the other things which are used to prevent leaks and keep out water,' he wrote, 'it still came in everywhere, so that there was nothing in the entire ship which was not wet – our beds and our belongings were sopping, our rations spoiled.'

A glance up on deck showed a situation no less dire. The wind shredded the mainsail, so the sailors lowered the yard and replaced it with a special storm sail, but the wind tore the ropes from their grasp and the force bent the composite mast, which creaked alarmingly almost to breaking point. It held, but Felix Fabri noted that at that moment, had the mast snapped, the ship was in its greatest danger. His faith was very much put to the test.

Fabri noted that, other than being caught in pitch darkness, what frightened him most about storms – and he encountered a few – was the immense noise. Stuck below decks, it was not just the wind or the sound of the crashing waves, but the unearthly creaking and groaning of the ship, which was loud and continuous and convinced him that something must be broken somewhere. Early in his first pilgrimage, he wryly recalled how he was asked in port what folly possessed him that he and his companions should wish to expose themselves to such risks. He was warmly encouraged to turn around and head back to Venice. Fabri was a rare beast – a landlubber who travelled extensively on the sea and who wrote about it. If he was ever frightened (and he had plenty of occasions to be), he did not betray his fear. His overriding excitement and joy at the world around him pervades all his written observations.

There are few fifteenth-century accounts of either land or sea travel, and direct comparisons are vanishingly rare. One exception, however, is a letter by the Italian-born Lazarus of Padway to a friend who was the Cistercian abbot of Buckland Abbey in Devon.[46] In it he notes that his journey from London to Cîteaux to attend the quadrennial Cistercian General Chapter in 1471 was long and arduous and, although mostly by land, included a Channel crossing in both directions. On the outward leg he sailed from Dover to Calais but was prevented from landing since England was at war with France. The ship anchored overnight before heading around the coast to Boulogne-sur-Mer. They then stayed overnight at Boulogne before heading north overland to Bruges and Flanders. At Bruges, he and John, his travelling companion, kicked their heels briefly and relaxed, potentially against the backdrop of the English court of Edward IV staying in exile there.

Resuming their journey, Lazarus and John were forced to skirt the edges of the French king's territory and passed through the duchies of Burgundy, Brabant and Lotharingia. He notes the cities and towns they stayed at and bemoans the many trials and tribulations they had to overcome to get to Cîteaux. There, at the General Chapter of the Cistercian Order, he gave a report on the state of the English province of Canterbury to the head of the order, who was allegedly moved to tears.

Describing the return leg in similar detail, and again trying to avoid danger zones, travelling where possible under safe-conduct passes, Lazarus notes that when they embarked at Calais, throwing in their lot with returning English merchants, they had already been delayed many days by adverse winds. They headed for Dover as part of a convoy, at which point he sets aside his long-winded Latin and his prose acquires a breathless matter-of-fact brevity: 'At length we were caught in a huge storm and, with all the ships tossed about we finally reached Sandwich, after which we made it to London on the third day.' He then notes, 'I would rather go to Rome or Jerusalem at such a time as this than make this journey in such a dreadful storm.' Rome and Jerusalem were major undertakings for anyone – even more so in dangerous times, as the effusive Fabri found – so the single experience of a Channel storm had clearly given Lazarus the fright of his life.

William Shakespeare, at the end of the sixteenth century, wrote in *The Tempest*: 'Now would I give a thousand furlongs of sea for an acre of barren ground, long heath, brown furze, anything. The wills above be done! but I would fain die a dry death.' Later, in the eighteenth century, Dr Samuel Johnson would express similar sentiments: 'Being in a ship is being in jail with the chance of being drowned.' Seemingly all were agreed.

Lighthouses

From antiquity most had heard of the Pharos, the Great Lighthouse of Alexandria, one of the seven wonders of the ancient world. As a structure, it survived until the fourteenth century when age, earthquakes and disrepair saw it finally collapse. It was far from the only such structure in medieval Europe, there being such edifices at Coruña in Spain,[47] and the map of Olaus Magnus in 1539 depicts another at the mouth of the River Elbe in north-east Germany, on the approach to the Hanseatic port of Hamburg.

The supposed Roman lighthouse at Dover is much celebrated, but by the period of this book it had long ceased to shine, being run-down, as John Leland had noted around 1540. But even to focus upon these and give them the name lighthouse is to miss the point – they were not lighthouses as we know them today. The enlightened view of the later seventeenth century up to the present, focussed on the need to save lives from Davy Jones's locker, was just not current in the late medieval period. Lighthouses were erected to look out and guide ships toward what they marked. They generally stood by harbours, navigable channels and ports of call – not perilous stretches of coastline. The Roman *pharos* at Dover had been built next to the home port of the Classis Britannica, the Fleet of Britain, formed along the so-called 'Saxon Shore' to rid the Channel of pirates in the later Roman period, a thousand years before the period of this

'Lighthouse' depicted on a marshy island (Neuwerk) at the mouth of the River Elbe, Germany, on Olaus Magnus *Carta Marina* (1539). Thanks to Uppsala University Library.

book. It was a statement that said, 'Here is the Fleet, we are here, don't mess with us.' It also guided the fleet back to port in failing light or if they were in any way worse for wear. Such lighthouses, more properly called beacons, were little more than elevated braziers.

A tall beacon tower had stood high at St Catherine's on the Isle of Wight since the early fourteenth century, with a priest to tend the light. However, it was close to neither rocks nor the sea level, negating any value in warding off the unwary – it does not appear in late medieval portolans. Lights could be kept in church towers too, such as at Lynn Greyfriars and the so-called Boston Stump (St Botolph's), or at Winterton-on-Sea and Cromer – all prominent seamarks on England's flatter east coast, which lacks the distinctive rocky headlands of the south. Eminently visible during the day from a couple of miles out to sea, their value could be felt round the clock if they were also lit up from a high window or belfry, although a mere brazier probably cast a rather weak glow, and none in fog.

It is not a coincidence that St Andrew's Church in Fairlight, Sussex is common to the fifteenth-century portolans of both Mediterranean and Baltic mariners although there was no appreciable landing place; it marked passage on a journey. It was a prominent, visible seamark – and it is no coincidence that St Andrew, the very first apostle and brother of St Peter, both fishermen, himself became the patron saint of fishermen. Similarly, a tower on the Isle of Thanet is mentioned in Michael of Rhodes' portolan. It was almost certainly a church tower.[48] A tiny chapel stands on the cliffs at the inaccessible promontory of St Aldhelm's Head in Dorset, the rocky headland being the lowering seamark. It is mentioned on the fifteenth-century portolans listed above as a landscape feature, one of a long row along the south coast, but not the chapel, so the later tradition that it originally bore a light but later became a chapel is not easily proven. Its very inaccessibility on foot, even today, tends to militate against any ease of maintenance as a light. It remains a breathtaking elevated coastal location, even if it holds questionable value as a lighthouse.

At Ilfracombe in north Devon, and on a much smaller scale, there was (and is) a pleasant seaside town with its own fishing fleet. There lay one of the few English 'lighthouses' for which there is ample evidence, if only in the form of a small chapel on the eponymous 'Lantern Hill' which maintained a candle in its window to guide fishermen to harbour in failing light. On its other side lie rocks. Now a private house, the position is clearly

A Permanent Heavy Swell

Ilfracombe, North Devon: top left is the Lantern House, formerly a chapel, perched on Lantern Hill between the harbour entrance and the open sea. Here in the safe harbour the *Julyan* of Brittany was set upon. Photo by Walton Hudson (c. 1958).

a guiding beacon on which to steer, indicating to keep left for the harbour. Imagine the horror of the crew of the *Julyan* of Brittany, safely guided in this way but then attacked in the assured safety of the harbour by an English ship in 1483.[49] Ilfracombe harbour has a higher tidal range than anywhere around the Bristol Channel. Entry for the unwary could be a dangerous trap with the tide on the ebb. The *Julyan* may have sealed its own fate just by entering with no quick exit possible.

On the same coast is the Huer's hut at Newquay. It may have begun as a lighthouse or beacon as early as the fourteenth century and is on a similar, domestic scale to the Ilfracombe Lantern House. By the sixteenth century it became a lookout to follow the pilchard shoals along the Bristol Channel, directing the fishing fleet towards them.

At the western tip of Brittany lie two early lighthouses, probably built as much to warn of English raids as to alert ships to the rocky shore. One lies at the Pointe de Penmarc'h, raided by the English in 1403. The other is on another of Britanny's rocky promontories,

Seas of Plenty

The Huer's hut, Newquay, Cornwall, before modern conservation. Photo by Walton Hudson (*c.* 1958).

the Pointe St Mathieu, where a medieval four-square hulk of a stone building stands beside the ruins of the Benedictine church of St Mathieu, whose monks originally manned the light.

Recognition was key for ships at sea. Today we recognise certain flags flown by modern shipping, such as the White Ensign for Britain's Royal Navy, and the Red Ensign for British merchantmen. In early navigational maps countries often bears their national flag as a matter of recognition – for England the cross of St George, seen flying from the mainmast on Tudor ships. There is also the issue of 'flags of convenience' and the reader will recall how fifteenth-century masters could swap vessels in the Baltic to make the most of different cities' trading privileges at destination ports. We have seen how a Venetian galley that carried Felix Fabri was decked out in an array of flags that shouted out its allegiances – to church, state and family. When in convoy the Venetians used flags in a form of semaphore to keep station and ensure there were no collisions at sea or sudden taking of another's wind. At night this

A Permanent Heavy Swell

Above left: Pointe de Penmarc'h; *above right*: Pointe St Mathieu, both Finisterre (29), France. Both late medieval so-called lighthouses, since replaced (2006).

was replaced with a system of lanterns – running lights – varied in their placing and numbering, each agreed to send a special fleet commander's message to each member of the convoy, even down to 'Send a boat with your captain – I am convening an on-board conference on the flagship'.

But the problem with all these was that they were private signals. Only those in one's own pay, Venetian or otherwise, understood them. The same might be true for lights, such as the lights kept burning at the harbours of the Baltic members of the Hanse (and again shown on the map of Olaus Magnus) or the few occasions where we know lights were kept burning in crowded waterways, such as on the mid-stream islands in the Danish Sound off Helsingør. These were simply guides and pointers to keep the procession of ships moving along a bottleneck created by the Danes for levying tolls.

These hints at a maritime language were often unintelligible, then, and an absence of recognition could be disastrous, as Felix Fabri relates:

> ... to the port of the Colossus, which is in front of the city of Rhodes. It was night, about nine o'clock in the evening, and we could see whither we were going clearly, thanks to the brightness of the moon. When we attempted to enter the harbour, and our sailors were, after their fashion, noisily labouring to trim the sails, the people ashore lighted beacons on their towers, and made a great disturbance running to and fro on the walls, thinking us to be their enemies the Turks, and they alarmed us much by firing a big cannon at us. In great terror we also lit many lights and stood on the deck of the galley begging them not to hurt us, for that we were marked with the sign of the cross, and friends of Him crucified, whose enemies we knew well had but a short time before been laid low in this very place. When the guards of the harbour heard this, they turned away the engines which they had prepared to cast great stones at us and unstrung their bows.

It is for similar reasons that the Venetians on the Flanders-and-England run were instructed to keep their bows strung on entering port. It gave real meaning to 'Who goes there?' 'Advance and be recognised!'

Shipwreck, of course, continued at an alarming rate. For the unfortunate drowned who were washed ashore, there was usually a decent burial. There are several such graves in numerous coastal churchyards around the country, such as some notable nineteenth-century examples at Lydd in East Sussex. In late medieval England the cargoes of such wrecks, washed onto the strand or fished from the rocks, whether spoiled or not, were the property of the Crown, usually via the local lord – whoever held the local coastal manor on whose shore the flotsam and jetsam was cast. In notable cases the 'rights of wreck' were granted as a boon to a monastery, such as the Benedictines of Abbotsbury and Frampton in Dorset, Spalding in Lincolnshire or Wymondham in Norfolk, and also the Austin canons at Beeston in Norfolk and Breamore and Twynham in Hampshire. These all had 'rights of wreck' or 'tithes of wreck' granted to them, giving them the responsibility for searching wrecks, retrieving beached cargo, burying the dead and salvaging anything which might have any enduring value. The majority would still go to the king but a portion, the so-called tithe, would be retained by the monastery. Since in some cases monasteries also had responsibilities for maintaining coastal beacons, the awful prospect of the unscrupulous enticing the unwary onto the rocks with misleading lights is barely to be contemplated.

Even when wrecks, by their very nature, happened in filthy weather or at night, when no one had any business being out and about, word of their aftermath still spread abroad and found its way to official channels, however isolated their location. In 1402 a royal commission was set up to investigate a 'barge' with an Irish master bound for Genoa, laden with copper, tin, cloth of Lynn and other things including wool and merchandise, which set out around 1397 and was wrecked on the Isles of Scilly. A very mixed cargo, this would have been of particular interest to the Crown, not just because of the dues to be paid to the Exchequer on the wool and cloth but because the king himself held the rights to all tin-trading out of England. As ever, the king had the last word.

11

THE RISE OF AN ENGLISH MERCHANT FLEET

The English are very powerful at sea.
Venetian secretary in England, 1551

The English merchant fleet in the fifteenth century apparently lacked little compared to its continental neighbours except for larger, more robust vessels such as those Florence and Venice possessed –and, at first, comparable numbers, although shipbuilding was very much a growth industry at the start of the century. Smaller English ships were already numerous in the Baltic in the fourteenth century, there being allegedly 300 English vessels in Danzig alone in 1392.[1] The much-vaunted technological advances creeping north in the form of the Mediterranean lateen-rigged caravel, gradually supplanting – or at least influencing – the northern European cog and carrack designs were probably merely academic to the master of a leaky crayer out of Sandwich and running to Yorkshire once a month for sea coal or acting as a fare-coaster out of Hythe to Calais and back. Despite the obvious shortcomings, by the end of the fifteenth century English ships were seen as far north as the Lofoten Islands.

The Rise of an English Merchant Fleet

Although there were no commercial shipping lines or carriers such as we might understand today, there were dotted around small fleets which did sail under single family ownership. Thus, in the early 1480s, the Celys family plied the seas via their six ships out of at least five different east coast ports from Kent to East Yorkshire.[2] Likewise, the Canynges family dominated Bristol's trade for a generation. Nevertheless, many English merchants continued for generations to use foreign carriers, such as the fabulously wealthy Stephen Browne (d. 1463), who had the excuse of living almost next door to the Hanseatic Steelyard on Thames Street, London, where he kept a sumptuous house running down to the Thames, with its own wharf and crane. In 1438-39 he imported grain from Danzig in his Hanseatic neighbour's ships, saving London from famine when England's crops failed.[3]

Scattered references in continental archives put English vessels trading in the Mediterranean as early as the 1380s and 1390s. They were at Genoa and Ibiza in 1412 and off Morocco and Barbary regularly from the 1460s, when Edward IV is known to have been seeking a share of the Barbary market. There was sent a huge amount of our woollen cloth, usually under an Italian flag.[4] Robert Sturmy's pilgrimage ship out of Bristol was lost returning from the Near East in the mid-fifteenth century. Carus-Wilson, considering later fifteenth-century trade in and out of Bristol, suggested that 'it could be argued that John Cabot came to Bristol not to beguile simple provincials but to pick local brains'. In 1535 the Swedes impounded English vessels to prevent their use by a hostile Lübeck, while in the 1540s Spain was complaining of English attacks on their shipping lanes. In 1553 it was said that the French were basing their warship designs on those of the English. This reflected massive advances since the beginning of the century. How times had changed!

Edward IV knew the growing value of England having its own ships on which to rely, rather than foreign carriers. However, he was strapped for cash so in 1474 he went so far as to offer rewards to anyone who would build one. Two years later, true to his word, he rewarded a London mercer who had built a ship at his own expense – the *George Cobham*. On at least one occasion, Edward equipped at his own expense a vessel to go to Porto Pisano, where it was called 'the nef of the King of England'.[5]

A good ship might be expected to give twenty to thirty years' service if regularly maintained. Even leaking, rotten hulks, well past their best, continued in service and ships which stayed afloat seemingly by just prayer and luck continued to be competitively bought and sold. Renewing a mast, re-caulking seams, careening the hull or re-rigging might give an old ship another lucrative voyage. Eventually they were all either lost at sea or beached, where they then rotted, often dismantled for their reusable parts.

English trading fleets of all values, however well insured, often needed protection and 'keeping the seas' became an annual consideration as the fifteenth century wore on.[6] By the 1470s,

A typical end. A more recent vessel beached at Portbail, Normandy, Manche (50), France (2022).

The Rise of an English Merchant Fleet

armed merchantmen even accompanied the wool ships to Calais and Bruges. The Patent Rolls between 1476 and 1485 indicate that fishing fleets in the North Sea and off Iceland were accompanied by warships, a scenario re-enacted even in the 1970s during the so-called 'Cod Wars' with Iceland. 'Armed' is a relative term since most had few or no guns. There were rarely battles on the high seas, rather the skirmishes were at the mouths of harbours and estuaries, or even at anchorages where the quarry lacked sufficient wind for an escape. Control – and then only brief – was either wrested by way of a hefty (and very dangerous) shove or, if necessary, boarding with grappling hooks and a shower of crossbow bolts.

In practice, the effects of seakeeping were only brief. Real damage could only be done by turning such maritime protection into punitive coastal raids – organised piracy, as has been examined above. For those who might feel they did not need protection, a merchantman could in fact turn to piracy or privateering on a whim, perhaps taking a lead from foreign examples.[7] Otherwise, when some sea lanes became too dangerous, a merchant might adopt a flag of convenience. For instance, when the Baltic proved particularly difficult to access during the fifteenth century, English merchants sometimes took part-ownership of Hanseatic craft. In this way the *St Andrew* of Lübeck happened also to be the *Pretence* of London.[8] If this was not a pun, then it was as close as a merchant might get to thumbing his nose at the Baltic port authorities!

Whether deliberately or in acts of unthinking petulance, the English had an unnerving ability to disrupt the trade of others, dominating as they did the 'English' Channel.[9] During the principal reign of Henry VI (1422–60), over half of English trade was with Burgundy and this hardly fell away during the first reign of Edward IV (1460–71). England had the power to disrupt the trade of the Duke of Burgundy's territories (including Bruges) and a threat to the duchy's supply lines was a threat to its existence. This was most keenly felt when Edward IV, as brother-in-law to the duke, was hounded into a brief exile at Bruges in 1471 and Henry VI retook the throne, albeit shakily as a mere puppet. Edward's presence at Bruges, initially (and very properly) welcomed as a family member, quickly became an embarrassment as Bruges tried to continue trading with Henry's England on the same terms as if the court-in-exile did not exist.[10] Edward, appreciated as a learned and cultured king who conducted himself with decorum, was given a rapturous public send-off from Bruges as he returned with a Burgundian army to reclaim his throne. It was, however, a farewell tinged with relief at Bruges as 'free' trade resumed.

A prime example of a reliable English ship which gave at least the expected quarter-century's service was the *Trinity* of Bristol. In service on a route that took it to France, Spain and Portugal, it also visited North Africa and was in service from at least 1464. Surviving documents, particularly the ship's purser's accounts, tell of its routes and cargoes until 1481.[11]

With a burden of roughly 300 tons, the *Trinity* was among the biggest and best of Bristol's own shipping, carrying a crew of twenty-eight. On 14 October 1480, this ageing but reliable ship left Kingroad for Spain with an outbound cargo of which we know very little, save that it included a small number of cloths carried just for its young purser, John Balsall.

In the wake of England's loss of Bordeaux in 1453, the *Trinity*, along with all other English ships, had to seek specific French licence to trade in Aquitaine, almost certainly on the wine run. The crew was fortunate to receive papers, and in March 1466, perhaps finding French wine too difficult a commodity, the *Trinity* was clearly venturing further south when it returned from Lisbon on the first of numerous voyages of up to six months at a time, unloading 90 tons of salt, 66 tuns of (Portuguese) wine, 30 tuns of olive oil, 14 tuns of fruit (probably dried figs in time for Easter),

5 tons of wax and small consignments of dyeing grain, honey, soap, sugar, vinegar and resin.

In May 1466 the *Trinity* was off again, back to Lisbon, laden with 700 cloths – an enormous amount for an English ship (from what records we have). In September 1470, it made the same journey with a much smaller cloth cargo. In 1472–73 at Bristol it unloaded wine, oil, soap and dyeing grain. Later, in 1479–80, it unloaded 76 tuns of wine, 182 tuns of olive oil and 3 tons each of sugar and wax along with a variety of small consignments, the property of no less than ninety-nine different shippers, thereby spreading the cost and the risk.

The *Trinity*'s outward route took it from Bristol to Minehead to pick up crew, on to Milford Haven and possibly Haverfordwest and then to Kinsale in Ireland, a town which did a flourishing trade with Bristol. Striking south, the crew then negotiated the Bay of Biscay and went on to Huelva in Andalusia, where they stayed four or five weeks before stopping at Puerto de Santa Maria and Gibraltar, where they took on a pilot and headed through the treacherous currents of the straits where Atlantic meets Mediterranean. From there it reached Oran, where there was a flourishing group of European merchants led by the Genoese, but with groups of Venetians, Spanish and Provençal French, importing northern European and English cloth and exporting cotton, sugar, pottery, silk and coral.

On the return leg the *Trinity* called once more at Puerto de Santa Maria where it was beached and heeled over for careening and re-caulking; it was about to re-enter the Atlantic, so it needed all the sleek, clean lines it could to make good speed. All ships needed to do this periodically and it seems many English ships regularly called there for this purpose. With at least some of the crew ashore, there may have been 'personnel problems', perhaps a bar room fracas, since the purser made payments for 'costs of the court'. Such problems were far from limited to one nation; in 1451, for instance, the Venetians had to make recompense for 'an outrage' committed in a convent in Lisbon by members of the Flanders galleys.[12] At sea once more, the vessel called at Palos and then made one last stop for supplies at the Berlingos Islands (off Cape Carvoeiro) before making for Bristol again via Kinsale.

Of course, the further English ships ventured, the more likely they were to be exposed to piracy and ambush. The Venetian consul at Naples reported in 1514 that an English ship, fully laden with merchandise, had been taken by Turks off Livorno. Given their own experiences, both in the Mediterranean and in the English Channel, it is unlikely that the Venetians even raised an eyebrow.[13]

A Census of Ships

In 1524–25, Henry VIII was wrapped up in widespread preparations to invade France (which in the end came to nothing). His paranoia at this time about *them* invading *us* gave him the opportunity to commission surveys of what support he could expect and where it lay, hoping to use such findings to bolster his naval power.

One of these surveys was a list of the trading ships that he could call upon – an embryonic merchant navy. It is preserved in the British Library, part of a volume which, although damaged by fire in the eighteenth century, survives well enough to let us assess the dispositions and tonnages around some of the country. It is a curious document, and the ships named may be just those that happened to be in port at the time.[14] I have preserved the subheadings of the document:

[Shypes of Southampton] The *Gret Galey*, 800 tons; The *Mary Koste*; The *Peter Pomgarnet*; The *St Nicolas*; The *Lesser Barke*, 180 tons; The *Katheryn Forster*; The *Mary George*; The *Swepstake*; The *Swallow*, 240 tons.

The Rise of an English Merchant Fleet

Schypes of London The *Mary Grace*; The *Mary Gloria*, 300 tons; The *Margaret Bonaventure*, 190 tons; The *Nicolas Drap*, 180 tons; The *Swift*, 180 tons; The *Christopher Davy*, 160 tons; The *Christopher Adrian*, 150 tons; The *George Stoye*, 120 tons, The *Maudeleyn*, 120 tons; The *Mary Grace Heneage*, 110 tons; The *Lyvernand Schipp*, 110 tons; The *Harry Tothill*, 90 tons; The *Powes*, 90 tons; The *Powle*, 80 tons; The *Date Prow*, 70 tons.

Shippes of Brestow The *newe shipp*, 200 tons; The *Mary Towers*, 160 tons; The *Mathew*, 130 tons; The *Edwarde*, 110 tons

Then follow 12 lines (each one a named ship) that are illegible due to damage to the manuscript. It takes up thereafter:

S[hippes of Gippe]swyck [Ipswich] The *Barbara*, 100 tons; The *Edward*, 100 tons; The *James*, 90 tons; The *John Evangeliste*, 80 tons; The *Nicholas Cornelis*, 75 tons; The *Mary Shipp*, 76 tons; The *John Peter Fermor*, 70 tons

Yarmouth The *Mary* [of Lynn], 70 tons; The *George* (of Blakeney Haven), 110 tons; The *Peter*, 90 tons; The *Mary*, 80 tons

Lynn The *John* [of Patrington?]; The *Mary James*, 80 tons; The *Trinity*, 100 tons; My Lord Wyldys Barke, 70 tons; The *Antony* of Mr Palmard, 60 tons; The *James* [of Boston], 80 tons; The *Thomas* [of Hull], 100 tons

Although incomplete, the list is a useful snapshot. It is hardly systematic, since it takes no account of what was at sea at the time, either outward or returning, but it does record what are clearly coasters, visiting from another English port nearby. Some ships belong privately to members of the nobility or are foreign vessels (Nicolas

Cornelis) or are foreign owned (Wyldys), both probably being Dutch Easterlings. Whatever the survey's shortcomings, it represents a slice of the merchant navy tied up in some of the principal ports on the south and east coast on one day in 1524. Others are in fact warships already part of Henry VIII's fleet from at least 1518.

The usefulness of these new-found ships needed to be exploited. Henry might need them at any moment if an invasion of France was to take place. Thus, a system was devised in which each newly inventoried vessel would be joined in a threesome with another two vessels, usually warships on the 1518 list (and others that had since been built or co-opted). Each would act as a supply-and-stores ship – a *'vittelar'* (victualler) – in a manner that presaged the modern Royal Fleet Auxiliaries which today operate out of Falmouth (RFA Bay Class vessels). The smallest ship noted was the *Hynde* (24 tons) and, but for a few of 40–60 tons, most were 75 tons or more, many well over 100 tons. These were seemingly either balingers or larger ships with proven oceangoing capabilities. Two, the *Baptiste* of Harwich and the *Barbara* of Ipswich (100 tons), are noted as 'St Andrew Ships', which suggests they were fishing boats. But the absence of small vessels, such as crayers, suggests that for the most part local coasters and ferries were left uncounted in their home ports, carrying out their usual runs. To split responsibilities, the ships – probably plus their *vittelars* – were divided to take responsibility for the summer months (ten vessels) and the winter months (ten vessels), probably to allow for a repair season. This was certainly a step forward for the navy, but it took some very capable merchant ships out of the business of trading for who knew how long. Unwittingly (or very consciously but without remorse), Henry was hampering the good offices of a generation of England's home-grown traders and shippers.

In this way the *Barbara* out of Yarmouth (100 tons) became *vittelar* to the *Gabriell Royall* (600 tons), plus forty mariners, while the identically named *Barbara*, out of Ipswich (100 tons), became *vittelar* to the *Nicholas* out of Southampton (possibly 180 tons) and the *Swallow* (240 tons) plus thirty mariners. The question now arises, however – were they merchant ships or were they warships? For a while they might serve two masters – commerce and the navy. Ultimately, they were whatever the king wanted them to be. It was all his business.

The Flanders Galleys Affair[15]

> *You must accommodate us with these galleys of yours for this expedition of ours.*
> Chancellor of Charles V to the Venetians, 8 June 1522

In a bid to add depth to his supply and transport capabilities, Henry VIII, just like his father before him, looked beyond his own merchant shipping to that of his trading partners. Whether he was being practical, avaricious or petulant is a moot point, and while he ran the risk of alienating those partners, those who remained in English waters were already by this time in dire financial straits. He ran the risk of tipping them over the edge.

The problem emerged not in England, but in mid-Biscay, on St Nicholas Eve (6 December) 1521, when the Flanders galleys, out late in the year, were caught in a storm. Two of them, veering west, made Plymouth but the third, under Captain Antonio Donato, was blown well off course and put in at St Sebastian, France. There the Donato galley, as it became known, was impounded by the hostile French, who confiscated its sail, rudder and guns. This news reached Plymouth just after Christmas. By the end of January 1522, Henry VIII threatened to seize Biscayan ships and merchandise if the galley was not released. Although it got its sails, rudder and guns back it was then blockaded in port by as many as nineteen vessels. It was eventually allowed to depart, but only after four months, arriving in Southampton in May. That was just the beginning.

The English king proceeded at the end of May to Dover with his special guest, the Emperor Charles V, King of Spain, to inspect his new flagship, the *Henry Grace à Dieu*. He wished to honour his guest (and thus Spain) with a lavish send-off, to include all three of the Flanders galleys, crewed by Englishmen (and a few Venetians). The galleys were by this time fully laden at Southampton and in no fit state to act as extravagant royal barges propelled by inexpert seamen speaking a different language to their Adriatic counterparts. Cardinal Wolsey seemed to suggest a compromise: the galleys would simply accompany the royal party as far as Brest as an armed convoy escort, past hostile northern French ports. The Venetians objected to both ideas, noting the need to unload, cross the Channel, return and reload before departing.

When the emperor's sympathetic chancellor clearly agreed with Henry, the Venetians unloaded and made ready, setting their cargoes aside in Southampton warehouses, but no sooner had they done this than Henry had their guns removed and transferred to English ships nearby. All three galleys, 600 tons apiece, remained embargoed as letters went to and fro between the three protagonists and the Venetians, who were trying to remain unbiased. Fearing a yawning lacuna in the remnants of their maritime wool trade, the Venetians made a rare concession to allow their cargoes from England to be shipped overland at reduced freight costs or in other continental ships.

In September it was first noted that bored, impecunious Venetian crewmen were beginning to drift away, despite (or perhaps because of) the delights of Southampton. Absconding rowers had, however, always been a problem to Venice, while they kicked their heels in a foreign port. However, it was also noted that Cardinal Wolsey was also placing restrictions on all exports, regardless of the carrier, to deny the Venetians any opportunity and keep up the pressure. The Venetians were beginning to get very worried, and in November the Doge himself wrote to both Henry and Wolsey. Early in the new year, 1523, Venice seemed helpless as it noted France was reputed to be preparing to send a fleet to the Far East to bring back spices, pulling the rug from under Venetian feet. This may have been alarmist diplomacy, since it would suggest to Henry that his enemy France might wrest control of the spice trade, in which case England would lose out. England, of course, knew well they could get their spices at this stage from Antwerp or Lisbon; if the Venetians believed their own propaganda, then they were deluding themselves that they still had any real control as they had once known it.

The impasse continued, and as the situation relating to France receded – the French king being ill and inclined to make peace – some movement seemed to be forthcoming. Rumours of the impending release of the galleys began to circulate in March, including repairs which were necessary after their extended overwintering without proper attention. The crews had apparently mostly departed (although this was so regular a complaint that it suggests most were still around) and they were only left with half their guns. Meanwhile Venice sought to get its stored wool purchases shipped out in six vessels of other nationalities, including Ragusan, Florentine and Genoese, but of these ships two were said to have foundered at sea (for which there was no evidence), two were said to have run aground and been wrecked (equally lacking evidence), one put back into Southampton unable to make headway against adverse winds, and the sixth was detained in Brittany. These were likely tall stories designed to elicit sympathy. In fact, it seems that everything remained in the warehouses in Southampton since it was announced at the beginning of June that the galleys would again be laden and released by the middle of that month.

On the 22 June 1523, the galleys, newly released and repaired, lay off St Edward's on the east coast of Southampton Water,

Netley Abbey, Southampton, Hampshire. For generations all comers would have followed a familiar Cistercian Latin Mass here where they were habitually given hospitality (2023).

perhaps to pick up their remaining crew. On the 30th, after a year and a half as political pawns, they finally set sail.[16]

Venice continued to trade, of course, and the English operation still seemed to be in rude health, since in 1526 it bailed out its financially embarrassed Beirut counterpart, which was in huge debt. In 1525 an embargo was laid upon all foreign vessels in English ports, followed by the detention of all ships and vessels so that they could be used to take troops to France. Although late in 1525–26 the Treaty of Richmond brought a temporary end to all the Anglo-French sabre-rattling, Venice's trading base had been irreparably damaged at a time when few could afford the financial discomfort and the breach of trust. Although the Venetians did eventually return in 1530, their dealings with England had been soured, and in financial terms they were forced to ever row harder. The last Venetian state fleet left England in 1533.

Endings and Continuity

It has been my choice to draw this book to a close around 1540. The reasons for this are numerous. Of course, all history goes on, and there is continuity everywhere, so there wasn't so much an end as a series of economic downturns which must have felt like something was seriously wrong across England, if not Europe too. John Leland noted it in a dozen or more places. The world – and England with it – was changing, and the marketplace was no different. Trade never stopped, of course, only evolved, and at that time drastically so, at a time when seemingly everything about England was shifting and old certainties were disappearing. Links with Europe continued but were perhaps less well defined. Families continued old allegiances, not least among a staunchly Catholic recusant community.

Xenophobia certainly never ceased, although the focus of English ire shifted eventually from France to Spain in the reigns of Mary and Elizabeth I, despite French spies being ever-present. Foreign traders in English ports, especially from Catholic countries, continued to be wary of their safety. The Protestant Reformation left England with a renewed northern European feeling, hostile to the Catholic south, just as the same wave broke over northern France, Flanders and the Netherlands, redrawing borders across the Channel along religious lines and driving Protestant refugees to England in their droves.

On a trading basis, by 1540 the Italians no longer sent their state vessels to England, although the Venetians had lingered and stuttered until 1533, long deprived of their spice monopoly. The Florentines and Genoese had stopped coming a generation before. Each was under pressure at home and abroad. Those were the state-owned fleets, of course – private merchants continued to run the risks, as they had always done – the last private Venetian vessel trading for wool out of Southampton was to sink off the Isle of Wight in 1587.

The Hanseatic League had been largely left trailing by the emergence of new markets, not least in the New World. It failed to adapt as the markets moved south and east – to Antwerp, Nuremburg and Basel among others – away from England. The league continued to trade formally in England for only a few more years.

When Henry VIII broke from Rome in 1534, he brought the entire English nation into disrepute in the eyes of the Catholic Church – and in the obedient eyes and ears of Europe's royal houses. Furthermore, Henry's Dissolution of the Monasteries in 1536–39 robbed England and Wales of some 800 monastic establishments whose commerce had – for centuries – been a prime mover in local economies across the land, thereby stripping communities of long-established landowners, ready building sites, places of learning, discerning consumers, shipowners and travellers, and importers of vast quantities of wine and fish especially. Although finances had been strained for a while, not least for the Cistercians, they had all been an integral part of the establishment – no more. Their ultimate allegiance was to Rome, and that now became their undoing. Ironically, we know that at the start of the run of demolitions, in 1537–38, Thomas Cromwell was guided by Giovanni Portinari, an Italian chief engineer, to demolish one of the bigger monastic churches at Lewes Priory (Cluniac), perhaps to show the English how it might be done!

From the 1520s, England's many provincial towns were increasingly falling on hard times, not helped by crop failures at the start of that decade and a further visit of the plague in 1525. For some a deep economic malaise had commenced even earlier. The writings of John Leland show this was plain in many a high street, whether inland or at the ports, home to some 25 per cent of the country's population. In the 1540s a pamphlet called 'Discourse of the Commonweal' noted that decay beset the majority of all the towns of England, except for London. An Act of Parliament in 1540 called for the re-edifying of such towns. It listed, among others, Canterbury, Chichester, Colchester, Coventry, Hereford, Northampton, Oxford, Rochester, Salisbury, Southampton, Stafford, Winchester and Worcester. So many had held monastic houses at their heart. London alone, the only true cosmopolitan city in the land, had the strength in depth to hold its own. Much provincial port trade shifted to the capital, to the further detriment of those provincial harbour towns.

Thus, many ports failed to escape the downward spiral. When he visited Bridgwater in the early 1540s, John Leland noted: 'There hath faullen yn ruine and sore decay above 200 houses yn the ttoun of Bridgwater in tyme of rememberaunce.'[17] The reader will have noted a similar fate at Boston and others on the east coast, increasingly shorn of their Hanseatic links.

Coventry, 'beloved of merchants', is a perfect example of the downturn, although even here there were individual plots and perhaps even enclaves which felt it less acutely. Landlocked at the heart of the kingdom, the city had risen to its unusual political and economic prominence during the fifteenth century. It had hosted three sessions of parliament, in 1403, 1456 and 1460. In the whole period covered by this book, Leicester was the only other city to achieve this expensive accolade, and then only once, in 1414. Ever a Lancastrian city, Coventry voted regular financial help to the increasingly cash-strapped Henry VI and the city enjoyed its heyday on his watch. It was at the centre of anti-Italian agitation, although it lived by Italian-carried woad and alum for its cloth. Although Edward IV was much cooler toward the city than Henry had been, he honoured it by holding his 1467 Christmas Court in its Benedictine cathedral priory.

Plague hit the city hard in 1468 and 1475. Occupied by Warwick the Kingmaker, the city was briefly invested by Edward IV in 1471, but he backed off as the city was described as 'strong and well-walled' in that year. When its trade exporting sky-blue cloth nosedived, its alum supply gone, the Yorkist crown failed to help. When Henry Tudor won his crown at Bosworth in 1485, Coventry clamoured to be the first to welcome this Lancastrian victory and entertained the new king lavishly. But the Tudor dynasty put an end to the Wars of the Roses and Coventry's former partisan support became irrelevant. John Leland wrote of the city: 'The towne rose by makynge of clothe and capps, that now decayenge the glory of the city decayethe.'[18]

In a lay subsidy in the 1520s it had over 500 houses lying empty against a population of about 6,000. In 1525, another plague year, Coventry rebelled and Cardinal Wolsey was licensed to put down the insurrection, which he did without mercy. In the ultimate renter's market, tenants could simply threaten to move to an empty property and rents tumbled. The 12-metre-wide, 3-metre-deep city ditch, representing half the city's defences, was filled with rubbish in this period as civic pride gave way, insistent instructions to clean it out being ignored. Similar ordure is known to have affected even London's ditch, nicknamed Houndsditch due to all the dead dogs thrown in, and that of Southampton, which ran with raw sewage.[19] The realm was ailing badly.

The Dissolution of the Monasteries was a dire body blow to many urban centres, by then experiencing rampant inflation. Most towns and cities lost at least one monastery, exacerbating the existing downward trend. Some had been avid consumers of foreign goods to the end, as had their civic fathers who, by 1540, fell into ruin. Even major marketplaces became squalid and noisome, such as that at Peterborough, for which both documentary and archaeological evidence is in full agreement.[20] The situation was little different in other towns – some had begun a steep decline much earlier, in the fifteenth century. When looked at in detail, the reasons for each are varied and the words expended by historians and archaeologists numerous, not all in

The Rise of an English Merchant Fleet

agreement. Some urban plots, blocks and whole urban streets were allowed to fall into total decay before anything like a resurgence can be discerned many decades later. The mid-sixteenth century was a pivot around which English urban fortunes turned. Only London prospered throughout, partially carrying the rest into a new, post-medieval world.[21]

Changes to the seashore ruined countless ports as silt and shingle blocked harbours, havens and inlets. Sandwich, Rye, Winchelsea and Chester fought and lost, as did the undoubted queen of the European port markets, Bruges, when in 1520 a great storm threw thousands of tons of sand across its approaches and blocked off trade via the Zwin forever. Although Antwerp had already assumed its mantle to some extent, Bruges went into a long sleep. A few ports, like Yarmouth, battled on. Some, like Boston, would eventually see a resurgence, but not for some time.

Meanwhile, Henry VIII remained fearful of a French invasion. His chain of artillery castles and fortlets along the south and east coasts stands as a reminder of his distrust of his neighbours, but alongside this in the 1540s he pressed most of the English merchant fleet into military service. It marked the end of their distinct late medieval trading years and the beginning of a period of anti-continental (or anti-Catholic) antagonism that started with the Crown and filtered down to the populace, ending perhaps only in Drake's defeat of the Spanish Armada under Queen Elizabeth in 1588. That famous, weather-assisted victory did at least ensure that, as the *Libelle* had once encouraged, we were for the moment 'maysters of the narrowe see'.

The economic malaise which affected much of England in the mid-sixteenth century was by no means universal. The uppermost echelons of society remained relatively unaffected, or at least maintained an outward show that little was amiss. In July 1517, only a few months after the great riots across London against foreigners, Henry VIII held a welcome procession and reception for a visit by the King of Spain. No expense was spared and the meal to which the assembled company sat down lasted for seven hours. At the end of it, Francesco Chieregato, apostolic nuncio in England, who partook of the banquet but seemingly also witnessed the riots, wrote to the Marchioness of Mantua and concluded his letter: 'The wealth and civilization of the world are here: and those who call the English barbarians appear to me to render themselves such. I here perceive very elegant manners, extreme decorum, and very great politeness.'[22]

Henry knew how to put on a good show. It is gratifying to realise that the people of this island, despite some utterly questionable welcomes to visitors and trading partners, could occasionally make a half-decent impression. After all, the show must go on.

NOTES

Introduction

1. The poetry beginning each chapter has two origins: *The Faber Book of Modern Verse*, ed. Michael Roberts (1936), and *The Collected Poems of John Masefield* (1930). And William Shakespeare, of course.
2. Hugely entertaining and to be found in Stewart (1896), digitised at https://archive.org/stream/libraryofpalestio7paleuoft/libraryofpalestio7uoft_djvu.txt All further references to Fabri's observations relate to this energetic and extremely useful translation.
3. It is hereafter simply called 'the *Libelle*'. I have chosen to retain the original text with the author's distinctive spellings. They are quaint but broadly understandable.
4. Lines 1-4.
5. The reader is directed to the likes of Hutchinson (1994), Greenhill (1995), Martin (2001), Flatman (2009) and Adams (2013) if ship design and development is of prime importance to their enquiry.
6. A useful introduction to excavated wharf-side remains may be found in Steane (1984, 131ff), although much has been added since publication.

7. The *Libelle* was originally published in the Rolls Series in 1861 by Thomas Wright. Editions have since appeared in 1907 (Everyman's Library) and 1926 (Sir George Warner). Extracts of the relevant sections are quoted in this book in their original English.
8. Lines 5-7.
9. Lines 1092–6.
10. Lines 630-1.
11. See Soden (2005) for archaeology here.
12. The epithet by Simon FitzSimon/Simeonis, a well-travelled Irish Franciscan friar.

1 Movers and Shakers

1. For which see Seymour 1963.
2. For an overview of travel in all its forms in the Middle Ages, see Ohler 2010.
3. Legassie 2017, 173-4, quoting Petrarch, for which see Fantham 2017.
4. Scammell 1969, 389-90.
5. In part giving rise to huge respect for China and its measured, long view – ibid., 392-3.
6. Op. cit., 391.
7. Boxer 1969, 31.
8. Manning 1991, 89-90 & 38 with n129.
9. Long et al. 2009, vol 2, 611, 613, 617.
10. Cairo Genizah T-S Ar.41.81.
11. Long 2009, 44.
12. The tomb may have been moved from elsewhere in Southampton. See Rose 2007, 153 and n17.
13. Dulley 1966, 104; Holmes 1961, 208 n1.
14. Lines 818-9.
15. See below. For the original Latin letter, Talbot 1967. For more on Lazarus see Chapter 11.
16. Harris 1935, xxii.
17. Carus Wilson 1967, 92-3.
18. Williamson 1913, 455.

Notes

19. Brown 1864, docs 580, 1340.
20. Neale 2000, 235 [418]. Although John Harvey notably published William Worcestre's *Itineraries* (1969), I am particularly indebted to Frances Neale for her noteworthy scholarship and translation of William Worcestre's scattered and disjointed notes on his time in Bristol, never written up in his generation.
21. Brown 1864, 750, 752.
22. Parry 1967, 42.
23. Boxer 1969, 21-2.
24. For more detail, see Hampden 1970.
25. Power 1937, 136.
26. Neale 2000, 263 additional leaves p10 [441].
27. Exwood and Lehmann 1993, 103.
28. Neale 2000, 141 [246].
29. Nichols 1854, 78.
30. Devon 1837, 341-2, 348 and Hardy 1835, 320ff (where the name of the master, vessel type, its name and home port of every ship requisitioned is given, from Barnstaple to Scarborough; Dordrecht, Haarlem, Middelburg etc.). For anyone interested specifically in medieval ships – all by name – this second source is a revelation.
31. Shakespeare: Henry V, Act III Prologue.
32. Nicholas 1830 (1972 facsimile), xcix-c.
33. Devon 1837, 402-3.
34. Devon 1837, 474 (31 Henry VI – 1453).
35. Devon 1837, 373 (10 Henry V – 1422).
36. See Daubney (2009); also West Midlands Archaeology for a typical find 53 (2011, 37-8).
37. Brown 1864, doc 209.
38. Brown 1864, doc 298.
39. Ross 1975, 351. Ross is a hugely valuable and understandable source for Edward IV's reign, just as Griffiths (1981) is for Henry VI.
40. Halliwell 1839.
41. A description by Polydore Vergil (for which see Soden 2013, 56).
42. Ross 1975, 386.

43. For the Breton exile see Soden (2013) or, with greater context, Sara Elin Roberts (2015).
44. Horrox 1987, 213.
45. See Chapter 11.
46. The so-called 'Device' castles, for which see Morley (1976).

2 'Cherysshe marchandyse'

1. Lines 53-63, 70-79.
2. Martin and Martin 2004, 184-5; Pearce in Dyson et al. 2011, 234.
3. Lines 58-60.
4. Soden 2013, 41-51.
5. Power 1937, 142 &188 n64.
6. Jahnke 2015, 227. Jahnke's work and the papers in the parent volume by Harreld (2015), are indispensable for understanding the Hanse in the light of the latest thinking, not least as put forward in Lloyd (1991) and in Friedland and Richards (1998).
7. Zimmern 1891, 100.
8. Jahnke 2015, 218.
9. In relation to the study of this trade, I highlight the tremendous published research of Wendy Childs.
10. Devon 1837, 328.
11. 1926, lines 120, 130-2.
12. 1992, 199.
13. Wolff 2003, 66.
14. Brown 1864 [838], [852].
15. Brown 1864, [863].
16. Brown 1864, [890].
17. Brown 1867, 167.
18. Line 159.
19. Lines 176-7.
20. Sir John Capgrave in Hingeston 1858, 284.
21. Soden 2013, 56-60.
22. Buttler and Given-Wilson 1979, 144.
23. Bridbury 1955.
24. Walker 1998, xxiv.

Notes

25. Harris 1935, xxii.
26. Flavin 2004.
27. Gasquet 1904, 171.
28. Hamilton-Thompson 1920, 194 et passim.
29. Neale 2000, 79 & 147 [123 & 251].
30. Lines 798-801.
31. For some aspects of compass navigation see Rose 2007, 39-62.
32. Hockey 1975, 37.
33. ibid.
34. Bond 2001, 73.
35. Donaldson et al. 1980, 86-96.
36. Dyer 1988, 30.
37. Hockey 1975, 37.
38. Gardiner, Stewart and Priestley-Bell 1998.
39. Allen and Pettit 1997.
40. Gardiner 1997; Riddler 2010.
41. Fryde 1983, 293.
42. Brown, 1864, 3 [11]; Fryde ibid., 292.
43. Lines 333-6
44. Wolff 2003.
45. Fryde 1983, 353.
46. Fryde 1983, 317.
47. Coleman 1963.
48. Fryde 1983, 330.
49. Mallett 1967, 126.
50. Twemlow 1933, 231.
51. Line 344 onwards.
52. Wolff 2003, 7.
53. Mallett 1967.
54. Fryde 1983, 325.
55. Published in full in the original Italian in Mallett (1967). I have found no English translation. Although the diary is well annotated, I have had to be circumspect with this very old Italian. Google Translate helps.
56. Mallett 1967, 236-40.

57. Lines 630-1.
58. Mallett 1967, 133-4, n2.
59. op. cit., 1967, 127.
60. Mallett 1967, 98; Fryde 1983, 333.
61. Lines 344-51
62. Homer, Odyssey XV, 415-6 – Ἔνθα δε Φοινικες ναυσικλυτοι ἤλυθον ἄνδρες,/τρωκται, μυρι' ἄγοντες ἀθυρματα νηι μελαινῃ.
63. Wolff 2003, 72.
64. Brown 1864, 3 [11].
65. Brown 1864, 7 [23].
66. Wolff 2003, 6.
67. Law 1992, 161.
68. Brown 1864, 38-9 [130].
69. Brown 1864, 39-40 [134].
70. Wolff 2003, 3.
71. Brown 1864, 43 [153].
72. ibid., 44-5 [158].
73. op. cit., 46, [165].
74. op. cit., 48 [168].
75. Hardy 1835, 320-9.
76. Brown 1864, 58 [214-5]
77. ibid., 86 [343, 346].
78. ibid., 115-6 [397, 399].
79. Wolff 2003, 8.
80. ibid., 2003, 100.
81. A Genizah is a lockable room at a synagogue –in this case in Old Cairo – in which are kept the accumulated letters, writings, accounts, receipts etc. of a Jewish business community which bear the name of God and are, for that reason, to be preserved beyond the sight of prying or unbelieving eyes. I was privileged to see a remarkable selection of the surviving 200,000 Cairo Genizah documents at an exhibition at Cambridge University Library in 2018.
82. Soden 2013, 41-51.
83. Brown 1864, 148 [492].
84. ibid., 115 [397].

85. ibid., 141 [473].
86. ibid., 175 [544-5] and 204 [606].
87. ibid., 214 [627].
88. op. cit., 212-3 [621-3, 625].
89. op. cit., 217 [639].
90. op. cit., 252-3 [735].
91. op. cit., 260 [750] & 262, [752].
92. op. cit., 1864, 185, [561-2].
93. Brown 1867, 349-65 [841].
94. ibid., 1867, 45 [102].
95. op. cit., 353, [7].
96. op. cit., 143-4 [336].
97. op. cit., 580 [1340].
98. op. cit., 1867, 31-2 [66].
99. op. cit., 1867, 34-9.
100. Brown 1869, 95 [139].
101. ibid., 489 [1141].
102. ibid., 324 [697].
103. ibid., 502 [1163].
104. Soden 2013, 22.
105. Zimmern 1891, 98.
106. Johnson in Soden 2020, 77-9.
107. Zimmern 1891, 181-3.
108. Lloyd 1991, 372.
109. ibid., 371.
110. Zimmern 1891, 98.
111. Harreld 2015, 129.
112. 1891, 187-90.
113. Harreld 2015, 158; Zimmern 1891, 195.
114. ibid., 137.
115. Lloyd 1991, 368.
116. ibid., 375-6.
117. Richards 1998, 17.
118. Ellmers 1998.
119. Richards 1998, 19; Jenks 1998, 100.

120. Colvin 1916, 74-5. The reader should take care with Colvin and remember the difficult years in which he was writing. Resentment of all things German was widespread at the time.
121. Colvin 1916, 72.
122. Jenks 1998, 102.
123. Lloyd 1991, 363.
124. Jahnke 2015, 239.

3 Sea Lanes and Sailing Routes

1. Scammell 1969, 404-5.
2. Mallett 1967.
3. Long, 2009.
4. ibid; Mallett, 1967.
5. To be found marked in the table as follows:

> * Tower on the Isle of Thanet – This is probably either the church tower of St Mary the Virgin, Minster, or St Lawrence's, Ramsgate. Both were major focal seamarks once visible from sea level at the Sandwich entrance to the Wantsum Channel which separated Thanet from the mainland. It is possible that the Venetians in 1434-45 used the Wantsum Channel to progress on to London with the village of Minster on the Starboard side, or if the latter, then a transit via the outside of Thanet was more likely, with Ramsgate off the port side.

> # 'Wormy land', a direct translation of *Terra Vermegia*, suggests that they did indeed use the rapidly silting Wantsum Channel if heading for London. Directly to their starboard would have been a fourteenth-century earthen bank which projected south from Ebbsfleet, an ideal candidate for 'wormy land' where its blocking effect would have exacerbated the silting. For those vessels which after Sandwich made for Sluys, the port of Bruges, a course out into the English Channel would put first the wormy land and then Ramsgate to their port side. The Wantsum Channel was badly silted by 1485 when a bridge replaced the previous ferry, and no further navigation was possible. It must have been problematic for

some time before that and only passable year on year to vessels with smaller and smaller drafts.
6. Breusing 1876.
7. Stahl 2009, 377 – f125b.
8. Long et al. 2009, 327.
9. ibid., 381.
10. Breusing 1876. See the table above for Koppmann's seamarks.
11. I am greatly indebted to Gunnar Sundelin and Charlotta Due for a facsimile of this map and Olaus Magnus' notes. The original is accessible on the Uppsala University Library website via their 'Alvin' platform (Alvin – Carta Marina et descriptio septemtrionalium terrarum (alvin-portal.org)). Otherwise see Ehrensvärd (1995) for its place in European cartography.
12. Fudge 2017, 256-7 (in Degn 2017).
13. Fortunately tolls survive for 1497, 1500, 1503, 1528, 1536-40, for which see www.soundtoll.nl
14. Mallett 1967.
15. Brown 1864, 141 [473]; 148 [492].
16. Brown 1867, 34-9.
17. Long et al. 2009, 345.
18. Rose 2007, 152.
19. Le Crotoy, Baie de la Somme (Dépt. 80). Devon 1837, 435.
20. Nichols 1854, 67-8.
21. Reddaway and Ruddock 1969.
22. Dell 1966, xli and Appendix III.
23. ML Cotton MS Otho E IX f57v, lists each one by name and gives its skeleton crew.
24. Horrox 1987, 215.
25. Devon 1837, 446.
26. BL Cotton MS Otho E IX f63r-67r.
27. Devon 1837, 400.
28. Adlard Coles 1973.
29. De Selincourt 1953, 81.
30. ibid., 66-8.
31. ibid., 19-20.

32. These, and other pertinent ship dimensions, are to be found in Martin (2001, Appendix 3).
33. Adlard Coles 1973, 165-70.
34. *The Scotsman* & *New York Times*, 23 March 2023, et passim. There are many photos of the calamity on the internet.
35. Such a contraption is illustrated in a later fifteenth-century painting by the School of Botticelli – *The judgement of Paris* c1445-1500 – Private Collection, Cini Foundation, Venice. It is depicted in Martin (2001, 124, fig 110).
36. Another depiction of the process can be seen in Herri Met de Bles' painting Paysage côtier avec Saint Augustin – Rome, Gallerie Colonna. (Illustrated in the museum and gallery catalogue: Fables du Paysage Flamand – Exposition au Palais des Beaux-Arts de Lille, p4). William Schellinks also depicts the process going on in the shallower reaches of Falmouth harbour in a drawing of 1662, now in the Austrian National Library, Vienna and accessible via their website (www.onb.ac.at).

4 Destination England and Wales

1. Power 1937, 136.
2. No doubt there are omissions. For any reader wishing to concentrate on waterfront archaeology, a huge and now very detailed subject, they might begin with the 1988 Council for British Archaeology [CBA] conference (Wood et al., 1991). For professional levels of detail, beyond most publications, the reader is referred to the various county-based Historic Environment Records (HERs) which collate and manage excavation and other fieldwork data on the historic environment. For initial access to a baseline of HER data, the Heritage Gateway website presents the best way in (http://www.heritagegateway.org.uk).
3. BL Cotton MS Otho E IX f80r-f80v
4. BL Cotton MS Otho E IX: f81r, 81v, 82r. I am immensely grateful to my friend Dr Sara Elin Roberts of the University of Chester for helping me with the identifications and getting the Welsh spellings correct! As a medieval specialist and fluent speaker of her mother tongue, her help was invaluable.

Notes

5. The full list: St Dwynwen, Malltraeth (muddy), Aberffraw, Crigyll Bay, Cymyran Bay, Rhoscolyn, St Bride, Holyhead, Classelyn, Carmel Head-The Skerries, Llanbadrig, Cemaes Bay, Cemlyn Bay, Mill Bay, Amlwch, Llaneilian, Saynt Hillary, Dulas Bay, Reedewarth Bay, and Dinas Sylwy. In Caernarvonshire: Abergele Roads, Morvarrandy in Creuddyn (Llandudno), Conwy, Aber Arendy, Carnarvon, Dinas Dinlle, Dinllaen, Abergierch, Ysgaden, Porth Gwylan, Porth Ychan, Traeth Penllech, Colman Bay, Porth Veryn, Porth Iago, Porthor & Bardsey Island (a centre of pilgrimage), Porth Meudwy, Aberdaron, Rygull, St Tydwal islands, Abersoch, Castell March, Tydwal Bay, Pwllheli. In Merionethshire: Llanfihangel y Traethau next to Dyfi, Aber Artro, Barmouth and Aberdyfi in Ardudwy.
6. Fryde 1983, 312ff.
7. Coleman 1963.
8. Devon 1837, 429.
9. Toulmin Smith 1964, 5 volumes. By volume and page only thereafter in the above text.
10. Neale 2000, Referred to as 'William Worcestre' hereafter.
11. Exwood and Lehmann 1993, referred to as 'William Schellinks' hereafter.

5 West Coast Ports

1. Toulmin Smith (1964), vol. V, 40–41 – hereafter referenced merely by volume and page.
2. Bliss and Twemlow 1902, 533.
3. Rosser 2016, 44.
4. Devon 1837, 281.
5. III, 91.
6. ibid., 92
7. ibid., 85
8. As for Chapter 4, note 3: 1524 list of harbours, creeks, and roads in Anglesey, Caernarvon and Merionethshire *where any shippe or ballinger or other vessel may enter or land* survives in the BL (Cotton MS Otho E IX, ff81r-82v). The list's purpose is unclear. Again, my thanks to Dr Sara Elin Roberts. If I have misunderstood anything, I apologise!

9. Soden 2013, 132 & 136.
10. III, 132
11. ibid., 134
12. Ex inf Dr Sara Elin Roberts.
13. As the 1524 list, above (f81v).
14. III, 88
15. Devon 1837 339.
16. III, 76–7
17. As the 1524 list, above (f82r).
18. III, 65
19. Neale 2000, 79 & 147 [123 & 251].
20. III, 116
21. ibid., 61
22. ibid., 30
23. ibid
24. Thanks to Dr Sara Elin Roberts for her helpful correspondence on these more southerly havens. On some we remained undecided. It is never certain how many ears, mouths and pens, and how many languages, the original went before Wagenhaer's final map of 1585 was labelled. Some defy even the subtleties and nuances of linguistics.
25. III, 22
26. ibid., 14
27. Twemlow 1912, 486.
28. V, 90-91
29. Exwood and Lehmann 1993, 102.
30. Worcestre's notes are quite disjointed. I am indebted to the scholarship of Frances Neale whose overview and translation of Worcestre's disparate and (mostly) Latin notes is a considerable boon (Neale 2000).
31. The treadwheel-crane was very probably of a type like that found in a number of continental towns, appearing in contemporary and later paintings of 1551 in Bruges [*Portret van Jan van Eyewerve* by Pieter Pourbus (1523-84)] and of c1785 in Haarlem [*De Waag en de Daamstraat te Haarlem* by Wybrand Hendriks (1744-1831)]

and in a vintage model in the STAM Town Museum in Gent (photographed for this book). Examples are also portrayed by Peter Breughel the elder (1526-69) [*The Tower of Babel* (Vienna)] and Tobias Verhaecht (1561-1631) [*Countryside with Tower of Babel (Antwerp)*]. Treadwheels for such cranes have survived indoors in the towers at Beverley Minster (Yorks) and at Peterborough Cathedral (Cambs), while one *ex-situ* example is conserved in Chesterfield Museum (Derbys). A surviving crane in Hamburg was photographed by Jordan (2004, plate 34).

32. Devon 1837, 502.
33. Harreld 2015, 158; Zimmern 1891, 195.
34. Jenks in Friedland and Richards 1998, 102.
35. Flavin 2004, 37.
36. I, 167; III, 22
37. I, 299
38. ibid., 317-8
39. Nichols 1854, xxxii.
40. I, 318

6 South Coast Ports

1. I, 319
2. ibid., 321-2
3. For which see, for instance, Morley 1976. These were Henry VIII's so-called 'Device' Forts and Blockhouses around our coasts and even up the River Thames. However, their constructions all postdate this book's period, if only just.
4. Exwood and Lehmann 1993 125.
5. I, 323
6. ibid., 203-4
7. Nichols 1854, xxxii.
8. Horrox 1987, 240.
9. Exwood and Lehmann 1993, 117.
10. I have other photos by Walton Hudson showing both ships in the background. However, on none of them can the name of the second ship anchored behind be made out. It seems to be of a

similar type judging from its size and the similarity of its upper works. The *Ampleforth* was a British steel screw steamer cargo ship of two decks (6,327 tons, measuring 420' x 54'8" and with a summer draught of 26'6½"). It could muster 11 knots. Its first appearance in Lloyd's register, newly built as *Empire Zephyr*, is in 1940-41 where its official given number is 168675, which stayed with it through all name-changes. It was built by Charles Connell & Co Ltd of Glasgow in 1941, but as the *Empire Zephyr*, an Empire-class cargo steamer built for the Ministry of War Transport (War emergency-type). In 1946 it was sold and renamed *Valewood* for the Kelston Steamship Company. In 1949 it was sold again to the Ampleforth Steamship Company and renamed again – *Ampleforth*. Moored at Fowey and photographed here in summer 1959, *Ampleforth* was assigned to be broken up, which took place beginning 12 August at Port Glasgow, Greenock. In the photo it was probably only days or weeks away from its final journey to the breaker's yard. Its registered owners in 1959 were Charles Cravos & Co of Cardiff (Lloyd's register).

11. I, 323
12. ibid., 324
13. ibid., 214
14. Exwood and Lehmann, 115.
15. Manning 1991, 256 for a contemporary description.
16. Nichols 1854, 66.
17. I, 220
18. Horrox 1987, 236 for royal grants to the 'new toure for saufe gard of the said towne'.
19. op. cit., 113.
20. I, 223-4
21. ibid., 232
22. op. cit., 111.
23. I, 244
24. Horrox 1987, 235-6.
25. Exwood and Lehmann 1993, 129.
26. I, 250

27. ibid., 304
28. Exwood and Lehmann 1993, 129.
29. I, 253
30. ibid., 255
31. Wood et al. 1991.
32. I, 254-5
33. Horsey 1992.
34. Hockey 1975. The three mid-thirteenth-century abbey ships were named *Salvata*, *la Mariote* and *la Stelle*.
35. Prof Colin Platt's 1973 work on Southampton remains the best history, unalloyed with archaeology. That edited by Hicks (2015), with numerous contributors, is a magisterial and superbly illustrated survey of imports through Southampton, based upon the port books and similar documentation. This is a must for anyone interested primarily in the imports themselves.
36. I, 275-7
37. ibid
38. ibid., 278-9
39. Mallett 1967, 239: '*Sabato mattina adi 3 ci trovamo sopra l'isola di Vicche, e 'l vento torno a sciloccho e levante, per che ci convene mutare proposito et tornamo in porto presso ad Antona circha 8 miglia, in sul'isola di Vicche che ssi chiama Calzadores.*' Thanks to Google Translate for their help with this very old Italian.
40. I, 279
41. Exwood and Lehmann 1993, 139.
42. Platt 1973, Mallett 1967.
43. Ross 1975, 359.
44. Victoria County History: Hants, Vol 2.
45. Riley 1864, doc 261.
46. Brown 1864, doc 616.
47. I, 282-4
48. Devon, 1837, 351, 354, 355.
49. Allen and Pettit 1997, 236-7.
50. Exwood and Lehmann 1993, 141.
51. Victoria County History: Hants, Vol. 2.

52. Long et al. 2009, 361.
53. Brown 1864, 176, doc 547.

7 Channel Coast Ports

1. The Kentish Knock is a shoal about 30 km east of the mouth of the River Thames
2. Dulley 1966, 103.
3. IV, 113-4
4. Martin and Martin 2004, 21.
5. Exwood and Lehmann 1993, 179.
6. I, 203
7. Dell 1966, xxxiv.
8. Brown 1864, p57, doc 209.
9. IV, 67
10. Gardner et al., 1998.
11. IV, 67
12. Riley 1864 II, 267.
13. IV, 64-5
14. Dulley 1966, 104.
15. IV, 64
16. Dulley 1966, 106.
17. IV, 49-51, 64
18. ibid., 48
19. ibid
20. ibid., 62
21. Parkin 1984.
22. Dulley 1966, 105.

8 London, East Anglia and the North-East

1. In place of Leland and his near contemporaries, I have been accompanied by *The Book of The Thames* (Hall 1859, 495-515), which notes some of the older features visible from the river's lower reaches. I have included only the medieval here. At that date, for the most part, the banks remained un- or under-developed and the authors helpfully added contemporary engravings from the water.

Notes

2. The church ruins stand within a late Roman 'Saxon Shore' fort, in the care of English Heritage. The site was the backdrop to the Air Ministry testing Barnes Wallis' bouncing bomb in the shallows adjacent, a scene memorably re-enacted in the 1955 film *The Dam Busters*.
3. Brown 1864, 72-3, doc 292.
4. ibid., 77, doc 310.
5. Exwood and Lehmann 1993, 46.
6. Kingsford 1925.
7. Devon 1837.
8. Nicholas 1972.
9. Exwood and Lehmann 1993, 162.
10. See Amor 2011 for a detailed study of Ipswich.
11. See Butcher 2016 for detailed study of Great Yarmouth.
12. See Ayers 2008 for a detailed study of Norwich.
13. Gaimster 1994.
14. Exwood and Lehmann 1993, 158, 160-61.
15. Riley 1864 II, 273.
16. Lloyd 1991, 368.
17. Jenks in Friedland et al. 1998, 103.
18. Breusing 1876, Koppmann voyage – No 14 p63, Items 15-16:

    '15. *Item van Ossenborch to Wintertune dat is 3 mylen. De Ossenborch staet up eyn hoch schone cleff, unde ys ene halve myle lank. Unde van Ossenborch to Wintertune dat sint alle santdunen by den strande, unde dat lant strecket van den Schylde went to Wintertune sutost unde nortwest, unde is en reyne strant by den land so na, sat men dar up scheten mach.*'

    '16. *Item Wintertune dat is eyn grot dorp unde licht vaste by de see, unde dar staet en grot stuff toren unde twe scharpe torne, de sal men bringen by suden dat dorp unde gan dan ostsutost in de see.*'

    My thanks to my wife for her translation from Low German.
19. Carus Wilson 1962, 201.
20. Richards in Friedland and Richards, 1998, 17.
21. Exwood and Lehmann 1993, 154-5.
22. I, 114, 181

23. V, 33
24. ibid., 34
25. IV, 181
26. For this slump, even at Boston, see Rigby 1985.
27. I, 55
28. ibid., 48-9
29. Childs 1984; a translated section in Rosser 2016, 108-11 for instance.
30. I, 61
31. ibid., 60-61
32. ibid., 61
33. I, 51
34. ibid
35. V, 48
36. IV, 117-8
37. V, 59-60

9 Sating Appetites

1. For a reasoned summary of imports from the Mediterranean: Table number 5 in Brown (1864), cxxxv-cxxxix. For sites with excavated imports the reader might like to first visit http://www.heritagegateway.org.uk in order to search county Historic Environment Records, the most accessible fruit of half a century of excavation, mostly planning-driven.
2. See, for instance Bond, in Keevill et al., 2001, 54-87.
3. Gasquet 1904, 167.
4. Reddaway and Ruddock 1969, 5-6.
5. Twemlow 1933, 273.
6. Mertes 1988, 218.
7. Such as the phenomenal menu provided for the enthronement of the Archbishop Neville of York, held at Cawood Castle, Yorkshire, in 1465.
8. Woolgar 1999, 23-4; Soden 2007, 214-5.
9. For which see Hicks (ed.) 2015.
10. Harris 1984.
11. Swabey 1999, 86-7.

12. Jolliffe 1967.
13. Soden 2013, 35-7.
14. Soden 1995, 12.
15. Butler and Given-Wilson 1979, 375.
16. ibid., 144.
17. Soden 2013, 22.
18. Ross 1975, 369.
19. Soden 2005, plate 26.
20. Hamilton Thompson 1920, 235, 266 & 270.
21. Prologue, lines 225-9
22. BL Cott MS Vesp E IX fo 100.
23. Devon 1837, 274.
24. ibid., 499.
25. op. cit., 495 & 500.
26. Fryde 1983, 315.
27. Devon 1837, 353.
28. ibid., 319.
29. Jenkins 2003, 338-40.
30. Williamson 1913, 511-14.
31. Andrews 1947, 40.
32. Rigby 2005.
33. Devon 1837, 457.
34. Broberg in Ersgård 1992, 56-75.
35. Archaeology Warwickshire, 2022 *Burton Dassett Excavations: A Digital Supplement to 'Burton Dassett Southend, Warwickshire: a Medieval Market Village'*, N. Palmer and J. Parkhouse [dataset]. York: Archaeology Data Service [distributor] https://doi.org/10.5284/1083492).
36. Devon 1837, 382.
37. Andrews 1947, 46.
38. Harris 1984.
39. See Vlierman 1993, 69-76 for an example.
40. Gairdner 1858, throughout.
41. Blatherwick and Bluer 2009.

42. The late Geoff Egan, pers. comm.
43. Pearce 2011.
44. Long 2009, 56.
45. Soden 2006, 176.
46. The reader is referred to Hurst et al. (1987) for a brilliant and detailed survey of excavated imported pottery across the country. More particularly, for Southampton, see Brown (1993, 77-81).
47. Gaimster 1994, 287.
48. Soden 2020.
49. Templeman 1944, 153-60.
50. Hulton 1999.
51. Coppack and Keen, 2019, 103-6, 321, 395-7.
52. Soden 1995, Woodfield 1981, Coppack and Keen 2019, Pearce 2011.
53. 'in loco fratrum minorum' – Talbot 1967, 59-60.
54. Shepherd in Soden 1995, 117-8.
55. Sutton 1982, 56-7, 60.
56. Tracy 1999, 97-8.
57. Holliday 1874.
58. Rosser 2016, 108-10.
59. My thanks to Brian Dix for bringing this strange story to my attention many years ago.

10 *A Permanent Heavy Swell*

1. Bradley 2012, xiii. The admirable work of Helen Bradley is key to understanding the rather xenophobic 'Views of Hosts' and her publication of these is indispensable.
2. ibid., xxii.
3. op. cit., xi.
4. Brown 1864, 84-5.
5. Brown 1867, 631, doc 1472 [Appendix].
6. ibid., docs 879, 887, 910.
7. Ross 1975, 359.
8. Tracy 1999, 98.
9. Ross 1975, 352.
10. ibid., 358-9.

Notes

11. Hingeston 1858, 234, 276.
12. Riley 1864 II, 273.
13. Hingeston 1858, 284; Manning 1991, 256.
14. Brown 1864, doc 760.
15. ibid., doc 625.
16. Toulmin Smith 1964, I, 191.
17. For pirates in general throughout this period, see Meier 2006.
18. Riley 1864 II, 275.
19. ibid., 285.
20. Long et al. 2009, 329.
21. Devon 1837, 467.
22. Fryde 1983, 330.
23. 102-5, 108-11: ... *stridens Aquilone procella/velum adversa ferit, fluctusque ad sidera tollit./Franguntur remi, tum prora avertit et undis/dat latus, insequitur cumulo praeruptus aquae mons./ ... /Tris Notus abreptas in saxa latentia torquet/saxa vocant Itali mediis quae in fluctibus Aras,/dorsum immane mari summo* ...
24. Acts Ch27: v13-44; by his own admission, he had been shipwrecked three times.
25. Jonah Ch1: v4-6
26. Matthew Ch8: v23-27, *inter alia*
27. Cairo Genizah Or.1081JI.
28. Soden 2009, 92.
29. For which see Flatman 2011.
30. Mallet 1967, 93.
31. Brown 1864, 217 doc 639.
32. Riley 1864 II, 275.
33. Brown 1856, 489 doc 1141.
34. Mallett 1967 231-2, n2.
35. ibid., 238, n4.
36. Hingeston 1858, 288; Riley 1864 II, 267.
37. Neale 2000, 89 & 143.
38. Brown 1864, 46 doc 163.
39. Brown 1864, doc 890.
40. Brown 1864, 42 doc 93.

41. Toulmin Smith 1964, I 216.
42. Brown 1864, 311 doc 864-870.
43. Homer, *Odyssey* III, 302, ἤλατο ξὺν νηυσὶ κατ' ἀλλοθρόους ἀνθρώπους.
44. Brown 1864, 326 doc 890 of Oct 1506.
45. Scammell 1972, 404.
46. For which see Talbot 1967, 46-50.
47. Long et al. 2009, 353.
48. ibid., 373.
49. Nichols 1854, xxxii.

11 *The Rise of an English Merchant Fleet*

1. Ramsey 1957, 98.
2. Power 1937, 136.
3. Kingsford 1925, 140. Browne's house contained (148-151) a hall of 40'x24', parlour, buttery, pastry, kitchen, four chambers, bulting house, house of easement, chapel, garners, mews, cloth house, gatehouse, waterhouse.
4. Scammell 1972.
5. Ross 1975, 352.
6. Richmond 1967.
7. Scammell 1972, 396.
8. ibid., 387.
9. Palmer 1968.
10. Soden 2013.
11. Reddaway and Ruddock 1969.
12. Brown 1864, 75.
13. Brown 1867, 173.
14. BL Cotton MS Otho E IX – the whole available as a digital download from the British Library website. There are eighty-eight named ships in the relevant folios of this volume dating between 1518 and 1525; but for the fire damage to the MS, the number would probably be at least half as many again.
15. Brown 1869, various docs 381-700.

16. ibid., 323, 325, docs 694, 700. Despite being part of the rather restrictive Cistercian order, Netley was a place of welfare for foreign mariners, a fact noted only a few years later at the Dissolution. So too Quarr Abbey on the Isle of Wight, in similar circumstances.
17. Toulmin Smith 1964, I, 163.
18. ibid., II, 108.
19. For Coventry, see Mason, McAree and Soden 2017.
20. Morris 2017.
21. Generally, for this decay see Dobson in Holt and Rosser 1990, Clark and Slack 1976. For Coventry see Phythian-Adams 1979.
22. Brown 1867, 400.

BIBLIOGRAPHY

Adams, J, 2013 *A maritime archaeology of ships: innovation and social change in medieval and early modern Europe*, Oxford: Oxbow

Adlard Coles, K, 1973 *The Shell Pilot to The South Coast Harbours*, London: Faber & Faber

Allen, M J, and Pettit, P B, 1997 A medieval wooden harpoon from the south coast of England. *Medieval Archaeology* **41**, 236-9

Amor, N R, 2011 *Late medieval Ipswich: trade and industry*, Boydell and Brewer

Andrews, H C, 1947 *The chronicles of Hertford castle*, Hertford

Anon 1968 Ships and shipping in early modern Europe, *The Historical Journal* **II**, no 2 372-5

Ayers, B, 2008 *Norwich: the archaeology of a fine city*

Beltrame, C, Gelichi, S, and Miholjek, I, 2014 *Sveti Pavao Shipwreck: a 16th-century Venetian merchantman from Mljet, Croatia*, Oxford: Oxbow

Bickley, F D, 1900 *Little Red Book of Bristol* (2 vols), Bristol

Blatherwick, S, and Bluer, R, 2009 *Great Houses, moats and mills on the south bank of the Thames; Medieval and Tudor Southwark and Rotherhithe*, Museum of London Archaeology Monograph **47**

Bibliography

Bliss, W H, and Twemlow, J A, 1902 *Calendar of entries in the Papal Registers of Great Britain and Ireland, Papal Letters* vol **IV**: 1362-1404, HMSO

Bliss, W H, and Twemlow, J A, 1904 *Calendar of entries in the Papal Registers of Great Britain and Ireland, Papal Letters* vol **V**: 1396-1404, HMSO

Bogucka, M, 1973 Amsterdam and the Baltic in the first half of the seventeenth century, *Economic History Review* 2nd series **XXVI**, no 3 Aug 1973, 433-7

Bond, J, 2001 Production and consumption of food and drink in the medieval monastery, in Keevill, G, Aston, M, and Hall, T, 2001 *Monastic Archaeology – papers on the study of medieval monasteries*, 54-87, Oxbow

Bovill, E W, 1968 *The golden trade of the Moors*, OUP

Boxer, C R, 1969 *The Portuguese seaborne empire 1415-1825*, London: Hutchinson

Bradley, H, 2012 The views of the hosts of alien merchants 1440-1444, *London Record Society* **46**, Boydell

Breusing, A, 1876 *Das Seebuch von Karl Koppmann. Mit einer nautischen Einleitung von Arthur Breusing. Mit Glossar van Christoph Walther*, Bremen

Bridbury, A R, 1955 *England and the salt trade in the later Middle Ages*, Oxford

Broberg, B, 1992 *The Late-medieval towns of Sweden – an important research resource*, in Ersgård et al., 1992, 56-75

Brown, D H, 1993 The imported pottery of late medieval Southampton, *Medieval Ceramics* **17**, 77-82; Journal of the MPRG

Brown, R, 1864 *Calendar of state papers and manuscripts relating to English affairs existing in the archives and collections of Venice and in other libraries of northern Italy;* **I**: *1202-1509*, London

Brown, R, 1867 *Calendar of state papers and manuscripts relating to English affairs existing in the archives and collections of Venice and in other libraries of northern Italy;* **II**: *1509-1519*, London

Brown, R, 1869 *Calendar of state papers and manuscripts relating to English affairs existing in the archives and collections of Venice and in other libraries of northern Italy;* **III**: *1520-1526*, London

Burkhardt, M, 2015 Kontors and outposts, in D J Harreld (ed.), 2015, *A companion to the Hanseatic League*, 127-61, Leiden: Brill

Burwash, D, 1969 *English merchant shipping 1460-1540*, Newton Abbott

Butcher, D, 2016 *Medieval Lowestoft*, Boydell and Brewer

Buttler, L, and Given-Wilson, C, 1979 *Medieval Monasteries of Great Britain*, London: Michael Joseph

Carus-Wilson, E M, 1962 The medieval trade of the ports of The Wash, *Medieval Archaeology* **6**, 182-201

Carus-Wilson, E M, 1967 *Medieval merchant venturers; Collected studies*, London: Methuen

Childs, W R, 1978 *Anglo-Castilian trade in the later Middle Ages*, Manchester UP

Childs, W R, 1982 Ireland's trade with England in the later Middle Ages, *Irish Economic and Social History* **IX**, 5-33

Childs, W R, 1984 (ed.) *The Customs Accounts of Hull 1453-1490*, Yorks Archaeol. Record Series **144**

Childs, W R, 1992 Anglo-Portuguese trade in the fifteenth century, *Royal Historical Society Transactions 6th series*, **2**, 195-220

Childs, W R, 1993 Imports of Spanish pottery to England in the later Middle Ages, *Medieval Ceramics* **17**, 35-8; Journal of the MPRG

Clark, P, and Slack, P, 1976 *English towns in transition 1500-1700*, OUP

Clarke, H, 1973 King's Lynn and east coast trade in the Middle Ages, in Blackman, D J, 1973 Marine archaeology, *Proceedings of the 23rd Symposium of the Colston Research Society*

Coleman, O, 1960-61 *The Brokage books of Southampton 1443-4*, 2 vols, Southampton Record Series **IV, VI**

Coleman, O, 1963 Trade and prosperity in the 15th century: some aspects of the trade of Southampton, *Economic History Review* (New Series), **16**, 9-22

Colvin, I D, 1915 *The Germans in England 1066-1598*, London

Coppack, G, and Keen, L, 2019 *Mount Grace Priory excavations of 1957-1992*, Historic England/English Heritage; Oxbow

Daubney, A, 2009 The circulation and prohibition of Venetian Soldini in late medieval England, *British Numismatic Journal* **79**, 186-98

Bibliography

Davey, P, and Hodges, R, 1980 *Ceramics and trade*, University of Sheffield

Degn, O (ed.), 2017 *The Sound Toll at Elsinore; politics, shipping and the collection of duties 1429-1857*, Museum Tusculanum Press/Danish Society for Customs and Tax History

Dell, R F, 1966 *Rye shipping records 1566-1590*, Sussex Record Society

Devon, F, 1837 *Issues of the Exchequer from Henry III to Henry VI inc, with Appendix (The Pell Records)*, London

Dobson, R B, 'Urban decline in late Medieval England', in Holt and Rosser, 1990, 265-86

Donaldson, A M, Jones, A K G, and Rackham, D J, 1980 Incorporating Barnard Castle Co Durham. A dinner in the Great Hall: report on the contents of a 15th-century drain, *Journal of the British Archaeological Association* **CXXXIII**, 86-96

Douët d'Arcq, M L, 1851 *Comptes de l'Argenterie des Rois de France en XIV-ème siècle*, Societé de l'Histoire de France

Dulley, A J F, 1966 Four Kent towns at the end of the Middle Ages, *Archaeologia Cantiana* **81**, 95-108

Dyer, C, 1988 The consumption of freshwater fish in medieval England, in M Aston (ed.), Medieval fish, fisheries and fishponds in England, *BAR British Series* **182**, 27-38

Dyson, T, Samuel, M, Steele, A and Wright, S M, 2011 *The Cluniac priory and abbey of St Saviour, Bermondsey, Surrey; excavations 1984-95*, English Heritage; MoLA Monograph 50

Ehrensvärd, U, 1995 *Mare Balticum: The Baltic – Two Thousand Years*, Helsinki

Ellmers, D, 1998 Late medieval harbours: function and construction, in K. Friedland and P. Richards, 1998 *Essays in Hanseatic History: The King's Lynn Symposium 1998*, 37-50, Dereham

Ersgård, L, Holmström, M and Lamm, K (transl. Clarke, H), 1992 *Rescue and Research: Reflections of society in Sweden 700-1700 AD*, Stockholm

Exwood, M, and Lehmann, H L (transl. & ed.), 1993 *The journal of William Schellinks' travels in England 1661-1663*, Camden 5th Series Volume 1, Royal Historical Society

Fantham, E, 2017 *Francesco Petrarca, Selected Letters* (2 vols), Harvard UP

Flatman, J, 2009 *Ships and shipping in medieval manuscripts*, British Library

Flavin, S M, 2004 *The development of Anglo-Irish trade in the 16th century*, University of Bristol MA Dissertation

Friedland K, and Richards, P, 1998 *Essays in Hanseatic History: The King's Lynn Symposium 1998*, Dereham

Fryde, E B, 1983 *Studies in medieval trade and finance*, Hambledon Press

Fudge, J D, 2017 The sound passage – comparing 16th century tolls and customs as sources for northern shipping, in Degn 2017, 247-66

Gaimster, D, 1994 The archaeology of post-medieval society, c1450-1750: Material culture studies in Britain since the war, in B Vyner (ed.), 1994 *Building on the past – papers celebrating 150 years of the Royal Archaeological Institute*, RAI 1994, 283-312

Gairdner, J (ed.), 1858 *Historia Regis Henrici Septimi, a Bernardo Andrea Tholosate conscripta*, Rolls Series, HMSO, London

Gardiner, M, 1997 The exploitation of sea-mammals in medieval England: bones and their social context, *Archaeological Journal* **154**, 173-95

Gardiner, M, Stewart, J, and Priestley-Bell, G, 1998 Anglo-Saxon whale exploitation: some evidence from Dengemarsh, Lydd, Kent, *Medieval Archaeology* **42**, 96-101

Gasquet, Abbott 1904 *English monastic life*

Gelichi, S, 2014, Other pottery finds, in Beltrame et al., 105-9

Good, G, Jones, R H, and Ponsford, M W, 1991 *Waterfront Archaeology. Proceedings of 3rd International conference on waterfront archaeology held at Bristol 23-26 Sept 1988*, Oxford: Alden Press

Gras, N S B, 1918 *The Early English customs system*, Harvard UP

Greenhill, B, 1995 *The evolution of the sailing ship 1250-1580*, Keynote studies from The Mariner's Mirror, London

Griffiths, R A, 1981 *The reign of King Henry VI*, Ernest Benn

Gröner, E, 1942 *Die Handelsflotten der Welt* (Edition of 1/11/42), Oberkommando der Kriegsmarine

Hall, S C, and A M, 1859 *The Book of The Thames from its rise to its fall*, 1977 ed. Charlotte James, Twickenham

Bibliography

Halliwell, J O (ed.), 1839 *A chronicle of the first thirteen years of the reign of King Edward the fourth by J Warkworth*, Camden Society: 1st series, 10

Hamilton Thomson, A (ed.), 1920 The building accounts of Kirby Muxloe Castle, 1480-1484, *Trans Leicestershire Archaeol Soc*, **XI**, 193-345

Hampden, J (ed.), 1970 *Richard Hakluyt – The Tudor Venturers*, Folio Society

Harding, V A, 1987 Some documentary sources for the import and distribution of foreign textiles in later medieval England, *Textile History* 18 1987 205-18

Hardy, T D, 1835 *Rotuli Normanniae I: 1200-1204 & 1417*, Records Commission

Harreld, D J, 2015 *A companion to the Hanseatic League*, Leiden: Brill

Harris, M D (ed.), 1907-13 *The Coventry Leet Book*

Harris, M D (ed.), 1935 Register of the Guild of the Holy Trinity, St Mary, St John the Baptist and St Katherine of Coventry, *Dugdale Society* 13

Harris, M (ed.), 1984 The account of the great household of Humphrey 1st Duke of Buckingham for the year 1452-3, *Camden Society 4th Series* **29**: *Camden Miscellany* **28**, 1-57, Royal Historical Society

Harvey, J, 1969 *William Worcestre's Itineraries*, Oxford: Clarendon Press

Hicks, M (ed.), 2015 *English inland trade 1430-1540: Southampton and its region*, Oxbow

Hingeston, F C, 1858 *The Chronicle of England by John Capgrave*, Rolls Series

Hinton, R W K, 1956 The Port Books of Boston 1601-40, *Lincolnshire Record Society* 50

Hockey, S F, 1975 The account-book of Beaulieu Abbey, *Camden Society 4th Series* 16, Royal Historical Society

Hollett, D, 1995 *The conquest of the Niger by land and sea, from the early explorers and pioneer steamships to Elder Dempster and Company*, Abergavenny

Holliday, J R, 1874 *Maxstoke Priory*, Birmingham and Warwickshire Archaeological Society Transactions 56-105

Holmes, G A, 1960 Florentine merchants in England 1346-1436, *Economic History Review*, new series **13**, 193-208

Holt, R, and Rosser G, 1990 *The medieval town – a reader in English Urban History 1200-1540*, Longman

Holmes, G A, 1961 The Libel of English Policy, *English Historical Review* **76**, 193-216

Horrox, R (ed.), 1987 *Financial memoranda of the reign of Edward V, Longleat Misc Manuscript Book 2*, Camden 4th series **34**, Camden Miscellany **29**, London: Royal Historical Society

Horsey, I P, 1992 *Excavations in Poole 1973-83*, Dorset Natural History and Archaeological Society

Horsey, I P, and Jarvis, K S, 1984 The Studland Bay wreck – an interim report on a medieval vessel of c1500 with a cargo of Spanish pottery, Dorset Archaeology in 1984 – *Dorset Natural History and Archaeological Society Proceedings* **106**, 124

Hurst, J G, Neal, D S, and Van Beuningen, H J E, 1987 *Pottery produced and traded in North-West Europe 1350-1650*, Rotterdam Papers **VI**

Hulton, M, 1999 Coventry and its people in the 1520s, *Dugdale Society* **38**

Hutchinson, G, 1991 The early 16th century wreck at Studland Bay, Dorset, in R. Reinders and K. Paul (eds) *Carvel construction techniques* 171-5, Oxbow Monograph **12**

Hutchinson, G, 1994 *Medieval ships and shipping*, Leicester UP

Jahnke, C, 2015 The Baltic trade, in D J Harreld 2015, 194-240

Jenkins, D (ed.), 2003 *The Cambridge History of western textiles*, Cambridge UP

Jenks, S, 1998 Lynn and the Hanse, in K Friedland and P Richards, 1998 *Essays in Hanseatic History: The King's Lynn Symposium 1998*, 94-114, Dereham

Johnson, E, 2020 Animal bone, in Soden, I, 2020

Jolliffe, J (ed. & transl.), 1967 *Froissart's Chronicles*, London

Jordan, P, 2004 *North Sea Saga*, Harlow

Kingsford, C L, 1925 A London merchant's house and its owners 1360-1614, *Archaeologia* **74**, 137-58, Oxford

Bibliography

Kralj, V Z, 2014, A transport of Iznik pottery, in Beltrame et al., 64-104

Krüger, K, 1998 Church and church business in Hanseatic agencies, in K Friedland and P Richards, 1998 *Essays in Hanseatic History: The King's Lynn Symposium 1998*, 81-93, Dereham

Law, J D, 1992 The Venetian mainland state in the fifteenth century, *Royal Historical Society Transactions 6th series*, 2, 153-74

Legassie, S A, 2017 *The medieval invention of travel*, Chicago UP

Lloyd, T H, 1991 *England and the German Hanse 1157-1611: a study of their trade and commercial diplomacy*, Cambridge UP

Long, P O, McGee, D, and Stahl, A M (ed.), 2009 *The book of Michael of Rhodes, a fifteenth-century maritime manuscript, Vol 2: Transcription and Translation*, MIT

Long, P O (ed.), 2009 *The book of Michael of Rhodes, a fifteenth-century maritime manuscript, Vol 3: Studies*, MIT

Longfield, A K, 1929 *Anglo-Irish trade in the 16th century*, London

Mason, P, McAree, D, and Soden I, 2017 *Coventry's medieval suburbs: Excavations at Hill Street, Upper well Street and Far Gosford Street 2003-2007*, Museum of London Archaeology/University of Leicester/Archaeopress

Mallett, M E, 1967 *The Florentine galleys in the 15th century, with the diary of Luca di Maso dagli Albizzi, Captain of the Galleys 1429-1430*, Oxford: Clarendon Press

Manning, J J (ed.), 1991 *The first and second parts of John Hayward's The Life and Raigne of King Henrie IIII*, Camden 4th Series, Vol **42**, London: Royal Historical Society

Martin, D, and Martin, B, 2004 *New Winchelsea, Sussex: a medieval port town*, English Heritage

Martin, L R, 2001 *The art and archaeology of Venetian ships and boats*, London

McGee, D (ed.), 2009 *The book of Michael of Rhodes, a fifteenth-century maritime manuscript, Vol 1: Facsimile*, MIT

Meier, D, 2006 *Seafarers, merchants and pirates in the Middle Ages*, Woodbridge: Boydell

Mertes, K, 1988 *The English noble household 1250-1600*, Oxford: Blackwell

Milne, G, with Flatman, J, and Brandon, K, 2004 The 14th century merchant ship from Sandwich: a study in medieval maritime archaeology, *Archaeologia Cantiana* 124, 227-63

Moore, E W, 1985 *The fairs of medieval England: an introductory study*, Studies and Texts 72, Toronto

Morley, B M, 1976 *Henry VIII and the development of coastal defence*, HMSO

Morris, S, 2017 *The history and archaeology of Cathedral Square, Peterborough*, Museum of London Archaeology/Archaeopress

Neale, F (ed.), 2000 *William Worcestre: the topography of medieval Bristol*, Bristol Record Society 51

Newton, A P, 1930 *Travel and travellers of the Middle Ages*, London

Nicholas, D, 1997 *The later medieval city 1300-1500*, London

Nicholas, N H, 1972 (facsimile of 1830 ed) *Privy purse expenses of Elizabeth of York; wardrobe accounts of Edward IV, with a memoir of Elizabeth of York, and notes*, London: Frederick Muller

Nichols, J G, 1854 *Grants etc. from the Crown during the reign of Edward the Fifth*, Camden Society Old Series 60, New York: AMS Press, 1968

Ohler, N, 2010 *The medieval traveller*, Woodbridge: Boydell

Olsen, J E, 2017 The right usual waterway – the sound toll in the fifteenth century, in Degn 2017, 29-44

Palmer, J J N, 1968 *Review* of Thielemans, M-R, 1966 Bourgogne et Angleterre. Relations politiques et économiques entre Pays-Bas bourgognons et l'Angleterre 1435-1467, *The Historical Journal* II, no. 1 185-87

Parry, J H, 1967 *The Spanish seaborne empire*, London: Hutchinson

Parkin, E W, 1984 The ancient port of Sandwich, *Archaeologia Cantiana* 100, 189-216

Pearce, J, 2011 Medieval and Post-medieval pottery, in Dyson et al., 214-36

Phythian-Adams, C V, 1979 *Desolation of a city: Coventry and the urban crisis of the later Middle Ages*, Cambridge

Platt, C, 1973 *Medieval Southampton: the port and trading community AD1000-1600*, London

Power, E, 1937 *Medieval people: a study of communal psychology*, Penguin/Pelican Books

Bibliography

Pye, M, 2021 *Antwerp, The Glory Years*, Allen Lane

Quinn, D B, and Ruddock, A A, 1938 *The port books or local customs accounts of Southampton for the reign of Edward IV*, Southampton Record Society 38

Rabb, T K, 1966 Investment in English overseas enterprise 1575-1630, *Economic History Review 2nd Series*, **XIX no 1**, April 1966, 70-81

Ramsey, G D, 1957 *English overseas trade during the centuries of emergence*

Reddaway, T F, and Ruddock, A A (eds), 1969 The accounts of John Balsall, Purser of the *Trinity of Bristol*, 1480-1, *Camden Society 4th Series Volume 7, Camden Miscellany* **24**, 1-28, London: Royal Historical Society

Richards, P, 1998 Town and harbour: the hinterland and overseas trade of King's Lynn 1205-1537; an introduction, in K Friedland and P Richards, 1998 *Essays in Hanseatic History: The King's Lynn Symposium 1998*, 10-21, Dereham

Richardson, D, 2009 Cultures of exchange: Atlantic Africa in the era of the slave trade, *Royal Historical Society Transactions* 6th Series, **19**, 151-80

Richmond, C F, 1967 English naval power in the fifteenth century, *History* **52**, no 174, 1-15

Riddler, I, 2010 'Whale chopping board' in Atkins, R, & Popescu, E, 2010 Excavations at the hospital of St Mary Magdalene, Partney, Lincolnshire 2003, *Medieval Archaeology* **54**, 204-70

Rigby, S H, 1985 Sore decay and fair dwellings: Boston and urban decline in the later Middle Ages, *Midland History* **10**, 47-61

Rigby, S H, 2005 *The overseas trade of Boston in the reign of Richard II*, Lincoln Record Society 93

Riley, H T (ed.), 1864 *Thomae Walsingham, quondam monachi S. Albani, Historia Anglicana* II: 1381–1422, Rolls Series

Roberts, S E, 2015 *Jasper, the Tudor Kingmaker*, Fonthill Media

Rose, S, 2007 *The medieval sea*, Hambledon Continuum

Ross, C, 1975 *Edward IV*, Book Club Associates

Rosser, G, 2016 *Towns in medieval England – selected sources*, Manchester UP

Ruddock, A A, 1944 Italian trading fleets in medieval England, *History* **19**, 192-202

Ruddock, A A, 1951 *Italian merchants and shipping in Southampton 1270-1600*

Scammell, G V, 1968 Ships and shipping in early modern Europe, *The Historical Journal* **11**, no 2, 372-5

Scammell, G V, 1969 The new worlds and Europe in the 16th century, *The Historical Journal* **12**, no 3, 389-412

Scammell, G V, 1972 Ship-owning in the economy and politics of early modern England, *The Historical Journal* **15**, no 3, 385-408

de Selincourt, A, 1953 *The Channel Shore*, London: Robert Hale

Seymour, M C, 1963 *The Bodley version of Mandeville's Travels*, Early English Text Society 253, London

Shepherd, J, 1995 *The Glass*, in Soden 1995, 117-120

Soden, I, 1995 *Excavations at St Anne's Charterhouse, Coventry, 1968-87*, Coventry Museums monograph

Soden, I, 2005 *Coventry – the hidden history*, Tempus; reprinted by The History Press, 2013

Soden, I (ed.), 2007 *Stafford Castle: Survey, excavation and research 1978-98, Volume II – the Excavations*, Stafford Borough Council

Soden, I, 2009 *Ranulf de Blondeville, the first English hero*, Amberley, Stroud and reprinted 2021 as *The first English hero – the life of Ranulf de Blondeville*

Soden, I, 2013 *Royal Exiles from Richard the Lionheart to Charles II*, Amberley, Stroud

Soden, I, 2020 *A tale (possibly) of John Garton, Pinner, and his neighbour in Coventry in the 1520s*, Archaeology Warwickshire Report 2005, to be found at: https://www.archaeologists.net/sites/default/files/2005%20PC10%20Coventry%20Parkside%202010%205_0.pdf

Stahl, A M (ed.), 2009 *The book of Michael of Rhodes, a fifteenth-century maritime manuscript, Vol 2: transcription and translation*, MIT

Steane, J M, 1984 *The archaeology of England and Wales*, University of Georgia Press

Stewart, A, 1896 *The wanderings of Felix Fabri*, London: Palestine Pilgrims Text Society

Bibliography

Studer, P (ed.) 1913 *The Port Books of Southampton*, Southampton Record Society

Sutton, A F, 1982 Christian Colborne, painter of Germany and London, died 1486, *Journal of the British Archaeological Assocation* **CXXXV**, 55-61

Swabey, F, 1999 *Medieval Gentlewoman – Life in a widow's household in the later Middle Ages*, Sutton Publishing

Talbot, C H (ed.), 1967 *Letters from the English Abbots to the chapter at Cîteaux 1442-1521*, Camden Society 4th series 4, London: Royal Historical Society

Templeman, G, 1944 Register of the Guild of the Holy Trinity, St Mary, St John the Baptist and St Katherine of Coventry: II, *Dugdale Society* 19

Thielemans, Marie-Rose, 1966 *Bourgogne et Angleterre: relations politiques et économiques entre les Pays-Bas Bourguignons et l'Angleterre 1435-1467*, Brussels

Thompson, J A F (ed.), 1988 *Towns and townspeople in the fifteenth century*, Alan Sutton

Toulmin Smith, L (ed.), 1964 *Leland's itinerary in England and Wales*, 5 Vols, Fontwell: Centaur Press

Tracy, C, 1999 The importation into England of church furniture from the continent of Europe from the late Middle Ages to the present day, *Journal of the British Archaeological Association* **CLII**, 97-149

Twemlow, J A, 1912 *Calendar of entries in the Papal Registers relating to Great Britain and Ireland, Papal Letters* **IX** (1431-1447), HMSO

Twemlow, J A, 1933 *Calendar of entries in the Papal Registers relating to Great Britain and Ireland, Papal Letters* **XII** (1458-1471), HMSO

Veale, E M, 2003 *The English fur trade in the later Middle Ages*, London Record Society 28

Vlierman, K, 1993 Late medieval pottery on Dutch shipwrecks and a well-dated inventory of the early 15th century, *Medieval Ceramics* **17**, 69-76; Journal of the MPRG

Walker, D (ed.), 1998 *The Cartulary of St Augustine's Abbey*, Transactions of the Bristol and Gloucestershire Archaeological Society 10

Warner, G, 1926 *The Libelle of Englysshe Polycye*
Whitfield, P, 2017 *Charting the oceans*, British Library
Wilhelmsen, L J, 1943 *English textile nomenclature*, Bergen
Willan, T S, 1938 *The English coasting trade 1600-1730*, Manchester University Press
Williams, G A, 1963 *Medieval London: from commune to capital*, University of London, Athlone Press
Williams, N J, 1951 Francis Shaxton and the Elizabethan port books [of Lynn], *English Historical Review* **66**
Williamson, J A, 1913 *Maritime enterprise 1485-1558*, Oxford
Wolff, A, 2003 *How many miles to Babylon? Travels and adventures to Egypt and beyond, from 1300 to 1640*, Liverpool University Press
Wood, G L, Jones, R H, and Ponsford, M W, 1991 *Waterfront Archaeology: Proceedings of the third International Conference, Bristol 1988*, CBA Research Report **74**
Woodfield, C C, 1981 The finds from the Free Grammar School at The Whitefriars, Coventry, c1545-1557/8, *Post Medieval Archaeol.* **15**, 81-159
Woolgar, C M, 1999 *The great household in late medieval England*, Yale UP
Wright, T (ed.), 1861 The Libelle of Englysshe Polycye, in *Political Poems and Songs*, Rolls Series II
Zimmern, H, 1891 *The Hansa towns*, London

Also available from Amberley Publishing

THE FIRST ENGLISH HERO

THE LIFE OF RANULF DE BLONDEVILLE

IAIN SODEN

Available from all good bookshops or to order direct
Please call **01453-847-800**
www.amberley-books.com